READINGS IN PHILOSOPHY OF RELIGION
SECOND EDITION

W9-AUK-386

EDITED BY
MICHAEL BERGMANN

Copley Custom Textbooks

An imprint of XanEdu Custom Publishing

ISBN 13: 978-1-58152-370-6
ISBN 10: 1-58152-370-X

Third Printing, July 2007

Acknowledgments:

pp. 1–11: "The Cosmological Argument" by William Rowe. Copyright © 2001 by William Rowe. Reprinted by permission of the author via the Copyright Clearance Center.

pp. 12–24: From *Metaphysics* by Peter van Inwagen. Copyright © 1993 by Perseus Books Group. Reprinted by permission of the publisher via the Copyright Clearance Center.

pp. 25–49: From *Reason for Hope Within* by J. A. Cover. Copyright © 1999 by William B. Eerdmans Publishing Co. Reprinted by permission of the publisher.

pp. 50–64: As appeared in *American Philosophical Quarterly* October, 1979. Copyright © 1979 by North American Philosophical Publications. Reprinted by permission of the publisher via the Copyright Clearance Center.

pp. 70–78: As appeared in *NOUS*. Copyright © 1981 by Blackwell Publishers.

pp. 79–99: From *Philosophy of Religion: A Contemporary Introduction* by Keith Yandell. Copyright © 1999 by Routledge, N Y. Reprinted by permission of the publisher via the Copyright Clearance Center.

pp. 100–105: From *Interpretations of Religion* by John Hick. Copyright © 1991, 1999 by Yale University Press. Reprinted by permission of the publisher via the Copyright Clearance Center.

pp. 106–125: From *Rationality of Belief and the Plurality of Faith* by Alvin Plantinga. Copyright © 1995 by Cornell University Press. Reprinted by permission of the publisher via the Copyright Clearance Center.

pp. 126–151: From *God Matters: Readings in the Philosophy of Religion* edited by Raymond Martin and Christopher Bernard. Copyright © 2003 by Scott A. Davison. Reprinted by permission.

pp. 152–164: From *Rationality, Religious Belief and Moral Commitment* edited by Robert Audi and William Wainwright. Copyright © 1986 by Robert Audi and William Wainwright. Reprinted by permission of the editors.

Contents

The Cosmological Argument

William L. Rowe

Since ancient times thoughtful people have sought to justify their religious beliefs. Perhaps the most basic belief for which justification has been sought is the belief that there is a God. The effort to justify belief in the existence of God has generally started either from facts available to believers and nonbelievers alike or from facts, such as the experience of God, normally available only to believers. In this and the next two chapters, we shall consider some major attempts to justify belief in God by appealing to facts supposedly available to any rational person, whether religious or not. By starting from such facts, theologians and philosophers have developed arguments for the existence of God, arguments which, they have claimed, prove beyond reasonable doubt that there is a God.

STATING THE ARGUMENT

Arguments for the existence of God are commonly divided into *a posteriori* arguments and *a priori* arguments. An *a posteriori* argument depends on a principle or premise that can be known only by means of our experience of the world. An *a priori* argument, on the other hand, purports to rest on principles all of which can be known independently of our experience of the world, by just reflecting on and understanding them. Of the three major arguments for the existence of God—the Cosmological, the Design, and the Ontological—only the last of these is entirely *a priori*. In the Cosmological Argument one starts from some simple fact about the world, such as that it contains things which are caused to exist by other things. In the Design Argument a somewhat more complicated fact about the world serves as a starting point, the fact that the world exhibits order and design. In the Ontological Argument, however, one begins simply with a concept of God. In this chapter we shall consider the Cosmological Argument; in the next two chapters we shall examine the Ontological Argument and the Design Argument.

Before we state the Cosmological Argument itself, we shall consider some rather general points about the argument. Historically, it can be traced to the writings of the Greek philosophers, Plato and Aristotle, but the major developments in the argument took place in the thirteenth and in the eighteenth centuries. In the thirteenth century St. Thomas Aquinas put forth five distinct arguments for the existence of God, and of these, the first three are versions of the Cosmological Argument.[1] In the first of these he started from the fact that there are things in the world undergoing change and reasoned to the conclusion that there must be some ultimate cause of change that is itself unchanging. In the second he started from the fact that there are things in the world that clearly are caused to exist by other things and reasoned to the conclusion that there must be some ultimate cause of existence whose own existence is itself uncaused. And in the third argument he started from the fact that there are things in the world which need not have existed at all, things which do exist but which we can easily imagine might not, and reasoned to the conclusion that there must be some being that had to be, that exists and could not have failed to exist. Now it might be objected that even if Aquinas' arguments do prove beyond doubt the existence of an unchanging changer, an uncaused cause, and a being that could not have failed to exist, the arguments fail to prove the existence of the theistic God. For the theistic God, as we saw, is supremely good, omnipotent, omniscient, and creator of but separate from and independent of the world. How do we know, for example, that the unchanging changer isn't evil or slightly ignorant? The answer to this objection is that the Cosmological Argument has two parts. In the first part the effort is to prove the existence of a special sort of being, for example, a being that could not have failed to exist, or a being that causes change in other things but is itself unchanging. In the second part of the argument the effort is to prove that the special sort of being whose existence has been established in the first part has, and must have, the features—perfect goodness, omnipotence, omniscience, and so on—which go together to make up the theistic idea of God. What this means, then, is that Aquinas' three arguments are different versions of only the first part of the Cosmological Argument. Indeed, in later sections of his *Summa Theologica* Aquinas undertakes to show that the unchanging changer, the uncaused cause of existence, and the being which had to exist are one and the same being and that this single being has all of the attributes of the theistic God.

We noted above that a second major development in the Cosmological Argument took place in the eighteenth century, a development reflected in the writings of the German philosopher, Gottfried Leibniz (1646–1716), and especially in the writings of the English theologian and philosopher, Samuel Clarke (1675–1729). In 1704 Clarke gave a series of lectures, later published under the title *A Demonstration of the Being and Attributes of God*. These lectures constitute, perhaps, the most complete, forceful, and cogent presentation of the Cosmological Argument we possess. The lectures were read by the major skeptical philosopher of the century, David Hume (1711–1776), and in his brilliant attack on the attempt to justify religion in the court of reason, his *Dialogues Concerning Natural Religion*, Hume advanced several penetrating criticisms of Clarke's arguments, criticisms which have persuaded many philosophers in the modern period to reject the Cosmological Argument. In our study of the argument we shall concentrate our attention largely on its eighteenth century form and try to assess its strengths and weaknesses in the light of the criticisms which Hume and others have advanced against it.

The first part of the eighteenth-century form of the Cosmological Argument seeks to establish the existence of a self-existent being. The second part of the argument attempts to prove that the self-existent being is the theistic God, that is, has the features which we have noted to be basic elements in the theistic idea of God. We shall consider mainly the first part of the argument, for it is against the first part that philosophers from Hume to Bertrand Russell have advanced very important objections.

In stating the first part of the Cosmological Argument we shall make use of two important concepts, the concept of a *dependent being* and the concept of a *self-existent being*. By a *dependent being* we mean *a being whose existence is accounted for by the causal activity of other things.* Recalling Anselm's division into the three cases: "explained by another," "explained by nothing," and "explained by itself," it's clear that a dependent being is a being whose existence is explained by another. By *a self-existent being* we mean *a being whose existence is accounted for by its own nature.* This idea, as we saw in the preceding chapter, is an essential element in the theistic concept of God. Again, in terms of Anselm's three cases, a self-existent being is a being whose existence is explained by itself. Armed with these two concepts, the concept of a dependent being and the concept of a self-existent being, we can now state the first part of the Cosmological Argument.

1. Every being (that exists or ever did exist) is either a dependent being or a self-existent being.
2. Not every being can be a dependent being.

Therefore,

3. There exists a self-existent being.

Deductive Validity

Before we look critically at each of the premises of this argument, we should note that this argument is, to use an expression from the logician's vocabulary, *deductively valid*. To find out whether an argument is deductively valid, we need only ask the question: If its premises were true, would its conclusion have to be true? If the answer is yes, the argument is deductively valid. If the answer is no, the argument is deductively invalid. Notice that the question of the validity of an argument is entirely different from the question of whether its premises are in fact true. The following argument is made up entirely of false statements, but it is deductively valid.

1. Babe Ruth is the president of the United States.
2. The president of the United States is from Indiana.

Therefore,

3. Babe Ruth is from Indiana.

The argument is deductively valid because even though its premises are false, if they were true its conclusion would have to be true. Even God, Aquinas would say, cannot bring it about that the premises of this argument are true and yet its conclusion is false, for God's power extends only to what is possible, and it is an absolute impossibility that Babe Ruth be the president, the president be from Indiana, and yet Babe Ruth not be from Indiana.

The Cosmological Argument (that is, its first part) is a deductively valid argument. If its premises are or were true, its conclusion would have to be true. It's clear from our example about Babe Ruth, however, that the fact that an argument is deductively valid is insufficient to establish the truth of its conclusion. What else is required? Clearly that we know or have rational grounds for believing that the premises are true. If we know that the Cosmological Argument is deductively valid, and can establish that its premises are true, we shall thereby have proved that its conclusion is true. Are, then, the premises of the Cosmological Argument true? To this more difficult question we must now turn.

PSR and the First Premise

At first glance the first premise might appear to be an obvious or even trivial truth. But it is neither obvious nor trivial. And if it appears to be obvious or trivial, we must be confusing the idea of a self-existent being with the idea of a being that is not a dependent being. Clearly, it is true that any being is either a dependent being (explained by other things) or it is not a dependent being (not explained by other things). But what our premise says is that any being is either a dependent being (explained by other things) or it is a self-existent being (explained by itself). Consider again Anselm's three cases.

a. explained by another
b. explained by nothing
c. explained by itself

What our first premise asserts is that each being that exists (or ever did exist) is either of sort *a* or of sort *c*. It denies that any being is of sort *b*. And it is this denial that makes the first premise both significant and controversial. The obvious truth we must not confuse it with is the truth that any being is either of sort *a* or not of sort *a*. While this is true it is neither very significant nor controversial.

Earlier we saw that Anselm accepted as a basic principle that whatever exists has an explanation of its existence. Since this basic principle denies that any thing of sort *b* exists or ever did exist, it's clear that Anselm would believe the first premise of our Cosmological Argument. The eighteenth-century proponents of the argument also were convinced of the truth of the basic principle we attributed to Anselm. And because they were convinced of its truth, they readily accepted the first premise of the Cosmological Argument. But by the eighteenth century, Anselm's basic principle had been more fully elaborated and had received a name, the *Principle of Sufficient Reason*. Since this principle (PSR, as we shall call it) plays such an important role in justifying the premises of the Cosmological Argument, it will help us to consider it for a moment before we continue our enquiry into the truth or falsity of the premises of the Cosmological Argument.

PSR, as it was expressed by both Leibniz and Clarke, is a very general principle and is best understood as having two parts. In its first part it is simply a restatement of Anselm's principle that there must be an explanation of the *existence* of any being whatever. Thus if we come upon a man in a room, PSR implies that there must be an explanation of the fact that that particular man exists. A moment's reflection, however, reveals that there are many facts about the man other than the mere fact that he exists. There is the fact that the man in question is in the room he's in, rather than somewhere else, the fact that he is in good health, and the fact that he is at the moment thinking of Paris, rather than, say, London. Now, the purpose of the second part of PSR is to require an explanation of these facts, as well. We may state PSR, therefore, as the principle that *there must be an explanation (a) of the existence of any being, and (b) of any positive fact whatever*. We are now in a position to study the role this very important principle plays in the Cosmological Argument.

Since the proponent of the Cosmological Argument accepts PSR in both its parts, it is clear that he will appeal to its first part, PSRa, as justification for the first premise of the Cosmological Argument. Of course, we can and should enquire into the deeper question of whether the proponent of the argument is rationally justified in accepting PSR itself. But we shall put this question aside for the moment. What we need to see first is whether he is correct in thinking that *if* PSR is true then both of the premises of the Cosmological Argument are true. And what we have just seen is that if only the first part of PSR, that is, PSRa, is true, the first premise of the Cosmological Argument will be true. But what of the second premise of the argument? For what reasons does the proponent think that it must be true?

4

The Second Premise

According to the second premise, not every being that exists can be a dependent being, that is, can have the explanation of its existence in some other being or beings. Presumably, the proponent of the argument thinks there is something fundamentally wrong with the idea that every being that exists is dependent, that each existing being was caused by some other being which in turn was caused by some other being, and so on. But just what does he think is wrong with it? To help us in understanding his thinking, let's simplify things by supposing that there exists only one thing now, A_1, a living thing perhaps, that was brought into existence by something else, A_2, which perished shortly after it brought A_1, into existence. Suppose further that A_2 was brought into existence in similar fashion some time ago by A_3, and A_3 by A_4, and so forth back into the past. Each of these beings is a *dependent* being, it owes its existence to the preceding thing in the series. Now if nothing else ever existed but these beings, then what the second premise says would not be true. For if every being that exists or ever did exist is an A and was produced by a preceding A, then every being that exists or ever did exist would be dependent and, accordingly, premise two of the Cosmological Argument would be false. If the proponent of the Cosmological Argument is correct, there must, then, be something wrong with the idea that every being that exists or did exist is an A and that they form a causal series. A_1 caused by A_2, A_2 caused by A_3, A_3 caused by A_4 . . . A_n caused by A_{n+1}. How does the proponent of the Cosmological Argument propose to show us that there is something wrong with this view?

A popular but mistaken idea of how the proponent tries to show that something is wrong with the view, that every being might be dependent, is that he uses the following argument to reject it.

1. There must be a *first* being to start any causal series.
2. If every being were dependent there would be no *first* being to start the causal series.

Therefore,

3. Not every being can be a dependent being.

Although this argument is deductively valid, and its second premise is true, its first premise overlooks the distinct possibility that a causal series might be *infinite*, with no first member at all. Thus if we go back to our series of A beings, where each A is dependent, having been produced by the preceding A in the causal series, it's clear that if the series existed it would have no first member, for every A in the series there would be a preceding A which produced it, *ad infinitum*. The first premise of the argument just given assumes that a causal series must stop with a first member somewhere in the distant past. But there seems to be no good reason for making that assumption.

The eighteenth-century proponents of the Cosmological Argument recognized that the causal series of dependent beings could be infinite, without a first member to start the series. They rejected the idea that every being that is or ever was is dependent not because there would then be no first member to the series of dependent beings, but because there would then be no explanation for the fact that there are and have always been dependent beings. To see their reasoning let's return to our simplification of the supposition that the only things that exist or ever did exist are dependent beings. In our simplification of that supposition only one of the dependent beings exists at a time, each one perishing as it pro-

5

duces the next in the series. Perhaps the first thing to note about this supposition is that there is no individual A in the causal series of dependent beings whose existence is unexplained—A_1 is explained by A_2, A_2 by A_3, and A_n by A_{n+1}. So the first part of PSR, PSRa, appears to be satisfied. There is no particular being whose existence lacks an explanation. What, then, is it that lacks an explanation, if every particular A in the causal series of dependent beings has an explanation? It is the *series itself* that lacks an explanation. Or, as I've chosen to express it, *the fact that there are and have always been dependent beings*. For suppose we ask why it is that there are and have always been As in existence. It won't do to say that As have always been producing other As—we can't explain why there have always been As by saying there always have been As. Nor, on the supposition that only As have ever existed, can we explain the fact that there have always been As by appealing to something other than an A—for no such thing would have existed. Thus the supposition that the only things that exist or ever existed are dependent things leaves us with a fact for which there can be no explanation; namely, the fact that there are dependent beings rather than not.

Questioning the Justification of the Second Premise

Critics of the Cosmological Argument have raised several important objections against the claim that if every being is dependent the series or collection of those beings would have no explanation. Our understanding of the Cosmological Argument, as well as of its strengths and weaknesses, will be deepened by a careful consideration of these criticisms.

The first criticism is that the proponent of the Cosmological Argument makes the mistake of treating the collection or series of dependent beings as though it were itself a dependent being, and, therefore, requires an explanation of its existence. But, so the objection goes, the collection of dependent beings is not itself a dependent being any more than a collection of stamps is itself a stamp.

A second criticism is that the proponent makes the mistake of inferring that because each member of the collection of dependent beings has a cause, the collection itself must have a cause. But, as Russell noted, such reasoning is as fallacious as to infer that the human race (that is, the collection of human beings) must have a mother because each member of the collection (each human being) has a mother.

A third criticism is that the proponent of the argument fails to realize that for there to be an explanation of a collection of things is nothing more than for there to be an explanation of each of the things making up the collection. Since in the infinite collection (or series) of dependent beings, each being in the collection does have an explanation—by virtue of having been caused by some preceding member of the collection—the explanation of the collection, so the criticism goes, has already been given. As Hume remarked, "Did I show you the particular causes of each individual in a collection of twenty particles of matter, I should think it very unreasonable, should you afterwards ask me, what was the cause of the whole twenty. This is sufficiently explained in explaining the cause of the parts."[2]

Finally, even if the proponent of the Cosmological Argument can satisfactorily answer these objections, he must face one last objection to his ingenious attempt to justify premise two of the Cosmological Argument. For someone may agree that if nothing exists but an infinite collection of dependent beings, the infinite collection will have no explanation of its existence, and still refuse to conclude from this that there is something wrong with the idea that every being is a dependent being. Why, the proponent of the Cosmological Argument might ask, should we think that everything has to have an explanation? What's wrong with admitting that the fact that there are and have always been dependent beings is a *brute fact*, a fact having no explanation whatever? Why does everything have to have an explanation anyway? We must now see what can be said in response to these several objections.

Responses to Criticism

It is certainly a mistake to think that a collection of stamps is itself a stamp, and very likely a mistake to think that the collection of dependent beings is itself a dependent being. But the mere fact that the proponent of the argument thinks that there must be an explanation not only for each member of the collection of dependent beings but for the collection itself is not sufficient grounds for concluding that he must view the collection as itself a dependent being. The collection of human beings, for example, is certainly not itself a human being. Admitting this, however, we might still seek an explanation of why there is a collection of human beings, of why there are such things as human beings at all. So the mere fact that an explanation is demanded for the collection of dependent beings is no proof that the person who demands the explanation must be supposing that the collection itself is just another dependent being.

The second criticism attributes to the proponent of the Cosmological Argument the following bit of reasoning.

1. Every member of the collection of dependent beings has a cause or explanation.

Therefore,

2. The collection of dependent beings has a cause or explanation.

As we noted in setting forth this criticism, arguments of this sort are often unreliable. It would be a mistake to conclude that a collection of objects is light in weight simply because each object in the collection is light in weight, for if there were many objects in the collection it might be quite heavy. On the other hand, if we know that each marble weighs more than one ounce, we could infer validly that the collection of marbles weighs more than an ounce. Fortunately, however, we don't need to decide whether the inference from 1 to 2 is valid or invalid. We need not decide this question because the proponent of the Cosmological Argument need not use this inference to establish that there must be an explanation of the collection of dependent beings. He need not use this inference because he has in PSR a principle from which it follows immediately that the collection of dependent beings has a cause or explanation. For according to PSR, every positive fact must have an explanation. If it is a fact that there exists a collection of dependent beings then, according to PSR, that fact too must have an explanation. So it is PSR that the proponent of the Cosmological Argument appeals to in concluding that there must be an explanation of the collection of dependent beings, and not some dubious inference from the premise that each member of the collection has an explanation. It seems, then, that neither of the first two criticisms is strong enough to do any serious damage to the reasoning used to support the second premise of the Cosmological Argument.

The third objection contends that to explain the existence of a collection of things is the same thing as to explain the existence of each of its members. If we consider a collection of dependent beings in which each being in the collection is explained by the preceding member that caused it, it's clear that no member of the collection will lack an explanation of its existence. But, so the criticism goes, if we've explained the existence of every member of a collection, we've explained the existence of the collection—there's nothing left over to be explained. This forceful criticism, originally advanced by Hume, has gained considerable support in the modern period. But the criticism rests on an assumption that the proponent of the Cosmological Argument would not accept. The assumption is that to explain the existence of a collection of things it is *sufficient* to explain the existence of every member in the collection. To see what is wrong with this assumption is to understand the basic issue in the reasoning by which the proponent of the Cosmological Argument seeks to establish that not every being can be a dependent being.

In order for there to be an explanation of the existence of the collection of dependent beings, it's clear that the eighteenth-century proponents would require that the following two conditions be satisified:

C1. There is an explanation of the existence of each of the members of the collection of dependent beings.
C2. There is an explanation of why there are *any* dependent beings.

According to the proponents of the Cosmological Argument, if every being that exists or ever did exist is a dependent being—that is, if the whole of reality consists of nothing more than a collection of dependent beings—C1 will be satisfied, but C2 will not be satisfied. And since C2 won't be satisfied, there will be no explanation of the collection of dependent beings. The third criticism, therefore, says in effect that if C1 is satisfied, C2 will be satisfied, and, since in a collection of dependent beings each member will have an explanation in whatever it was that produced it, C1 will be satisfied. So, therefore, C2 will be satisfied and the collection of dependent beings will have an explanation.

Although the issue is a complicated one, I think it is possible to see that the third criticism rests on a mistake: the mistake of thinking that if C1 is satisfied C2 must also be satisfied. The mistake is a natural one to make for it is easy to imagine circumstances in which if C1 is satisfied C2 also will be satisfied. Suppose, for example, that the whole of reality includes not just a collection of dependent beings but also a self-existent being. Suppose further that instead of each dependent being having been produced by some other dependent being, every dependent being was produced by the self-existent being. Finally, let us consider both the possibility that the collection of dependent beings is finite in time and has a first member, and the possibility that the collection of dependent beings is infinite in past time, having no first member. Using G for the self-existent being, the first possibility may be diagramed as follows:

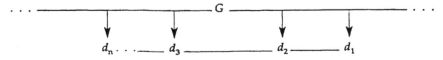

G, we shall say, has always existed and always will. We can think of d_1 as some presently existing dependent being, d_2, d_3, and so forth as dependent beings that existed at some time in the past, and d_n as the first dependent being to exist. The second possibility may be portrayed as follows:

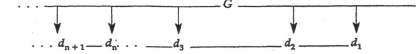

$$\ldots \quad d_{n+1} - d_{n} \ldots \underline{\hspace{2cm}} d_3 \underline{\hspace{3cm}} d_2 \underline{\hspace{2cm}} d_1$$

On this diagram there is no first member of the collection of dependent beings. Each member of the infinite collection, however, is explained by reference to the self-existent being G which produced it. Now the interesting point about both these cases is that the explanation that has been provided for the members of the collection of dependent beings carries with it, at least in part, an answer to the question of why there are any dependent beings at all. In both cases we may explain why there are dependent beings by pointing out that there exists a self-existent being that has been engaged in producing them. So once we have learned that the existence of each member of the collection of dependent beings has its existence explained by the fact that G produced it, we have already learned why there are dependent beings.

Someone might object that we haven't really learned why there are dependent beings until we also learn *why* G has been producing them. But, of course, we could also say that we haven't really explained the existence of a particular dependent being, say d_3, until we also learn not just that G produced it but *why* G produced it. The point we need to grasp, however, is that once we admit that every dependent being's existence is explained by G, we must admit that the fact that there are dependent beings has also been explained. So it is not unnatural that someone should think that to explain the existence of the collection of dependent beings is nothing more than to explain the existence of its members. For, as we've seen, to explain the collection's existence is to explain each member's existence and to explain why there are any dependent beings at all. And in the examples we've considered, in doing the one (explaining why each dependent being exists) we've already done the other (explained why there are any dependent beings at all). We must now see, however, that on the supposition that the whole of reality consists *only* of a collection of dependent beings, to give an explanation of each member's existence is not to provide an explanation of why there are dependent beings.

In the examples we've considered, we have gone *outside* of the collection of dependent beings in order to explain the members' existence. But if the only beings that exist or ever existed are dependent beings then each dependent being will be explained by some other dependent being, ad infinitum. This does not mean that there will be some particular dependent being whose existence is unaccounted for. Each dependent being has an explanation of its existence; namely, in the dependent being which preceded it and produced it. So C1 is satisfied: there is an explanation of the existence of each member of the collection of dependent beings. Turning to C2, however, we can see that it will not be satisfied. We cannot explain why there are (or have ever been) dependent beings by appealing to all the members of the infinite collection of dependent beings. For if the question to be answered is why there are (or have ever been) any dependent beings at all, we cannot answer that question by noting that there always have been dependent beings, each one accounting for the existence of some other dependent being. Thus on the supposition that every being is dependent, it seems there will be no explanation of why there are dependent beings. C2 will not be satisfied. Therefore, on the supposition that every being is dependent there will be no explanation of the existence of the collection of dependent beings.

The Truth of PSR

We come now to the final criticism of the reasoning supporting the second premise of the Cosmological Argument. According to this criticism, it is admitted that the supposition that every being is dependent implies that there will be a *brute fact* in the universe, a fact, that is, for which there can be no explanation whatever. For there will be no explanation of the fact that dependent beings exist and have always been in existence. It is this brute fact that the proponents of the argument were describing when they pointed out that if every being is dependent, the series or collection of dependent beings would lack an explanation of *its* existence. The final criticism asks what is wrong with admitting that the universe contains such a brute, unintelligible fact. In asking this question the critic challenges the fundamental principle, PSR, on which the Cosmological Argument rests. For, as we've seen, the first premise of the argument denies that there exists a being whose existence has no explanation. In support of this premise the proponent appeals to the first part of PSR. The second premise of the argument claims that not every being can be dependent. In support of this premise the proponent appeals to the second part of PSR, the part which states that there must be an explanation of any positive fact whatever.

The proponent reasons that if every being were a dependent being, then although the first part of PSR would be satisfied—every being would have an explanation—the second part would be violated; there would be no explanation for the positive fact that there are and have always been dependent beings. For first, since every being is supposed to be dependent, there would be nothing outside of the collection of dependent beings to explain the collection's existence. Second, the fact that each member of the collection has an explanation in some other dependent being is insufficient to explain why there are and have always been dependent beings. And, finally, there is nothing about the collection of dependent beings that would suggest that it is a self-existent collection. Consequently, if every being were dependent, the fact that there are and have always been dependent beings would have no explanation. But this violates the second part of PSR. So the second premise of the Cosmological Argument must be true: Not every being can be a dependent being. This conclusion, however, is no better than the principle, PSR, on which it rests. And it is the point of the final criticism to question the truth of PSR. Why, after all, should we accept the idea that every being and every positive fact must have an explanation? Why, in short, should we believe PSR? These are important questions, and any final judgment of the Cosmological Argument depends on how they are answered.

Most of the theologians and philosophers who accept PSR have tried to defend it in either of two ways. Some have held that PSR is (or can be) known *intuitively* to be true. By this they mean that if we fully understand and reflect on what is said by PSR we can see that it must be true. Now, undoubtedly, there are statements which are known intuitively to be true. "Every triangle has exactly three angles" or "No physical object can be in two different places in space at one and the same time" are examples of statements whose truth we can apprehend just by understanding and reflecting on them. The difficulty with the claim that PSR is known intuitively to be true, however, is that a number of very able philosophers fail on careful reflection to apprehend its truth, and some have developed serious arguments for the conclusion that the principle is in fact false.[3] It is clear, therefore, that not everyone who has reflected on PSR has been persuaded that it is true, and some are persuaded that there are good reasons to think it is false. But while the fact that some able thinkers fail to apprehend the truth of PSR, and may even argue that it is false, is a decisive reason to believe that PSR is not so obvious a truth as say, "No physical object can be in two different places in space at one and the same time," it falls short of establishing that PSR is not a truth of reason. Here, perhaps, all that one can do is carefully reflect on what PSR says and form one's own judgment on whether it is a fundamental truth about the way reality must be. And if after carefully reflecting on PSR it does strike one in that way, that person may well be rationally justified in taking it to be true and, having seen how it supports the premises of the Cosmological Argument, accepting the conclusion of that argument as true.

The second way philosophers and theologians who accept PSR have sought to defend it is by claiming that although it may not be known to be true, it is, nevertheless, a presupposition of reason, a basic assumption that rational people make, whether or not they reflect sufficiently to become aware of the assumption. It's probably true that there are some assumptions we all make about our world, assumptions which are so basic that most of us are unaware of them. And, I suppose, it might be true that PSR is such an assumption. What bearing would this view of PSR have on the Cosmological Argument? Perhaps the main point to note is that even if PSR is a presupposition we all share, the premises of the Cosmological Argument could still be false. For PSR itself could still be false. The fact, if it is a fact, that all of us *presuppose* that every existing being and every positive fact has an explanation does not imply that no being exists, and no positive fact obtains, without an explanation. Nature is not bound to satisfy our presuppositions. As the American philosopher William James once remarked in another connection; "In the great boarding house of nature, the cakes and the butter and the syrup seldom come out so even and leave the plates so clean."

Our study of the first part of the Cosmological Argument has led us to the fundamental principle on which its premises rest, the Principle of Sufficient Reason. We've seen that unless, on thoughtful reflection, PSR strikes us as something we see with certainty to be true, we cannot reasonably claim to know that the premises of the Cosmological Argument are true. Of course, they might be true. But unless we do know them to be true they cannot *establish* for us the conclusion that there exists a being that has the explanation of its existence within its own nature. If it were shown, however, that even though we do not *know* that PSR is true we all, nevertheless, *presuppose* PSR to be true, then, whether PSR is true or not, to be consistent we should accept the Cosmological Argument. For, as we've seen, its premises imply its conclusion and its premises do seem to follow from PSR. But no one has succeeded in *showing* that PSR is an assumption that most or all of us share. So our final conclusion must be that, with the exception of those who, on thoughtful reflection, reasonably conclude that PSR is a fundamental truth of reason, the Cosmological Argument does not provide us with good rational grounds for believing that among those beings that exist, there is one whose existence is accounted for by its own nature. And since the classical conception of God is of a being whose existence is accounted for by its own nature, apart from the exception noted, the Cosmological Argument fails to provide us with good rational grounds for believing that God exists.

Notes

1. St. Thomas Aquinas, *Summa Theologica*, 1a. 2, 3, in *The Basic Writings of Saint Thomas Aquinas*, ed. Anton C. Pegis (New York: Random House, 1945).
2. David Hume, *Dialogues Concerning Natural Religion*, pt. IX, ed. H. D. Aiken (New York: Hafner Publishing Company, 1948), pp. 59–60.
3. For a brief account of two of these arguments see the preface to my *The Cosmological Argument* (New York: Fordham University Press, 1998).

The Wider Teleological Argument

Peter van Inwagen

Our present picture of the cosmos has two main components: our picture of the nature of the elementary particles that make up the cosmos and the forces by which they interact (supplied by physics) and our picture of the large-scale structure and the history of the cosmos, from the Big Bang to the present (supplied by cosmology). These two components form a very tightly integrated whole. Each of these components involves a lot of numbers. The description of the particles and the forces, for example, involves a number called the fine-structure constant, which relates to the way in which electrically charged particles interact with the electromagnetic field. Other constants have to do with other kinds of interaction, such as gravity and special interactions that take place at very short range between some kinds of elementary particles. The description of the large-scale structure of the cosmos involves numbers like the number of elementary particles that belong to each "family" of particles allowed by theory. Lots of the numbers that are needed to describe the cosmos cannot be predicted theoretically. They are numbers that, as the physicists say, "have to be filled in by hand." That is, their values have to be established by the laborious process of measurement and experiment. There seems to be no necessity in the values that these numbers actually have. Therefore, it looks as if there are perfectly possible cosmoi (the plural of "cosmos") in which these numbers are different, and we can ask what those possible cosmoi would be like. And, because our present picture of the world is so precise and unified, we can often answer such questions. There is quite a lot that can be said in answer to a question like, What features would the cosmos have if the fine-structure constant had twice its actual value?

The interesting thing about the answers to these questions is that it appears that if the cosmos were much different at all, there would be no life (and therefore no rational animals). Small changes in various of these numbers would result in a cosmos that lasted only a few seconds or in which there were no atoms or in which there were only hydrogen and helium atoms or in which all matter was violently radioactive or in which there were no stars. In no cosmos of these sorts could there be life, and, as a consequence, in no cosmos of these sorts could there be human

12

beings or any other rational animals. (And there are many, many other ways in which small changes in certain of the numbers that describe the features of the cosmos would produce a cosmos that was inimical to life.)

Suppose we fancifully think for a moment of the cosmos as the product of a machine designed to produce cosmoi. The machine has a largish number of dials on it, perhaps twenty or thirty, and the overall features of the cosmos are the result of the ways the dials were set when the cosmos was produced. If they had been set in other positions, a different type of cosmos would have emerged from the machine. It seems to be the lesson of modern physics and cosmology that *many* statements like the following ones will be true: 'The pointer on dial 18 is set at .0089578346198711. If it had not been set at some value between .0089578346198709 and .00895783461987l2, there would be no carbon atoms and hence no life'; 'The pointer on dial 23 is set at 5.113446 and the pointer on dial 5 is set at 5.113449; if the values of the two readings had been exactly equal, there would have been no matter, but only radiation; if the two readings had differed by more than .000006, all stars would be of a type that would burn out before multicellular organisms could evolve on their planets.'[1]

The suggestive metaphor of a cosmos-producing machine with lots of dials on it that must be very precisely set if the machine is to produce a cosmos that could contain life (notice, by the way, that we say 'could contain' and not 'will necessarily produce') has led some writers to say that the cosmos is "fine-tuned" in such a way as to enable it to contain life. Only a vanishingly small proportion of the totality of possible cosmoi are suitable abodes for life, and yet the actual cosmos is one of these very few (in fact, not only is it a suitable abode for life, but it actually contains life; in fact, not only does it actually contain life, but it contains life that is rational; these features make it an even rarer specimen among the totality of possible cosmoi than a mere "life-permitting" cosmos; how *much* rarer is hard to say, but our present presuppositions about the emergence of life and the mechanisms of evolution say, in effect, "Not all that much rarer"). Why is the cosmos one of the few possible cosmoi that permit life? Why does the cosmos appear to have been fine-tuned by someone who had life in mind? Why are the numbers right for life?

One answer to these questions is provided by the so-called teleological argument. Late in the thirteenth century, Saint Thomas Aquinas presented the following argument for the existence of God:

> We observe that things that have no knowledge—objects that we find in the natural world, for example—sometimes act for an end. (That this is so is proved by the fact that they always, or nearly always, behave in the same

13

way, and this way is the way that will lead to the best result. It is evident from this that their behaving in these ways is due not to chance but to design.) But a thing that has no knowledge cannot act for an end unless it is directed by a being that has knowledge and intelligence, as an arrow is directed by an archer. There is, therefore, some intelligent being who directs all of those things in the natural world that act for an end, and we call this being God.

This argument has been variously called the teleological argument (from the Greek *telos*, meaning an end or goal), the argument from design ("due not to chance but to design"), and the analogical argument (because it proceeds by drawing an analogy between the apparently goal-directed behavior of things in the natural world—birds flying south for the winter or the leaves of a phototropic plant turning toward the sun—and the behavior of things designed or controlled by human begins: "as an arrow is directed by an archer").

It is commonly held that the teleological argument has been refuted by the Darwinian account of evolution—indeed by the very existence of the Darwinian account, whether or not we know it to be true. And this may very well be so if we take the scope of the argument to be limited to living organisms (that is, to those objects in the natural world whose features the Darwinian theory gives an account of). But what of the cosmos as a whole? If the cosmos is a very special cosmos among all possible cosmoi, and if it has every appearance of being a cosmos that has been designed to be an abode for life, might not the most obvious explanation of this appearance be that the appearance is reality? Might not the most obvious explanation of the fine-tuning of the cosmos be that it has *been* fine-tuned? That its large-scale features (if no others) have been carefully chosen and put into place by a conscious, purposive being who wanted to make an abode for living things? And if a conscious, purposive being designed the cosmos to be an abode for living things, and if, as we know it does, the cosmos also contains rational beings like ourselves—rational animals—is it not reasonable to infer further that the existence of those rational beings is a part of the purposes of the Designer (who is, after all, also a rational being and may therefore be presumed to take a special interest in rational beings)? . . .

It is consistent with the conclusion of the teleological argument that the Designer's purposes be analogous to a scientist's (we are part of a vast experiment) or a dramatist's ("All the world's a stage," in a sense that is uncomfortably close to the literal). Neither of these purposes would be possible for God: He does not need to conduct experiments, since, being omniscient, He knows how they would turn out without having to conduct them; being loving and good, He would not employ self-aware, flesh-and-blood beings for purely aesthetic purposes—all the more so because He would see all possible dramas laid out simultaneously and in their entirety in the infinite theater of His mind and could therefore have no reason for wanting to watch the actual performance of any play.

The teleological argument, therefore, does not claim to prove the existence of a being that is all-powerful or all-knowing or recognizes any moral obligations toward the rational beings whose existence it is responsible for. A moment's reflection will show that it cannot claim to prove the existence of a being that is infinite or necessarily existent or eternal. (As to eternity, it may be, for all the teleological argument can claim to show, that the Designer has been outlasted by its cosmos, just as the pharaohs have been outlasted by their pyramids.) It is consistent with the conclusion of the teleological argument that the creation of the cosmos was a cooperative endeavor involving the labors of many beings, like the construction of a ship by human beings. For all the teleological argument can claim to show, it may not only be that the cosmos is the work of many beings but also that these beings have to learn to build cosmoi by trial and error; it may be that somewhere outside our ken there are lying about a lot of "botched and bungled" cosmoi that represent their earlier and less successful attempts at a working cosmos; it may be that *our* cosmos is an "early draft" and that various of its more unfortunate features like disease and parasitism and natural disasters are due to their not yet having fully mastered the craft of cosmos building.

Let all this be granted, however, and it still seems to be true that the teleological argument does show that we should think of rational animals in a way somewhat like the way in which we should think of a cache of mysterious artifacts unearthed by an archaeologist: We may not know what their purpose is, but it is clear that they do have a purpose; they exist because some designers—known to us only through their productions—made them to fulfill that unknown purpose. (Of course, the above reflections do not show that no one could, or that no one does, know that purpose. There might be any number of ways of finding it out. Perhaps, for example, someone will devise some marvelously clever theory about a purpose that we might serve in the eyes of a cosmos-designer, a purpose that, when we consider it carefully, makes so many hitherto mysterious facts "fall into place" that we feel intellectually compelled to believe that this person has guessed the purposes of the Designer. An analogy might be the clever theory that Stonehenge is an astronomical observatory. Or the Designer might be able and willing to communicate with rational animals and might tell certain of them what end their kind serves. But no one *has* devised any compelling theory about the purpose behind our existence, and supposed revelations of the purposes of the Designer are so plentiful and so wildly inconsistent with one another that the metaphysician who does not desire a severely limited audience can make no use of them.) . . .

Some philosophers have argued that there is nothing in the fact that the universe is fine-tuned that should be the occasion for any surprise. After all (the objection runs), if a machine has dials, the dials have to be set *some* way, and any particular setting is as unlikely as any other. Since any setting of the dials is as unlikely as any other, there can be nothing more surprising about the actual setting of the dials, whatever it may be, than there would be about any possible setting of the dials if that possible setting were the actual setting. (Here is a parallel argument. If you toss a coin and it comes up "heads" twenty times in a row, you shouldn't be surprised. After all, you wouldn't be surprised if the sequence HHTTHTHTT- THTHHTTHTHT occurred, and that sequence and the sequence HHHH- HHHHHHHHHHHHHHHHHH both have exactly the same probability of occurring: 1 in 1,048,576, or about .000000954.) This reasoning is sometimes combined with the point that if "our" numbers hadn't been set into the cosmic dials, the equally improbable setting that did occur would have differed from the actual setting mainly in that there would have been no one there to wonder at its improbability.

This must be one of the most annoyingly obtuse arguments in the history of philosophy. Let us press the "parallel" argument a bit. Suppose that you are in a situation in which you must draw a straw from a bundle of 1,048,576 straws of different length and in which it has been decreed that if you don't draw the shortest straw in the bundle you will be instantly and painlessly killed: you will be killed so fast that you won't have time to realize that you didn't draw the shortest straw. Reluctantly—but you have no alternative—you draw a straw and are astonished to find yourself alive and holding the shortest straw. What should you conclude?

In the absence of further information, only one conclusion is reasonable. Contrary to appearances, you did *not* draw the straw at random; the whole situation in which you find yourself is some kind of "set-up"; the bundle was somehow rigged to ensure that the straw that you drew was the shortest one. The following argument to the contrary is simply silly. "Look, you had to draw some straw or other. Drawing the shortest was no more unlikely than drawing the 256,057th-shortest: the probability in either case was .000000954. But your drawing the 256,057th-shortest straw isn't an outcome that would suggest a 'set-up' or would suggest the need for any sort of explanation, and, therefore, drawing the shortest shouldn't suggest the need for an explanation either. The only real difference between the two cases is that you wouldn't have been around to remark on the unlikelihood of drawing the 256,057th-shortest straw."

It is one thing, however, to note that an argument is silly and another thing to say why it is silly. But an explanation is not hard to come by. The argument is silly because it violates the following principle:

> Suppose that there is a certain fact that has no known explanation; suppose that one can think of a possible explanation of that fact, an explanation that (if only it were true) would be a very *good* explanation; then it is wrong to say that that event stands in no more need of an explanation than an otherwise similar event for which no such explanation is available.[2]

My drawing the shortest straw out of a bundle of over a million straws in a situation in which my life depends on my drawing just that straw certainly suggests a possible explanation. If an audience were to observe my drawing the shortest straw, they would very justifiably conclude that I had somehow "cheated": they would conclude that I had had some way of knowing which straw was the shortest and that (to save my life) I had deliberately drawn it. (If I know that I *didn't* know which straw was the shortest—if I am just as astounded as anyone in the audience at my drawing the shortest straw—then the situation will not suggest to *me* that particular explanation of my drawing the shortest straw, but it will suggest the one that I have already mentioned, namely that some unknown benefactor has rigged the drawing in my favor.) But if an audience were to observe my drawing the 256,057th-shortest straw (and my consequent immediate demise), this would not suggest *any* explanation to them; no one would suppose—nor would it be reasonable for anyone to suppose—that I knew which straw was the 256,057th-shortest and that I deliberately drew it; nor would anyone suppose that someone had rigged the drawing to ensure my getting the 256,057th-shortest straw; nor would any other possible explanation come to anyone's mind.

We have seen that the setting of the cosmic dials does suggest an explanation: the dials were so set by a rational being who wanted the cosmos to be a suitable abode for other rational beings. Therefore, the critics of the teleological argument who say that one setting of the cosmic dials is no more remarkable than any other possible setting are certainly mistaken. We should note that our principle does not say that if one can think of a really good explanation for some fact, one should automatically assume that that explanation is correct; the principle says only that in such cases it would be a mistake simply to assume that that fact required no explanation. . . .

I will now turn to a reply to the teleological argument that I believe to be decisive. I said earlier that the common belief that the teleological argument had been refuted by the Darwinian account of evolution (or even by the *possible* truth of this account) was mistaken. It was mistaken because evolution is a phenomenon that occurs only within the realm of living things (or at least of self-reproducing things) and the version of the teleological argument we have been examining applies to the cosmos as a whole. And the cosmos is not a living thing or a self-reproducing thing: it is not the product of the operation of natural selection on ancestral cosmoi that reproduced themselves with variations in an environment that contained limited amounts of the resources needed for cosmic survival and reproduction. Nevertheless, the Darwinian account of evolution does have a feature that can be adapted to the needs of the present discussion. Darwin showed how it was possible, in certain circumstances, for chance to produce results that one might be initially inclined to ascribe to the purposive action of rational beings; some of the ideas on which this demonstration rests are so simple and general that they can be lifted out of the biological context in which Darwin applied them and applied to the apparent design exhibited by the cosmos.

An example will illustrate these ideas. Suppose that each of the citizens of Wormsley Glen has a job; and suppose that each of them has an alarm clock; and suppose that each alarm clock goes off at just the right time each day to enable its owner to get up and get to work on time. For example, Alice's clock goes off at 5:36 each morning; and if it went off even a few minutes later she would frequently be late for work; as it is, she breezes into the office just under the wire every day. And Tim's clock goes off at 6:07, which is just right for letting him sleep as late as possible and still get to work on time. (And so on and so on, for every citizen of Wormsley Glen. They all have clocks that enable them to arise at the optimum time, given the time they are expected at work, the amount of time they need to deal with their morning domestic chores, the amount of time they need to travel to work, and whatever other factors in their lives may be relevant to the times at which they have to get up in the morning.)

Here, we might suppose, is an obvious case of purposive design: on the back of each of the alarm clocks there is a little knob or something that regulates the time at which the alarm rings, and all of the citizens have calculated the times at which they have to get up and have set their individual alarms accordingly. But this is not so. The real explanation is different and rather unpleasant. Not so long ago there were hundreds of times as many people in Wormsley Glen as there are today. Each of them was issued an alarm clock that was unchangeably set to go off at some particular time each day, and no returns or trading allowed. The alarm settings were in every case entirely random, and this had just the consequence you would expect. Almost every alarm was set wrong (that is, was set for a time that was not the time at which its owner needed to get up), and these wrong settings, owing to the laissez-faire economic system that prevailed in Wormsley Glen, had disastrous consequences for their owners. Sally's was set for 11:23 A.M., and she was, as a consequence, consistently late for work and lost her job and starved to death. Frank's was set for 4:11 A.M., and, once it had gone off, he could either go back to sleep and be late for work or stay up and try to deal with the demands of his job (he was a brain surgeon) without having had a good night's sleep. He chose the latter course, but his being chronically short of sleep led him to make a few serious mistakes, and he had to be let go; shortly thereafter, he starved to death.

And that is what happened to everyone in Wormsley Glen who was issued a "bad" alarm clock. (Even those whose clocks were set just slightly wrong lost their competitive edge and were forced out of their jobs by more punctual and better rested rivals.) Wormsley Glen is no welfare state, and they're all dead of starvation now. Knowing this to be the case we can see that there is no conscious purpose behind the setting of Alice's or Tim's alarms. Each of them received an alarm clock that *just happened* to be set at the "right" time, and each of them therefore survived. And this is what happened with all of the other citizens of Wormsley Glen. It was statistically likely that a certain percentage of the original inhabitants would, simply by the luck of the draw, receive clocks that were set at the time that was right for them. And that is what happened: a certain not-at-all-surprising proportion of the original inhabitants got clocks that were set at the right time, and the unforgiving social arrangements of Wormsley Glen removed everyone else from the picture.

This story is a model for the sort of circumstances in which the action of chance can mimic the productions of a rational being. A rational being, as we have said, can be aware of non-actual states of affairs and can act on values that it happens to have in order to single out some of these states of affairs and cause them to become actual. The operations of chance cannot do that because chance is not, so to speak, aware of any non-actual states of affairs and chance has no values. What chance can sometimes do is to generate a large number of actual states of affairs, and it may happen that the world is arranged in such a way that it will proceed to eliminate from actuality all of them that do not satisfy some condition. The "surviving" states of affairs in the second case may very closely resemble the "chosen" states of affairs in the first. (I have talked of the operations of chance, but it might be better to follow Jacques Monod and talk of the "interplay of chance and necessity": chance generates a large set of actual states of affairs, and necessity eliminates all, or at any rate, most, of the ones that do not meet its demands.)

In our story of Wormsley Glen, chance produced a large number of actual "alarm-clock situations," and the grim necessities of Wormsley Glen then proceeded to eliminate from actuality all of them but a few that closely resembled the alarm clock situations that a rational being would have chosen from among possible alarm-clock situations to be actual. As rationality decides which possibilities are to be actual, so a non-rational cosmos or nature may decide which actualities (which of a set of actualities generated by chance and displaying a range of characteristics almost as broad as the range of characteristics displayed by the set of possibilities that rationality examines) are to remain actual.

According to Darwin, chance and nature have combined in just this way—but there are a few factors peculiar to the evolutionary process that are not represented in the schema laid out in the preceding paragraph— to produce the appearance of conscious design in living organisms. Chance produces random inheritable variations among the offspring of an organism, and nature (which, like Wormsley Glen, is no welfare state) tends to favor the preservation of those variations that contribute to an organism's ability to have descendants. The appearance of design in organisms is due to the accumulation of such useful (useful for having descendants) variations. Organisms are adapted to their environments— to the extent that they *are* adapted to their environments; adaptation is often imperfect—owing to the fact that the better adapted an organism is to its environment, the more likely it is to have descendants. It will be noted that our "alarm clock" story includes only some of the features of the Darwinian account of apparent design in living things: those that do not involve reproduction and inheritability.

The operations of chance can, moreover, produce an appearance of "design" (the appearance of a purposive choice among possibilities by a rational being) without actually eliminating anything from existence. To produce the *appearance* of design, it is necessary only to render those things whose features would count against a design-hypothesis unobservable. It is of course true that one very effective way to render something unobservable is to destroy it. But that is not the only way. I need not destroy any green things (or even change their colors) to prevent you from observing green things. I could also remove all green things from your vicinity, or move you to a region in which there happened to be only non-green things, or render you color-blind. This consideration suggests that chance could produce the appearance of design by generating a large number of actual objects under conditions in which some "observational selection effect" allowed observers to be aware of only a few of those objects, ones that had (more or less) the features that a rational being would have chosen to accomplish some purpose. (The meaning of 'observational selection effect' is best explained by an example. In 1936, *The Literary Digest* predicted on the basis of a poll conducted by telephone that Alf Landon would be elected president. But Roosevelt was elected by a landslide. It turned out that a vast number of Roosevelt supporters did not have telephones, for the poor tended both to support Roosevelt and not to have telephones. An observational selection effect had rendered a large body of voters "invisible" to the editors of *The Literary Digest*.)

It is the possibility of an interplay of chance and an observational selection effect that is the undoing of the teleological argument in the form in which we are considering it. In our initial statement of the teleological argument, we asked the following question: "Might not the most obvious explanation of the fine-tuning of the cosmos be that it has *been* fine-tuned?" If the answer to this question is No, then the teleological argument fails. And the answer to this question is No if there is even one other explanation of the fine-tuning of the cosmos that is at least as good as the explanation that it has been fine-tuned. And another explanation, one at least as good, is available: an explanation that appeals to the interplay of chance and an observational selection effect.

The alternative explanation goes like this. First, the cosmos is only one among a vast number of *actual* cosmoi. (If there are people who insist on using 'the cosmos' as a number for the whole of physical reality, we could accommodate them by saying instead that what appears to us to be the whole of the cosmos is in reality a very small *part* of the cosmos. The difference between the two statements seems to me to be merely verbal. I shall continue to talk of a multitude of cosmoi, and anyone who does not like my way of talking can easily translate it into talk of a multitude of parts of the one cosmos.)

These cosmoi exhibit a vast number of "cosmos-designs." To see what is intended by the statement, think of our cosmos-designing machine as containing a randomizing device. The randomizing device sets the dials on the machine at random. The machine turns out a cosmos. Then the randomizing device resets the dials and the machine turns out another cosmos, and so on through a very large number of resettings. Alternatively, we could suppose that there were an enormous number of cosmos-producing machines on each of which the dials were set at random and that each machine turned out one cosmos. (Compare the alarm clocks issued to the citizens of Wormsley Glen.) Since the dial settings are random, and since the existence of life is allowed by hardly any of the possible combinations of settings, only a very small proportion of these cosmoi will be suitable abodes for life. Most of them will last only a few seconds or will contain no protons or will contain no atoms or will contain only hydrogen and helium atoms or will be composed entirely of violently radioactive matter or will be devoid of stars or will contain only stars of a kind that would burn out before evolution could get started on their planets.

21

We suppose, however, that there are so *many* actual cosmoi that it is statistically unsurprising that there are a few of them that are possible abodes for life and in fact that it is statistically unsurprising that there are a few that actually contain life. The total number of cosmoi needed to render unsurprising the existence of even a few cosmoi that were suitable abodes for life would be enormous: perhaps comparable to the number of elementary particles in "our" cosmos, perhaps vastly greater than that. (It is hard to think of a reason to suppose that the number of actual cosmoi would have to be finite. If the number of cosmoi were infinite, it would certainly not be surprising that some of them were suitable abodes for life.) . . .

The final part of our alternative explanation of apparent cosmic design takes the form of an appeal to an observational selection effect: we cannot observe the cosmoi that are unsuitable for life. We cannot observe them because something restricts the scope of our observations to our own cosmos—the space-time curvature of our cosmos, or the simple fact that everything that is not a part of our cosmos is just too far away for us to see, or some other factor.[3] And any rational beings that there may be anywhere in the macrocosm (so to call the aggregate of all the cosmoi) will be in the same position as we. The members of every rational species anywhere in the macrocosm will be able to observe only the "insides" of their own cosmos. It will look to them as if they inhabited a cosmos that was both carefully designed to be an abode for life (it will have to be suitable for life, since they are in it) and unique (since they can't see any of the others). But this will be appearance rather than reality. It will be the result of the interplay between chance and an observational selection effect.

We can gain some insight into the way this reply to the teleological argument works if we look again at the case in which you would have been killed if you had not drawn the shortest straw from a bundle of 1,048,576 straws. You were (you remember) astonished to find that, lo and behold, you had drawn the shortest straw and were still there to be astonished. I said that the most reasonable thing for you to conclude would be that some unknown benefactor had rigged the drawing in your favor. And this is true provided that you know that your situation is unique. But suppose that you knew that your situation was not unique. Suppose that you knew that you were only one among many millions of people who had been placed in a situation in which they had to draw the shortest straw from a bundle of 1,048,576 or else to be instantly killed. In that case the most reasonable hypothesis would not be that an unknown benefactor had rigged the drawing in your favor. The most reasonable hypothesis would be that you were just lucky.

If someone tosses a coin exactly twenty times, and if there is no other occasion on which someone tosses a coin twenty or more times, it is most improbable that anyone will *ever* toss a coin "heads" twenty times in a row: the chances are 1 in 1,048,576. If millions of people toss a coin twenty times, it is likely that someone will toss "heads" twenty times in a row. If millions of millions of people toss a coin twenty times, it is a virtual certainty that someone will toss "heads" twenty times in a row. The odds are, of course, the same with respect to drawing the shortest straw from a bundle of 1,048,576 straws. If you draw the shortest straw from a bundle of that size, and if you know that millions of millions of other people have been drawing straws from a bundle of that size, you should reason as follows: "It was all but inevitable that a fair number of people would draw the shortest straw. Luckily for me, I happened to be one of that number." But if you draw the shortest straw and know that you were the only one engaged in such a drawing, you cannot reason this way, for you will know that it was *not* all but inevitable that a fair number of people would draw the shortest straw; on the contrary, you will know that it was all but inevitable that *no one* would draw the shortest straw. It is for that reason that you will have to turn to the alternative hypothesis that someone has rigged the drawing in your favor.

Now given our everyday knowledge of the world, it would never be reasonable for one to believe that millions of millions of other people were in circumstances that almost exactly duplicated one's own, and this would be true with a vengeance if one's circumstances were as bizarre as those laid out in the "straw-drawing" story. But suppose that the conditions of human life were very different from what they actually are. Suppose that you were in the circumstances of the hero of the straw drawing story and that *for all you knew* there were millions of millions of people in the same circumstances. Suppose that, as far as your knowledge went, the following two hypotheses were about equally probable.

• This is the only drawing, and someone has rigged it in my favor.
• This is only one among millions of millions of such drawings, in some of which the short straw is drawn.

What could you say then? Only this: that you didn't know whether you had an unobserved benefactor or whether you were "surrounded" by millions of millions of such drawings.

This, I believe, is exactly analogous to our situation with respect to the fine-tuning of the cosmos. As far as our present knowledge goes (aside from any divine revelation that certain individuals or groups may be privy to) we have to regard the following two hypotheses as equally probable:

• This is the only cosmos, and some rational being has (or rational beings have) fine-tuned it in such a way that it is a suitable abode for life.

- This is only one among a vast number of cosmoi, some few of which are suitable abodes for life.

We do not know whether the apparently purposive fine-tuning of the cosmos is reality or mere appearance, a product of chance and an observational selection effect.

Notes

1   These examples are entirely made up. They are meant only to give the reader a "feel" for the sensitivity of the existence of life to changes in the actual values of certain numbers, according to modern physics and cosmology. The reader who is interested in some real information on this topic should consult John Leslie's splendid book *Universes* (London and New York: Routledge, 1989).

2   The importance of this principle in discussions of the implications of the fine-tuning of the cosmos has been pointed out by John Leslie in *Universes* and other publications. Leslie calls the principle the "Merchant's Thumb" principle, on the basis of the following story. A merchant, displaying an expensive silk robe to a potential buyer, consistently keeps a hole in the robe covered with his left thumb. When he is accused of dishonestly concealing the hole from the buyer, his defenders point our that everyone's left thumb has to be *somewhere*. And so it does, but one can think of a very good explanation for its having been over the hole, and it is therefore wrong to proceed on the assumption that its having been over the hole requires no more explanation than its having been at any other particular place.

3   One possibility would be that, although there are many cosmoi, they exist "one at a time": a cosmos has a finite "lifetime" (the heavens will wear out like a garment, as the Psalmist says), and when it has passed away, another will somehow be born from its remains. And each cosmic "rebirth" has the effect of re-setting the dials.

Miracles and Christian Theism

Jan A. Cover

I. Introduction

Most Christians read their Bibles in a way that makes "believing in miracles" a pretty natural thing to do. Indeed most would regard belief in miracles to be part and parcel of embracing the Christian faith, echoing St. Paul's judgment that the bodily resurrection of Christ is an unnegotiable part of it (1 Cor. 15:17). If his resurrection is not just one more occurrence in the natural order of things, but instead an occurrence *contra natura* — as our Church Fathers would have described an exception to the stable and lawful order of nature — then so too, presumably, is Christ's revival of Lazarus' corpse after four days in the grave, and his turning water into wine at Cana, and his feeding a multitude in the wilderness from a few loaves and fishes. For most Christians, these and many other events recorded in Scripture are genuine miracles, accepted as such with the same readiness as they accept the biblical record to be an account of God's sovereign omnipotence generally and the divinity of Christ in particular.

There's no news in any of that. If the existence of miracles is what one would expect in a world into which God reaches down to make himself known, there seems at first glance little about miracles for the contemporary Christian to fuss over. *Philosophers* are of course free to puzzle over them. But armchair philosophizing aside, what of any consequence arises for the believer in respect to miracles?

Well, Christians aren't alone in the world. While Christians find believing in miracles a pretty natural thing to do, many others will express a good deal more skepticism about miracles. Some have claimed that belief in miracles is *irrational,* or more severely that miracles are *impossible.* And here the believer may well confess to being rather at a loss to explain such an attitude: what exactly is the source of such skeptical doubts about miracles, and what could motivate the claim that "believing in miracles is irrational" or that "miracles are impossible"? No doubt the parties to such doubts and claims as these are not believers. But to many thinking Christians this renders such doubts and claims all the more puzzling. For by their reckoning, miracles look to offer a veritable *argument* for God's existence, or at very least they serve as good evidence for it: miracles (the thinking Christian might say) point to God in just the way that any effect points to its cause.

These are the broader issues of concern to us in this chapter. To get a feel for things, let's consider straight off that last item — the simple idea that since miracles point to God, they serve as good grounds for believing (good evidence) that there is a divine being.

The idea is in a way too simple. Miracles point to God only if *there are* miracles. While the existence of miracles is pretty much what is to be expected by someone believing that ours is a world into which God has reached down to make himself known, the atheist or agnostic — who does not (yet) believe there exists any such God — can scarcely be supposed to share that expectation. So if anything like an "argument from miracles" is legitimately to play a role in Christian evidences (and this is something we have yet to determine), the reasons a believer might offer to the skeptic for judging this or that event to be miraculous oughtn't depend on a *prior commitment* to the existence of God. For such an argument to be successful, it must be possible to determine that something is indeed a miracle without first supposing that God exists. The thinking Christian, then, will know what conditions must be met if one is reasonably to believe that some event is indeed miraculous.[1] But one cannot evaluate the reasonableness of believing that some event is a miracle unless one knows what a miracle *is* — that is, knows what conditions an event must satisfy if it is to count as miraculous. The thinking Christian, then, will know what a miracle is.[2]

Three points about this little exercise we've just conducted: First, it is clearly an exercise in armchair philosophizing, and just as clearly it is the sort of thing we'd better not set aside. If the Christian faith is a reasonable one, then it will satisfy the objective demands of rational inquiry that believers and nonbelievers of intellectual good will and honesty alike strive to meet. Whatever our beliefs, it's no good defending them with bad arguments. This isn't to claim, of course, that some ivory-tower method of purely *a priori* theorizing (thinking hard with our eyes and ears closed) can settle the issue between believers and unbelievers. Nor is it to insist on what is sometimes called an "evidentialist" apologetics — according to which we are rational in believing some bit of the Christian faith only if we are in possession of some other belief or beliefs serving as evidence for them. Historically, thinking Christians have differed in their views about whether such an evidentialist approach is or isn't the best way to go. But *whatever* stance we might choose to take on the role of miracles in supporting the fundamental beliefs of Christianity, miracles are important not simply because they might help us defend the faith. And that is a second point: miracles have found a central place in Christian thought from St. Augustine down to the present day because they figure crucially in the larger story of God's relation to us, his creatures. The thinking Christian will want to understand that story, and to be able intelligently to express the place of miracles within it. Our little exercise above is a first step in that direction. It takes that step by slowing down long enough to distinguish carefully, as Augustine himself did, two central questions — arguably *the* two central questions — about miracles: (A) What are miracles? (that is the metaphysical question) and (B) On what grounds would one be rationally warranted in believing that there are miracles? (that is the epistemological question). Here then is the third point about our little exercise above. It sets for us something of an agenda, a pair of questions that must be added to those bothering many thinking Christians about the skeptical view of miracles generally.

We shan't aim for complete answers to all of these questions (alas there are many others) about the nature and evidential value of miracles, in this chapter. But since miracles are a fundamental part of the Christian faith, and since thinking Christians seek to clarify and defend the rationality of its most fundamental commitments, let's see what progress can be made in addressing some of them. Our ultimate goals are to determine to what extent some strong apologetic strategy — some argument from miracles to the existence of God — is workable, and to defend the rationality of believing in miracles. Along the way, we'll be able to address some important subsidiary questions that both believers and unbelievers are led to ask when thinking about miracles.

II. What Is a Miracle? The Standard Conception

It's a fact about language that words often get used in various ways. The deployment of "miracle" in common usage has come to permit such expressions as "her recovery was a miracle" or "it was a miracle that he wasn't seriously injured." Descriptions of this sort typically highlight the remarkable, unexpected nature of the event. Unbelievers and Christians alike admit that in a universe as complex and complicated as ours, there will arise remarkable and unexpected occurrences: those with welcome consequences may invite this loose description of "miracle" without any implication of religious significance or divine intervention. Where for many believers such usage will underscore the providential character of an event, serving perhaps to confirm or strengthen one's faith, the event in question (the astounding recovery or amazing lack of injury) might still be viewed as admitting of some explanation — however complicated, however elusive — in terms of natural causes. Such welcome but remarkable events, no less than an unexpected tragedy or unfortunate freak of nature, will have their place in the divine economy, an economy that God in his wisdom and power has woven into the fabric of nature itself.

So not all providential events are miracles. Let's stick with what would seem to be a clear case. A man of seeming good health suddenly takes seriously ill. Despite the prayers of his sisters, he soon thereafter ceases breathing, his heart stops, and he dies. He is buried in an earthen grave. Four days later, as the body begins to manifest signs of decay, a religious figure of devoted following arrives at the graveside. He weeps, but then declares with a loud voice, "Lazarus, come forth." The man emerges whole and living from the earthen grave.

Supposing (as believers do) that such an event occurs, what sort of special event is this?

On the *standard conception,* an event is a miracle only if it is contrary to the natural order. To say that an event is "contrary to the natural order" is simply to say that it is an exception to the regular order of natural occurrences. Dead people do not, in the natural course of events, come back to life. In the words of David Hume, the eighteenth-century skeptic and outspoken opponent of miracles, "A miracle is a violation of the laws of nature."[3]

If being a violation of at least one law of nature is necessary for an event's being a miracle, it is not enough. An event is a miracle, one is inclined to say, only if it is caused directly by God. That might prove to be a bit too strong, leaving no room for (say) Peter's healing the lame man (Acts 3:1-9) to count as the performance of a miracle. Let's say that an event is a miracle only if it is *caused by God either directly or through some divine agency,* leaving further details aside. (From such details it may well emerge that another condition will prove to be necessary: perhaps an event is a miracle only if it *serves as a sign to rational creatures that God is acting,* or more weakly only if it has some religious significance. To make our task manageable, we won't include this final condition in our working "definition" of a miracle below. No doubt it's very important.)

So we have at least two conditions that must be met in order for an event to count as a miracle, on the standard conception. To state it carefully:

An event *e* is a miracle only if:

(1) *e* violates at least one law of nature, and
(2) *e* is caused by God either directly or through some divine agency.[4]

III. What Does Reasonable Belief in Miracles Require?

Conditions (1) and (2) serve as our working definition of "miracle," on the standard construal. Now it's obvious that defining something — e.g. "dog," "Santa Claus," "water," "extraterrestrial" — doesn't get the thing (or things) into existence. The skeptic doubts that there *are* any miraculous events: she doubts that there are (or have been) any events satisfying our defining conditions (1) and (2). And believers think otherwise. Suppose, then, that the believer is confronted with (or is otherwise considering, perhaps in the form of historical testimony or an eyewitness report) some event that she takes to be a miracle. From our discussion so far, it is pretty clear that she will need to answer two questions concerning that event: (a) Is the event a violation of a law of nature (i.e., is it what we'll call an *anomalous event*)?[5] and (b) Is the event caused by God? That is, with our standard conception of a miraculous event in hand, a miracle will have to meet the *A*nomalous *E*vent condition (AE) and the *D*ivine *C*ause condition (DC). An event *e* is a miracle only if

(AE) *e* is an anomalous event, and

(DC) *e* is caused by God either directly or through some divine agency.

Now in the introduction to this chapter, we encountered two pressing concerns: the concern of many believers to deploy miracles in the role of a positive argument for the existence of God, and the concern of all thinking Christians to better understand the skeptical attitude of unbelievers. Let's set aside for now the most severe skeptical attitude, according to which miracles are impossible. If miracles are to figure in a strong Christian apologetic, in the form of an "argument from miracles," then the believer must acknowledge that even if the skeptic grants that miracles are *possible,* there may yet be challenges to believing rationally that miracles are *actual.* Here's a little challenge to the aim of giving an argument from miracles, just to get things started: notice that according to the divine cause condition (DC), there can be no miracles unless God exists. As a result, we can imagine one objecting that "there cannot be miracles which are evidence for God's existence, because accepting a description of an event as a miracle commits a man to accept[ing] the existence of God."[6] Our definition itself looks to beg the question against the unbelieving skeptic about miracles.

But is that right? Surely we can define "miracle" in a way that, should any occur, entails the existence of God, without begging the question in favor of theism generally or Christianity in particular. What is at issue between the believer and unbelieving skeptic, presumably, isn't *whether miracles are good evidence for theism or Christianity,* but *whether there is good evidence for miracles* in the first place. And traditionally, it is precisely (AE) — the existence of what we are calling an anomalous event — that is offered *as evidence for (DC)* — the existence of a divine cause. What the above objection teaches us, then, if it teaches us anything, turns out to be a reminder of something we encountered in our little opening exercise: if the believer aims to deploy a strong apologetic strategy, arguing from miracles to the existence of a divine being, then it must be possible for the skeptic to recognize evidence for, and form a reasonable belief about, the truth of (AE) without requiring prior evidence for the truth of (DC). The strong apologetic strategy requires unbiased — one might say "theistically neutral" — grounds for claiming that some event is anomalous.

So what evidential value *can* the believer fairly expect miracles to contribute in the Christian apologetic? The answer to this question, as we can now see, depends on how the Christian confronts a serious challenge from the skeptic. The challenge is twofold, directed at two distinct tasks in the effort to bring miracles into some strong apologetic service. One task is giving reasons for judging that an anomalous event has occurred; another task is showing that such an anomalous event points to God. So (AE) figures in the strong project of justifying Christian religious belief in two ways. For given some candidate-event *e,* one confronts two questions: first, Is (AE) indeed true? and second, Does the truth of (AE) establish the truth of (DC)? More carefully:

(I) Are there (theistically neutral) grounds on which to justify the belief that (AE) is true?

(II) Does the truth of (AE) serve as (theistically neutral) evidence for believing that (DC) is true?

The issue before us is whether the believer is well-placed to deploy miracles as evidence for believing in the existence of God. If the strong apologetic undertaking is to be workable, these central questions must each receive the answer "yes."

IV. Three Objections to Miracles

The stage is now properly set for confronting our two concerns — the concern of many believers to deploy miracles in arguing for the existence of God, and the concern of all thinking Christians to better understand the skeptical attitude of unbelievers. There are three basic objections that skeptics might raise in an attempt to explain why we are not (ever) able to answer "yes" to our two central questions above. The first two argue that we can never expect an affirmative answer to the first question. The latter argues that we cannot get an affirmative answer to the second question. In this section, we'll have a look at the objections themselves. The task of sections V and VI is to evaluate the prospects for a Christian apologetic of miracles in light of them.

(1) The Humean Objection

In his famous essay "Of Miracles,"[7] David Hume argued that it is never reasonable to believe that a miraculous violation of law has occurred. His argument begins with a reminder of how we do in fact seem to justify (to fairly *earn*, so to speak) our belief that something counts as a law of nature: observing that two kinds of objects or events repeatedly and regularly occur together (unsuspended objects and falling, say, or deaths and irreversible decay) counts as very strong evidence that "All Fs are Gs" is a genuine law (of gravity, or of irreversible biological decay).[8] Indeed the constant and repeated co-occurrence of such events amounts to what Hume would call a "proof" of the law. And that seems to be right; for surely we can't discover the laws of nature *a priori*, that is by simply thinking hard with our eyes and ears closed. Rather, we must do so empirically. Observing the uniform and regular behavior of objects and events provides the strongest evidence one could possibly have for judging some generalization of the form "All Fs are Gs" to be a law of nature.

What, then, should the rational person believe if confronted with testimony for an alleged miraculous rising from the dead (say) — an eyewitness report of even the strongest credentials amounting to its own "proof"? Well, we must weigh evidence against evidence, proof against proof. And here the evidence for it being true that all Fs are Gs must inevitably outweigh the evidence for it being true that there is an F that is not a G; for against the testimony of our witness stands the whole host of repeated experiences to the contrary, of regular and constant co-occurrences of Fs and Gs. Since (as Hume puts it) "the wise man always proportions his belief to the evidence," and since the testimonial evidence for a miracle can never outweigh the repeated observational evidence for a law of nature, no evidence will ever allow us rationally to believe a reported violation of law.[9] In short, one is never justified (warranted) in believing that (AE) is true for some event. The answer to our Question (I) is "no." That is Hume's Objection.

(2) The Wrong Laws Objection

But suppose that we can answer the Humean Objection, so that it's still an open question whether one might reasonably believe that a law of nature has been violated. Suppose that a candidate for such a case is in fact offered, i.e., that we have good grounds for believing some distinctive and unexpected event to have occurred. Shall we claim that the anomalous event condition (AE) is true and that some law is violated? Well, even if we are confronted with such evidence that *e* violates some accepted law of nature, the skeptic will encourage us to see that the most reasonable conclusion to draw — or anyway, an equally good conclusion to draw from the evidence — is *not* that a law of nature is violated, but rather that *what we took to be a law turns out not to be a genuine law of nature after all*. Remember: there is no *a priori* method of determining the correct laws of nature. Since the method of all working scientists is an empirical one, it must remain open to the empirical scientist to recognize evidence against proposed laws when it arises. And just as science itself works in part by rejecting supposed laws when the evidence no longer fits them, so the skeptic will argue that this unexpected event — the supposed miracle — is simply good evidence that *we have not understood the relevant laws of nature correctly*. Indeed, if we had properly latched on to the true laws of nature, then we should no longer judge the actual event *e* as contrary to them. *Nothing that actually happens is contrary to the truth.* So if the man really was dead and really did come to life, then surely there is something about the difficult and complex biology of human organisms we have yet to learn. Of course, were someone (the believer, say) *already* disposed to anticipate supernatural intrusions into the natural order — were one already inclined to see remarkable events like *e* as divine interventions — then they would more readily judge events of that remarkable sort to be genuinely anomalous violations of law. But the conditions for judging an event as genuinely anomalous must (recall) be unbiased, theistically neutral. So the skeptic is under no obligation whatever to do otherwise than regard an unexpected, heretofore unobserved event precisely as any empirical scientist would: *e* is at best evidence for the need to reconsider our present understanding of the powers in nature and the laws governing them. Once again, we cannot conclude that (AE) is true; again, the answer to our central Question (I) is "no." That is the Wrong Laws Objection.

(3) *The Non-Miraculous Anomaly Objection*

But suppose that we can adequately address both of these objections, so that the anomalous event condition (AE) *is* acknowledged to be true. That is, suppose we are warranted in believing *e* to be an event that violates a law of nature, and so can answer "yes" to Question (I). From the existence of such an anomalous event, can we infer the existence of a divine cause? Not at all straightaway, we can't. From the truth of (AE) we can infer the truth of (DC) *only if we are sure that every anomalous event must have a divine cause.* But since, for all we know, some events are anomalous precisely because they are radically spontaneous or otherwise uncaused events, there may be anomalous events that are not miracles.[10] Such events would be "non-miraculous anomalies." The skeptical worry here is an important one; for it is not at all clear on what grounds the believer could argue that such non-miraculous anomalies are impossible. An event's lacking a natural cause does not entail its having a supernatural cause. If non-miraculous anomalous events are possible, and if there is no unbiased, theistically neutral reason for saying "it's more likely that *e* has a supernatural cause than that *e* is radically spontaneous (random) or otherwise uncaused," then the evidential value of *e* emerges to be practically nil. A man rose from the dead. So? So it scarcely follows that God did it. We are thus without any good reason for judging the anomalous event to be evidence of the existence and activity of a divine being. (DC) cannot be thereby reckoned true, and the answer to our Question (II) is "no." That is the Non-Miraculous Anomaly Objection.

Here then are three significant challenges to the strong apologetic strategy of offering a positive "argument from miracles" in defense of the Christian faith. In the course of assessing these objections, we shall be able to consider again the nature of miracles (the metaphysical question), and to reevaluate the evidential worth of miracles in justifying Christian religious belief (the epistemological question). Let's begin with the Humean Objection, since it leads us pretty quickly to rethinking the first, metaphysical question — the one about *what miracles are.*

V. The Metaphysical Question:
A Response to Hume and a New Conception of Miracles

A. *A Response to Hume's Objection*

Recall again Hume's Objection. Miracles, if any there be, are violations of at least one law of nature — violations of at least one generalization about the course of events that we've expressed in the form "All Fs are Gs." The evidence we have for any law of nature, consisting in our empirical observation of the repeated and regular occurrence of Fs followed by Gs, amounts to what Hume calls a "proof" of the law. What then of someone's claim that (say) a person rose from the dead? Says Hume, we weigh evidence against evidence, proof against proof. And over against this testimony of our witness that there is some F that is not a G, stands all the weight of repeated experiences to the contrary, of that very evidence of regular and constant concurrence of Fs with Gs which proves our law that all Fs are Gs. Since the evidence of a violation will never be strong enough to outweigh the evidence for the law, and since the rational person is obliged to judge on the side of the greatest evidence, one is never justified in believing that the anomalous event *e* occurred: we are never in a position to assert that (AE) is true.

There are two things to point out about Hume's challenge, two important weaknesses. Let's consider these, approached here in the form of two objections: doing so will lead us readily into a more potent sort of Humean challenge — one providing us with a chance to think more clearly about the nature of miracles and laws.

First, Hume's Objection supposes that the only evidence one might have for a miracle is the testimony of someone's claim to direct observation. But there may be — indeed, typically will be — evidence of another, *indirect* sort; and such indirect evidence may well be strong enough to warrant our supposing the existence of a genuinely anomalous event as its best explanation. Let's consider a simple, more familiar example first. Imagine that a good friend and family man, Jones (as philosophers inevitably call him), is found lying dead on his bedroom floor. Here is a surprising event that we ache to have explained. Suppose someone tells us and the authorities that they saw Jones commit suicide. No detective worth his salt (nor you or I, for that matter) would stop with evidence of that sort, and call it a day. After all, the witness might be lying, or deluded, or have poor eyesight. Rather, the detective will seek out indirect evidence — Jones's own fingerprints on a gun lying nearby, a suicide note on the table, a host of antidepressant drugs in the medicine cabinet, and so on. Where the direct testimony of our witness might prove insufficient, further indirect evidence might prove overwhelming: indeed, the hypothesis that Jones committed suicide might well explain all the other, indirect evidence much better than any alternative hypothesis (murder in a bungled robbery attempt, say).

Now think about the case of a purported (i.e., supposed) miracle. Here too, quite apart from the direct testimony of a witness, there may well be many other such bits of indirect evidence that are best explained by the hypothesis that an anomalous event did indeed occur, and which might well be far stronger than the direct evidence. Thus, in addition to direct testimony for the claim that Christ arose ("I saw him in the garden and he spoke to me!") would be the empty tomb itself and the burial clothes, the despondency of the Christ's followers suddenly giving way to great cheer and a deep faith, and so on. Surely these things need explaining; and it may emerge that such bits of indirect evidence are much better explained by Christ's actual resurrection than by any competing hypothesis, and that such evidence is even stronger than the testimony of our witness. Hume's objection is one about the weight of evidence, and he has said nothing whatsoever about adding the weight of indirect evidence for a genuinely anomalous event.

Second, Hume's Objection appears on reflection to be much too strong. The evidence of past experience for some regularity of nature (all Fs are Gs) will, on his account, always be weightier than new contrary evidence for a violation. But if that were true as a general principle, it would seem to show that it is *never* rational to believe — on the basis of direct testimony or any other evidence — that an event which never occurred before has in fact occurred. But this, surely, is not at all plausible as a general principle. Indeed, were Hume's Objection against miracles taken seriously, it's partner objection — the Wrong Laws Objection — could never even arise: one could *never* have good reasons for saying (as scientists clearly sometimes must) that supposed scientific laws need to be revised on the basis of new, contrary evidence. Hume seems to think that the invariable experience of past occurrences must always win out, and that one could never have good grounds to revise laws in the way scientists actually do. And that, clearly, is much too strong. Hume has vastly overestimated the weight of past experience.

B. A More Potent Humean Objection

Recall from our introduction to this chapter a concern of many thinking Christians to understand the most severe form of skepticism about miracles, namely that they are impossible. One might understand Hume's stance on miracles to express exactly this form of severe skepticism. While this is perhaps not the most charitable way of reading Hume's own claims, an extreme skepticism is at least *beneath the surface* of what he says about miracles and their relation to laws of nature. For on reflection, it looks as if Hume has understood miracles and laws in a way that would render miracles impossible. Miracles, on the standard conception, are violations of at least one law of nature. But laws of nature are simply true statements of the uniform and regular behavior of natural objects and events. Were there no such uniform and regular behavior of the natural objects and events, we should have no grounds for calling those statements *laws* at all. Hence, our grounds for calling them laws are precisely our grounds for denying any event as miraculous.

Here then arises the more severe (we might still reckon it Humean) challenge to miracles: given the standard definition that miracles violate a law of nature, there are no miracles, *because they are impossible*. Let's state this argument more explicitly, as follows:

> We discover genuine laws of nature by discovering the orderly, regular behavior of natural objects, like dead bodies irreversibly decaying, and heavy bodies falling, and so on. It is a law of nature that (say) all metals are conductors of electricity, that all bodies on which no net forces are acting remain at rest or move at uniform velocity in a straight line,

and so on. In short, a law of nature is what is called a *true universal generalization,* of the form "All Fs are Gs" or "All so-and-sos do such-and-such." This is the standard account of a law of nature. Hence, anything that is a genuine law of nature has *no exceptions,* no counterinstances: if it really *is* a law of nature that all Fs are Gs, then there cannot be an F that is not a G. But a miracle is by definition a violation of a law of nature. Thus: if (i) nothing could be a law of nature unless it is unviolated, and (ii) no event could be a miracle unless it violates a law of nature, then no event could be a miracle. Miracles are impossible.[11]

That's a pretty scary argument. What should the thinking Christian make of it?

C. Miracles as Non-Violations of Law

Given the believer's commitment to miracles, it may be quite natural to respond as follows: "I smell a trick. It's all just a matter of definition, of how miracles are defined in relation to laws. If this really shows that miracles aren't possible, well, alright, so there are no 'miracles.' But it doesn't show that Christ didn't raise Lazarus from the dead, or that he didn't walk on the water, or that he didn't multiply the loaves and fishes. Call them what you want: no abstract philosophical argument like this can show that he couldn't raise Lazarus or walk on water, and that's all I need."

But hold on now: that's *not* all the believer needs. Not, at least, if the believer aims to deploy such remarkable events as these to any apologetic advantage — strong or otherwise — as evidence for the existence of God or the divinity of Christ. Whatever apologetic role we might want miracles to play, this response threatens to cut it off, by conceding that such events have no special status in relation to natural laws. If the believer simply gives up on insisting that miracles have some genuinely *anomalous status* in relation to laws of nature, then it becomes altogether unclear what there is about such events that points to something *outside* the natural order.[12] (Mere *rarity* won't do it.) And if miracles point to nothing outside the natural order, one can scarcely hope to use them to apologetic advantage. No: the believer needs to recognize in such events something distinctive in their relation to the natural course of law-governed events, something more than the quick response just offered acknowledges.

Let's take the severe skeptical argument seriously, as Christian philosophers universally have. If miracles are actual, as believers claim, then they *are* possible. Given the above argument for their impossibility, then, the available options are pretty clear, aren't they? There are two options, corresponding to the two main premises of the argument above — that (i) nothing could be a law of nature unless it is unviolated, and that (ii) no event could be a miracle unless it violates a law of nature. Since it is an unnegotiable part of the Christian faith that miracles are possible (since actual), the believer must deny one of these two premises. That is, the believer must either claim that laws of nature can be violated, or else claim that miracles are not violations of the laws of nature but are in some other way anomalous.

D. Salvaging the Possibility of Miracles

There is plenty to be learned from thinking about the second of these options — lots of fun metaphysics, if you want to think of it that way (or even if you don't), but more importantly, plenty to help us advance our thinking about the apologetic role of miracles. Let's see what can be said in reply to this severe skeptical argument against the possibility of miracles by taking the second route. Our task is to determine whether we can arrive at a coherent story about miracles that is different from the standard conception of them as violations of laws. Let's do it in two steps.

(i) An Assessment of the Problem

We can best start by asking how we got into this mess. (Let's hear nothing of it being the author's fault. The mess is an old and important one, and we are going to get out of it.) We got into the mess by adopting the standard picture of miracles, as violations of laws of nature. And where did that come from? Well, it came from two fundamental beliefs, shared by many theists and nontheists alike, which motivate the picture we've been working with up till now:

(a) Miracles, if any there be, are fundamentally divine interventions into the causal order of nature; and
(b) The concept of causality is fundamentally a concept of *lawlike regularity* among events.

Those might have seemed innocuous enough. Especially the first: the believer, surely, will be happy enough with (a) — with the idea that miracles are brought about by God in a supernatural way, from outside of nature. The challenge (the mess) confronting believers who also accept (b) is to explain the idea that something could be a law of nature despite having a miraculous violation: and as the above argument suggests, it's far from clear how a law could be a true statement of the form "All Fs are Gs" if there are cases of an F that *isn't* a G. We're trying to avoid that bugaboo. And it is important to see that we can. It is important to see that accepting (a) doesn't in any way *require* one to accept (b).

(ii) Accounting for Miracles Without (b)

On the Humean conception, we are led to think of causality in terms of lawlike regularity, and to think of miracles as *violations* of such laws. Is there some other way of thinking about causality, laws, and miracles that would avoid the challenge confronting us? There is. Consider first the idea of miraculous intervention itself. When we speak of God's miraculous activity in the natural order, we can, surely, understand such divine intervention not simply in terms of laws themselves as descriptions of the (otherwise) regular course of nature, but rather in terms of God's having the power *to bring about occurrences that cannot be caused by the natural forces operative in the created objects* left to themselves. That is to say — now following two Christian philosophers of a bygone age, St. Thomas Aquinas and G. W. Leibniz — that miracles are occurrences which are *beyond the natural power of any created thing to cause or bring about:* the natural forces operative in a human body dead for four days cannot cause that body to rise anew in living health. What God can cause is something the powers operative in the body itself *cannot* cause. And that is a somewhat different picture of causality and laws — a non-Humean picture. How so, exactly? Well, according to the Humean idea (b), causality is fundamentally a concept of lawfulness, and laws are simply descriptions of the regular behavior of objects and events. But on this alternative picture, causality is fundamentally a concept about the causal powers in things; and laws, accordingly, are not mere descriptions of regularities, but instead expressions of what the objects in nature are capable of producing in virtue of the powers they possess.

And so notice, then, how miracles are related to laws on this new, alternative picture. Miracles are not "violations" of the laws of nature at all. The laws of nature, recall, describe what objects in nature are capable of producing in light of the powers that they have. And miracles, recall, are occurrences that are beyond the natural power of any created thing to cause or bring about. Thus, miraculous events — those events not caused by the operation of natural powers in created objects — do nothing to threaten the truth of natural laws about natural causes. The idea of some event rendering a claim of the form "All Fs are Gs" false while that claim remains a law was the difficulty with accepting (b) above, the bugaboo we aimed to avoid. We can now see that believing in events having supernatural causes needn't saddle one with believing that there are *false laws of nature,* laws having exceptions. Miracles are so to speak "gaps" in nature, occurrences having causes about which laws of nature are simply silent. The laws are true, but simply don't speak to events caused by divine intervention. (Laws of nature are, after all, laws *of nature,* not supernature. As our Church Fathers might have expressed it, miracles can be *supra natura* without being *contra natura.*) In short, then, miracles are anomalous — non-nomological, non-lawlike — not because they violate laws of nature, but rather because the laws of nature don't speak to their causes at all.

So much for our rescue of the possibility of miracles. We've secured here a new picture of miracles, a better picture: we've secured it by getting a better picture of laws of nature and the relation of miracles to them. Our new picture, of miracles as anomalous events not violating laws of nature, pulls the teeth from any severe skeptical argument against the very possibility of miracles.

Thus we can, at last, judge the first of our three objections to miracles — the broadly Humean misgiving(s) — to be safely behind us. But what about the Wrong Laws Objection to miracles, and the Non-Miraculous Anomaly Objection? These are still on board. Let's consider them now, in the context of facing head-on our main question yet outstanding: What evidential role can believers fairly expect miracles to play in a Christian apologetic?

VI. The Epistemological Question: Miracles and Evidence

One shouldn't, I think — and now grant me, as you just have, the luxury of speaking in the first person — expect too much.[13] Recall again (from the introduction) that many Christians will confess to being perplexed when confronting someone who is utterly skeptical about miracles. Don't miracles point to God in the way any effect points to its cause? True enough, if miracles are impossible, then there is no hope of engaging such an argumentative strategy. But that severe skepticism is well behind us. Isn't there a positive "argument from miracles" to the existence of God, what we've called a strong apologetic strategy for showing someone that God exists? Thus we ended our introduction with this: "Our ultimate goals are to determine to what extent some strong apologetic strategy — some argument from miracles to the existence of God — is workable, and to defend the rationality of believing in miracles." What I should like to emphasize in these final sections is that those are indeed *two* goals, and that the success of defending a rational belief in miracles is *in no way* dependent upon the success of giving "an argument from miracles to the existence of God." The remaining objections to miracles — the Wrong Laws Objection and the Non-Miraculous Anomaly Objection — provide a good context in which to clarify these points. I shall recommend that while these objections may *have some force* against a strong apologetic of miracles, they have *little or no force* against a more moderate apologetic strategy, and that they *count not at all* against the rationality of believing in miracles. Let's gird up our loins one last time, and confront these objections.

A. Miracles: Possibility vs. Actuality

Miracles are not impossible. There is nothing incoherent about them, as the severe Humean skeptic might have it. But a *coherent* story about the world needn't be a *true* story: wide is the gate to coherence, and narrow the way to truth. Now according to the Wrong Laws Objection, any candidate *e* for an anomalous event — one which the laws of nature together with prior natural events cannot in any way explain — is at best evidence that we've gotten the laws of nature wrong. And according to the Non-Miraculous Anomaly Objection, even if that remarkable event *is* anomalous and falls outside the scope of the true laws of nature, it points to God only if every anomaly must have a divine cause (or, put another way, only if *non-miraculous* anomalies are impossible). Both of these objections, then, are directed squarely against the truth of the miracle claims of theism generally and Christianity in particular. How strong are these objections?

If the Humean Objection emerges as weak overall, the same cannot quite be said of these remaining objections. Recall again our working "definition" of a miracle: *e* is a miracle only if

(AE) *e* is an anomalous event, and
(DC) *e* is caused by God either directly or through some divine agency.

And recall again our two central questions: given some remarkable event *e*,

(I) Are there (theistically neutral) grounds on which to justify the belief that (AE) is true?
(II) Does the truth of (AE) serve as (theistically neutral) evidence for believing that (DC) is true?

The strong apologetic, aiming to argue from miracles to the existence of God, requires that each of these central questions receive the answer "yes." Confronting this apologetic is the skeptic who claims that, while miracles are possible, they are not actual — that belief in miracles is coherent but not true. Such a skeptic will think about miracles, perhaps, in much the way you and I are likely to think about (for example) UFOs and extraterrestrials. (The analogy isn't perfect, but few analogies are: maybe it'll help.) If someone aimed to offer a sort of "argument" for extraterrestrials — an argument from the reality of UFOs, say — then you and I, as fair-minded skeptics, can grant that such creatures are *possible* while nevertheless persisting in the rational belief that extraterrestrial creatures are *not actual*. Far from shrinking in the face of "evidence from UFOs," we have in place a much larger, overarching view of the world according to which such "evidence" from UFOs is really no evidence at all: however remarkable and curious those lights in the sky may be, we will persist in the belief that there is available some alternative, if perhaps complex, hypothesis that can more plausibly explain that phenomena. Of course if one were already disposed to believe in the existence of extraterrestrials, then one would more quickly judge the remarkable and curious events to involve some object from another planet. But that's scarcely a neutral stance, and the believer in extraterrestrials cannot expect you and I to share beliefs of that sort. Moreover, even if (for whatever reasons) we came to believe that such curious events *did* involve some object from outside our atmosphere, this alone does not show that there are sentient and intelligent creatures visiting us on earth aboard them. It's not at all easy to *show* that there are extraterrestrials.

Now our skeptic about miracles, while granting the *possibility* of genuinely anomalous events, may fairly persist in a view of the physical world according to which they are *not actual*. Among nonbelieving skeptics about miracles, it is very common to have in place a larger, overarching view of the world according to which each event that occurs is caused by prior events, in accordance with the laws of nature. Let's call this prevalent worldview *Naturalism*. And consider then some remarkable and unexpected event *e*. The naturalist, far from shrinking in the face of "evidence from remarkable and unexpected events," will presumably recommend what many see as the hallmark of a proper scientific methodology — expanding and revising our account of nature and the laws governing occurrences within it, in the face of new and contrary observations. Should some remarkable event *e* appear to have no explanation in terms of prior events and causal laws, the naturalist will encourage us to remember that it is in precisely this way that currently formulated *laws of science* are shown not yet properly to capture the genuine *laws of nature*. Putative evidence is always evaluated relative to some prior beliefs or worldview. So whatever "evidence from remarkable events" we might offer for *e* being an event having no cause in prior natural events, the naturalist skeptic will surely regard it as evidence that we have misunderstood the laws of nature. When regarded in this way, such an event *counts not at all* as evidence for the existence of genuine anomalies. Of course, if one were already disposed to believe in divine interventions into the natural causal order, one would more quickly judge *e* to be genuinely anomalous. But that's scarcely a neutral stance, and the believer in miracles can hardly expect the skeptic to share those beliefs. No remarkable event *all by itself* counts as unbiased, theistically neutral evidence for being genuinely anomalous. Thus the Wrong Laws Objection is always available to the skeptic. Given the demand for neutral evidence, the answer to our central question (I) looks to be "no."

Moreover, even if the skeptic were, for whatever reasons, to become convinced that some remarkable event was not caused by prior *natural* events, he might still insist that whatever *is* caused to occur is caused *by prior natural events*. That is, such a skeptic will be prepared to admit two options: either an event is caused or uncaused. If it is caused, its cause is *natural*. If it is uncaused, well then, of course, nothing caused it: the event is a radically spontaneous and inexplicable event. And here again, no such inexplicable event all by itself counts as unbiased, theistically neutral evidence for its having a divine cause. Thus our skeptic can fairly and rationally claim that the anomalous event is not miraculous: the Non-Miraculous Anomaly Objection is always available to the skeptic. So the answer to our central question (II) looks to be "no."

40

In short, there is no *forcing* one to accept the occurrence of miracles.

But of course, there is no *forcing* anyone to believe *anything*. The real question is what it is most reasonable to believe. While the Wrong Laws and the Non-Miraculous Anomaly objections are always at least *available* as options one might take, they may not always be the most *reasonable*, the most rational options to take. Let's pause briefly to reflect on what might be said against these options being the most reasonable options to take. Doing so will lead us to some final thoughts, in the direction of a more moderate apologetic strategy and the rationality of believing in miracles.

B. The Wrong Laws Objection

How reasonable the Wrong Laws Objection proves to be, in particular cases, will depend upon lots of details. Different cases of supposed anomalies will bring with them different details. Avoiding too many details, let's suppose that we grant the familiar demand for theistically neutral evidence (although soon, I shall urge that we needn't grant it). Even granting this demand, there may be cases of supposed anomalies where our remarkable event *e* turns out — after the most serious and persistent efforts to reformulate our scientific laws — stubbornly to resist any naturalistic causal explanation whatever. In such a case, we might think that the unity of science is better preserved by admitting that *e* is truly an anomaly than by working toward a radical revamping of scientific laws.

Suppose that a small group of unbelieving biologists and forensic scientists, all committed to Naturalism, were confronted with what, by any examination of the relevant facts, seems to be the raising of a man from the dead after four days in the grave. The accepted and successful laws of natural science cannot explain such an occurrence, and no diligent efforts to uncover new laws, or ingenious efforts to revamp existing ones, succeed in explaining the occurrence. Our scientists might persist in their commitment to Naturalism. If so, they can only judge their larger belief-system to be in pretty serious disarray. The truth about biology, whatever it is, must be reckoned quite different from what existing biological science tells us — a strained admission in light of the ability of existing science to explain all relevant biological phenomena *except* the man's rising. Moreover they are yet without any explanation whatsoever about the apparent anomaly. Now remaining in this state of "cognitive vertigo" is, surely, an option. And yet, in light of the evidence, one cannot help but think that our scientists' degree of (well-earned) confidence in the laws of science ought to be *higher* than their confidence in Naturalism.[14] They do of course *believe* that every event must be causally explainable in terms of prior natural events and the laws of nature; but — here is the *key* question — is it reasonable to continue believing this, in the face of an event that seems resistant to explanation by biological laws, given the otherwise great success of these laws?

41

That question is not easily answered. For our thoroughgoing naturalists, the anomaly has shaken their confidence in the established laws of science, but not their belief that every event has natural cause. (More than once, they will remind us, the history of science has witnessed such upheavals: in all such cases, the community of scientists, far from giving up their Naturalism, retrenched their efforts to work out a more adequate account of the world consistent with it.) Yet to many, it would — all things considered — seem far more reasonable to retain the existing canons of biology, and grant the following inference to the best explanation: the phenomenon is genuinely anomalous, and Naturalism is false.

One can't help but wish for some clearer way of deciding, on purely neutral grounds, when one stance is more reasonable than another. Which of the two stances, prior to any other considerations or details, is *in its own right* objectively more reasonable, or is more likely to be true — the idea of Naturalism, or the idea of events having no natural causes? I confess to thinking that there is no good answer to this question, no "right" answer that anyone who is rational would be obliged to accept.

C. The Non-Miraculous Anomaly Objection

Something similar arises in connection with the Non-Miraculous Anomaly Objection. Here, as with the Wrong Laws Objection, the believer might at least make progress without arriving at anything like a proof; and then, despite the progress, one may still confront residual worries about what is most reasonable to believe. Let's see why.

Suppose it were granted that some remarkable event *e* is genuinely anomalous. Such an anomalous event points to God (i.e., is genuinely miraculous) only if it has a divine cause. But as the Non-Miraculous Anomaly Objection is keen to remind us, we can prove that our anomalous event *e* has a divine cause only if we can give some proof against its having some other cause or indeed *no cause at all*. And this simply cannot be proven. The event could be anomalous precisely because it is a spontaneous, uncaused event. In other words, there is no direct, deductive proof of the divine cause condition (DC) from the anomalous event premise (AE). That's the challenge against being able to answer "yes" to our central question (II).

But perhaps all is not immediately lost here. The objection seems to require that the only available argumentative route to a conclusion — the only way of supporting some claim as reasonable to believe — is a deductive one, in the form of a genuine proof. Surely this is too strong. Even if there is *no deductive route* from (DC) to (AE), it hardly follows that there is *no route whatever* from (DC) to (AE) — no way at all in which an anomaly can serve as rational grounds or good evidence for believing that it has a divine cause. Indeed, much of legal and scientific reasoning takes the form of a (nondeductive) "inference to the best explanation." Long ago, astronomers came to realize that the orbit of Uranus exhibited unexpected deviations from their best calculations of what it should be. The best explanation — the only reasonable explanation, given everything else that was known about the solar system — was that there must exist a gravitational force exerted by some theretofore unknown (and as yet undiscovered) heavenly body, affecting the orbit of Uranus. That reasonable belief led astronomers to search for, and eventually discover, the planet we call Neptune. Or consider a miniature "legal" case — of two hopelessly failing students whose final exam papers are remarkably high-score 'A's. If, on inspection, both exams are exactly alike (even down to the few mistakes), then we can reasonably believe that our students have cheated: given the evidence, that is far and away the best explanation, the best inference to make. Now in both of these cases, as in a vast range of others like them, while we lack anything like a deductive proof, we nevertheless have very strong evidence grounding our inference to what best explains it. It is of course *possible* that (unlike all other planets) there is no gravitational explanation for the orbit of Uranus, or that the failing students suddenly knew the course material remarkably well and by chance inexplicably wrote the same things on their papers. But surely it is far and away more reasonable, given the evidence, to believe here that some other gravitational body exists, and that the students have cheated.

In the same way, while a positive "argument from miracles" may not be available to *prove* the existence of God, it may nevertheless be *more reasonable* to claim that e has a divine cause than to claim that e is spontaneous, inexplicable, uncaused. The occurrence of some remarkable event that is inexplicable in terms of past events and the laws of nature is perhaps good evidence that it was caused by something outside nature: perhaps the best explanation is that e is caused by God. Indeed many people would claim that the idea of an event being altogether *uncaused* (having no causal explanation whatsoever) is simply unreasonable.

That's fair enough. But is it right? How would one show, or plausibly defend, this view that the idea of an uncaused event is unreasonable? Indeed, how would one go about showing or defending even the weaker claim — that uncaused events are less reasonable than divinely caused events? While many of us do in fact find ourselves quite naturally believing this weaker claim, the skeptic might find himself quite naturally believing otherwise: to the skeptic, it seems more reasonable to accept the existence of an uncaused event than to accept the existence of an invisible divine cause. Which view, *in its own right,* all on its own, is objectively more rational, more likely to be true? Once again, I confess to thinking that there is no good answer to this question, no "right" answer that anyone who is rational would be obliged to accept.

Yet perhaps the challenge from Non-Miraculous Anomalies isn't so dim as all that. As before, different cases bring with them different details. Mightn't there be cases presenting us with *evidence,* quite beyond the anomalous event itself, for their having a divine cause? You can have evidence for my causing some occurrence if you see me bring it about. That sort of evidence won't be available in the case of an invisible God. But suppose that you know me and my inner character well — well enough to know that if you call me on the phone and ask that I send you $50, then you will receive the money from me. Should you ask me for money, receiving it is evidence that I sent it. Had you not asked, you almost certainly wouldn't have found an envelope with money taped to your front door: surely the best explanation for the money's appearing on your door is that I put it there. Elijah knew the inner character of the God of Abraham and Isaac well enough: he asked God to consume the bullock and stones and wood and water on Mt. Carmel, and fire came down from a cloudless sky to consume the altar. That, surely, is evidence of God's causing the fire. In this case at least, isn't it more reasonable to suppose that fire from a cloudless sky was caused by God, and less reasonable to suppose it was uncaused?

It sure seems so. The skeptic might, alas, wonder if the Elijah story is even true, and add that he himself has no evidence that any miracle like the one described in the case of Elijah has actually occurred. For better or worse, we have rather fewer examples of candidate miracles, nowadays, earning a spot in the broadcasts of reputable evening newscasts, to present to our skeptic. It *is* worth remembering that a strong apologetic of miracles, aiming to provide the skeptic with an "argument from miracles" to the existence of God, needs an event to offer up for discussion that the skeptic will accept as a candidate.[15] As we've said, there is no forcing one to believe in miracles. But our latest effort has been in the direction of cutting a path that could in principle be followed in arguing from the occurrence of a genuine anomaly to the existence of a divine cause. Whether our skeptic is well enough on board to grant the occurrence of a genuine anomaly will depend on the particular case at issue, and how well the Wrong Laws Objection can be met in that particular case. If, in light of our previous reflections, it can in that case be met, then our latest effort has shown that such a case might also point to a divine cause, even if the route to this conclusion is something weaker than a deductive proof — something rather more like an inference to the best explanation.

VII. Belief in Miracles and a Moderate Apologetic Strategy

So far as I can see, apologetics is about defending the rationality of the Christian faith, not *proving* it. There is probably no convincing proof for Naturalism, but it is not thereby irrational to believe that Naturalism is true. There is probably no argument for theism that every rational person must accept, but theism isn't thereby irrational to believe. Suppose the challenges from Wrong Laws and Non-Miraculous Anomalies cast some doubt on our confidence that questions (I) and (II) can readily be answered affirmatively. This result counts at most against what we have been calling the strong apologetic undertaking, of proving the existence of God by appeal to miracles: it tells not at all against the rationality of believing in miracles, nor against their deployment in a more moderate apologetic strategy. Let me close with some brief reflections on those issues.

My purpose is to address the two residual worries most recently nipping our heels — about the difficulty of judging one view to be objectively more reasonable or likely than another, and about the demand for theistically neutral evidence. Neither of these, on reflection, are genuine worries at all.

A. The Rationality of Believing in Miracles

The believer oughtn't shoulder the mistaken idea that the rationality of the Christian faith stands or falls with the success or failure of positive arguments proving the existence of God. Likewise, the Christian would be equally mistaken to suppose that the rationality of believing in miracles stands or falls with the success or failure of an argument showing that some event is indeed anomalous and has a divine cause. Let's think about the first of these, first. If the central apologetic task is one of defending the rationality of the Christian faith, then the thinking Christian is concerned with answering the charge that believing in God is somehow illegitimate — that in light of the evidence, accepting theism is in one way or another irrational, or less than fully rational. But what evidence *is* that, and what exactly makes believing theism in light of it irrational or unreasonable? The skeptic will say that theistic belief is unreasonable because it simply isn't very credible, isn't very likely to be true, given other accepted beliefs. But surely a lot rides on (i) what those other beliefs *are,* and (ii) how likely or reasonable *they* are said to be. Concerning (ii), I've already spilled the beans: few if any "deep" beliefs wear an obvious and objective degree of likelihood or reasonableness marked plainly on their sleeves. (Which is objectively more likely to be true — that time had a beginning, or that there is no beginning to time? Which, all on its own, is objectively more likely to be true — that in our heavenly abode we are souls or spirits, or that we have physical (if incorruptible) bodies? None of these wears an obvious and objective likelihood on its sleeve. None of these, *all on its own,* is objectively more reasonable, more likely.) This brings us straight to (i): What *are* these other beliefs, on the basis of which theism is judged to be not very likely true, not very credible? No doubt theism is not very likely, when judged from the basis of Naturalism. But the believer is scarcely obliged to judge the credibility of theism against the "evidence" of Naturalism. (No doubt the claim "Time had a beginning" is not very likely, when judged from the view that every event must be caused by a temporally earlier event. But one needn't believe that latter causal hypothesis: it isn't all on its own more objectively likely, something that anyone who is rational is obliged to accept.)

Is the believer rational in accepting theism? Well, the reasonableness or likelihood one associates with that belief will depend on the reasonableness or likelihood associated with other of his or her beliefs. Among these beliefs may be — *why not?* — the deliverances of religious experience, and/or the fine-tuning version of the teleological argument (say), and/or an acquired faith via general revelation, and/or the work of the Holy

Spirit. If the believer is in possession of no good reason for doubting the deliverances of one or another of these sources of belief, then their likelihood for that person will be sufficiently high to count for them as evidence for believing in theism.

Now return to miracles. The skeptic may insist that belief in miracles is unreasonable simply because it isn't very credible, isn't very likely to be true, given other beliefs about the world. As before, a lot rides on (i) what those "other beliefs about the world" *are,* and (ii) how likely or reasonable *they* are said to be. Concerning (ii), there is no obvious and objective degree of likelihood or reasonableness marked plainly on the sleeves of the naturalist claim that laws of nature have no "gaps," or that nature encounters no outside intervention. The likelihood that there are sometimes genuinely anomalous events, events having no cause in some prior natural event, will for the believer be judged on the basis of other beliefs she has, and the likelihood she attaches to them. Among these other beliefs may be — why not? — the deliverances of religious experience, and/or arguments for the existence of God, and/or an acquired faith via general revelation, and/or the work of the Holy Spirit. If the believer is in possession of good reasons for accepting (no outweighing reasons for rejecting) the deliverances of one or another of these sources of belief, then the likelihood of those beliefs, for that person, may be sufficiently high to count as good grounds for reckoning the belief in genuine anomalies to be very reasonable. Indeed, the contents of these other beliefs may be such as to invite the *expectation* of divine intervention. True enough: if what is counted as good grounds for believing some claim is to be judged on the basis of the likelihood or reasonableness of other, prior beliefs, then an unbeliever — sharing no such beliefs as those deliverances of religious experience and natural theology and faith might provide — may well lack sufficient grounds for believing in miracles. But the believer needn't be in that position. And the believer who isn't in that position, who aims to defend the rationality of believing in miracles, needn't presume the posture of "adopting" it by obliging the familiar demand for "theistically neutral evidence."

B. The Moderate Apologetic

These latest reflections suggest how in broad outlines one might conceive the relevance of miracles to a more attenuated, moderate Christian apologetic. The evidential contribution of miracles, rather than figuring at the front end (the beginning) of an effort to demonstrate the existence of a divine being, will instead figure in the middle of an effort to establish the warrant for other central religious beliefs — the Christian plan of salvation generally, say, or the divinity of Christ in particular. At the front end will be located those of one's beliefs already enjoying sufficiently high likelihood, thanks to the arguments of natural theology or to religious experience or general revelation or the work of the Holy Spirit. Here the believer may have sufficient (and let's call it what it is — *theistic*) evidential grounds not simply for judging miracles to be possible, but to be expected from a Creator having those attributes such beliefs give reason to believe he has. And since Hume's argument against testimony is no longer in place, the believer may safely enlist the evidence of historical testimony as well. The route taken by this moderate apologetic is thus from theistic belief (supplemented by historical testimony or not), to rational belief in miracles, to belief in the authority and truth of claims to which miracles are a confirming witness. The raising of Lazarus, the walking on water, the multiplication of loaves and fishes — all alike serve as confirming evidence that Jesus of Nazareth is who he said he is, namely the divine Son of God.[16]

Many further questions remain, about the stronger positive argument from miracles and the moderate apologetic strategy lately suggested. The purpose of this chapter has been to point the thinking believer in the direction of these questions, to illustrate how philosophical reflection is fruitfully brought to bear in approaching them and their forerunners, and to recommend that, in light of its inherent difficulty, thinking Christians approach an "apologetic from miracles" with a refined mixture of intellectual humility and tenacity. There is no forcing one to believe in miracles. But neither is there any reason to shrink from seeing in events like the resurrection evidence of God's reaching down to make himself known to creatures.

I am very grateful to Michael Murray for working patiently to turn a difficult ancestor of this chapter into something less difficult. If it is still too hard, that is entirely my fault. I'm also indebted to my colleagues Mike Bergmann (a thinking Christian) and Martin Curd (a thinking skeptic) for talking with me at length about miracles.

Notes

1. That is to say, the thinking Christian will have paid some attention to the *epistemology* of miracles. "Epistemology" is just the complicated-sounding (but etymologically well-deserved) word that philosophers have long attached to the study of knowledge — to the study of what makes a true belief sufficiently warranted or justified (well-earned, you might say) to count as knowledge. Given its currency in apologetic discussions, we might as well have it in our vocabulary.

2. That is to say, the thinking Christian will have paid some attention to the *metaphysics* of miracles. 'Metaphysics' is just a complicated-sounding (and etymologically not-very-well-deserved) title that philosophers have long attached to the study of what there is and the nature of what there is. Given its currency, we might as well have this word in our vocabulary too.

3. David Hume, *An Enquiry Concerning Human Understanding*, 3rd ed., edited by L. A. Selby-Bigge and P. H. Nidditch (Oxford: Clarendon Press, 1975), 114. From the same paragraph: "It is no miracle that a man, seemingly in good health, should die on a sudden. . . . But it is a miracle, that a dead man should come to life. . . ." We'll encounter presently Hume's reason for claiming that one should never believe such accounts as the Lazarus story. (What we called an "exception" Hume has called a "vio-

lation." Those mean the same thing. Don't think of a violation of a law as something *naughty*. Think of it as an exception.)

4. Thus David Hume's "accurate definition" includes both conditions: a miracle is *"a transgression of a law of nature by a particular volition of the Deity, or by the interposition of some invisible agent"* (*An Enquiry*, 115, n. 1). Don't fret over the little *"e"* in our formulation, needed to render the definition perfectly general. It's just a placeholder, to be filled in by any event whatsoever. It functions rather like "something" and "it" in English when we define (say) "dog" by claiming that "Something is a dog if and only if it is a member of the family *canidea*."

5. "Anomalous" literally means non-lawful, from *a-* ("not-") and *nomos* ("law").

6. Apparently one needn't imagine this objection: the quoted misgiving is offered on p. 7 of Richard Swinburne's *The Concept of Miracles* (London: SCM Press, 1964), as grounds for taking seriously the claim that such a definition of "miracle" ". . . seems to place a restriction on the use of the term not justified in general by practice."

7. The essay comprises Section X of Hume's *An Enquiry*, 109-31.

8. Here again, don't fret over the "Fs" and "Gs." They're just placeholders, needed to render the form in which we state a law of nature perfectly general, to be filled in with descriptions of objects or events. "All Fs are Gs" is thus a sort of shorthand for "All metals are conductors," or for "All unsupported bodies are falling bodies," or the like.

9. Hume's argument begins with "a reminder of how we justify our belief that some generalization of the form 'All Fs are Gs' is a law of nature," namely by repeated observation of the regular conjunction of Fs with Gs. Leaving an assessment of Hume's argument for a later section, two points are worth noting here. First, it may be objected that Hume is just wrong about this "reminder" — that in fact scientists don't proceed in this way at all, and that his argument is fundamentally flawed from the outset. The objection is correct this far: while it is agreed on nearly all hands that Hume is right to say that our justification for postulating some candidate L as a law of nature is nondeductive in character, it remains a point of controversy to what extent scientists rely on the form of "enumerative induction" that Hume offers here — as opposed to some alternative "abductive" inference to the best explanation. (The matter is complicated in part by the difficulty of always clearly distinguishing methods of discovery from methods of justification, and by the fact that the formulation of many laws involves idealizations relative to actual data.) But, second, even if we can't rely on Hume (who was no philosopher of science) to accurately describe scientists' warrant for proposing the laws they do, he is still very much correct in claiming that we do indeed *possess* the evidence of repeated and regular conjunction of Fs with Gs: and this provides the force of his point that such evidence always outweighs the single-case evidence for it being true that there is an F that is not a G. For more on laws of nature, including Humean and competing accounts, see chapter 7, "Laws of Nature" (pp. 805-901) of Martin Curd and J. A. Cover, *Philosophy of Science: The Central Issues* (New York & London: W. W. Norton and Company, 1998).

10. Alternatively, for all we know the event *was* caused — but by Satan or some angel. That is another problem we shan't dwell on, in this chapter: we'll suppose that non-miraculous anomalies are uncaused events. Sort of like flukes of nature.

11. Representatives of this line of argument can be found in Nicholas Everitt, "The Impossibility of Miracles," *Religious Studies* 23 (1987): 347-49 and in Alastair McKinnon, "'Miracle' and 'Paradox'," *American Philosophical Quarterly* 4 (1967): 308-14.

12. The point being made here was encountered earlier in Section II, with the words "traditionally, it is precisely (AE) — the existence of what we are calling an anomalous event — that is offered as evidence for (DC) — the existence of a divine cause."

13. Most chapters in this volume are written in the first person. I adopt the first person here, in part to indicate that many believers are (I gather) inclined to be rather more optimistic than I about the role of miracles in a Christian apologetic. They won't reckon anything in the remainder of this chapter to be outright false; they'll just read it as being too pessimistic. At least the record is straight: from here on out I'm speaking for myself, as most authors have spoken through their entire chapters.

14. Indeed, it is presumably because the general run of natural scientists abhor such cognitive vertigo that, given their commitment to Naturalism, they are keen to deny the historical basis of the biblical testimony to miracles in the first place. The historical reliability of the biblical record is, alas, another question we haven't pursued here: see footnote 15.

15. A tall order, perhaps, if we aim to enlist the help of Elijah. I've studiously avoided the question of how one should go about establishing the inspiration and authority of the biblical record and its reliability as a true statement of past events. The second of these won't follow straight from the first: we'd need other premises (on which fair-minded believers have disagreed) about literal reading and inerrancy and more. I have no expertise on such matters, and shan't pronounce on it. I have no expertise on the first issue (of inspiration and authority) either, but will pronounce on it this far: the divine authority of Scripture seems to me not something that one could really establish at all. Some of us came to believe it at our parents' knee. (But then, how'd *they* come to know it?) To accept the authority of Scripture on the authority of my parents will work all right as an explanation of why I *do* believe it, but hardly works as a justification of the belief itself (why I *should* believe it). My own view is that no amount of historical scholarship can establish the inspiration and authority of scripture. We've got historical evidence about the life of President Washington sufficient to underwrite the belief that he owned slaves; but what sort of evidence could there be about God inspiring the Gospel writers (say) or the selection of the Canon that would underwrite belief in those? (Here I commend to the reader the later chapters of Alvin Plantinga's *Warranted Christian Belief* (Oxford University Press, forthcoming), and his discussions there of the Principle of Dwindling Probabilities. My suspicion is that Plantinga is right: our warrant in believing the Bible to be the authoritative Word of God owes to the work of the Holy Spirit. Full stop, pretty much.)

The Problem of Evil and Some Varieties of Atheism

William L. Rowe

THIS paper is concerned with three interrelated questions. The first is: Is there an argument for atheism based on the existence of evil that may rationally justify someone in being an atheist? To this first question I give an affirmative answer and try to support that answer by setting forth a strong argument for atheism based on the existence of evil.[1] The second question is: How can the theist best defend his position against the argument for atheism based on the existence of evil? In response to this question I try to describe what may be an adequate rational defense for theism against any argument for atheism based on the existence of evil. The final question is: What position should the informed atheist take concerning the rationality of theistic belief? Three different answers an atheist may give to this question serve to distinguish three varieties of atheism: unfriendly atheism, indifferent atheism, and friendly atheism. In the final part of the paper I discuss and defend the position of friendly atheism.

Before we consider the argument from evil, we need to distinguish a narrow and a broad sense of the terms "theist," "atheist," and "agnostic." By a "theist" in the narrow sense I mean someone who believes in the existence of an omnipotent, omniscient, eternal, supremely good being who created the world. By a "theist" in the broad sense I mean someone who believes in the existence of some sort of divine being or divine reality. To be a theist in the narrow sense is also to be a theist in the broad sense, but one may be a theist in the broad sense—as was Paul Tillich—without believing that there is a supremely good, omnipotent, omniscient, eternal being who created the world. Similar distinctions must be made between a narrow and a broad sense of the terms "atheist" and "agnostic." To be an atheist in the broad sense is to deny the existence of any sort óf divine being or divine reality. Tillich was not an atheist in the broad sense. But he was an atheist in the narrow sense, for he denied that there exists a divine being that is all-knowing, all-powerful and perfectly good. In this paper I will be using the terms "theism," "theist," "atheism," "atheist," "agnosticism," and "agnostic" in the narrow sense, not in the broad sense.

I

In developing the argument for atheism based on the existence of evil, it will be useful to focus on some particular evil that our world contains in considerable abundance. Intense human and animal suffering, for example, occurs daily and in great plenitude in our world. Such intense suffering is a clear case of evil. Of course, if the intense suffering leads to some greater good, a good we could not have obtained without undergoing the suffering in question, we might conclude that the suffering is justified, but it remains an evil nevertheless. For we must not confuse the intense suffering in and of itself with the good things to which it sometimes leads or of which it may be a necessary part. Intense human or animal suffering is in itself bad, an evil, even though it may sometimes be justified by virtue of being a part of, or leading to, some good which is unobtainable without it. What is evil in itself may sometimes be good as a means because it leads to something that is good in itself. In such a case, while remaining an evil in itself, the intense human or animal suffering is, nevertheless, an evil which someone might be morally justified in permitting.

Taking human and animal suffering as a clear instance of evil which occurs with great frequency in our world, the argument for atheism based on evil can be stated as follows:

1. There exist instances of intense suffering which an omnipotent, omniscient being could have prevented without thereby losing some greater good or permitting some evil equally bad or worse.[2]
2. An omniscient, wholly good being would prevent the occurrence of any intense suffering it could, unless it could not do so without thereby losing some greater good or permitting some evil equally bad or worse.

3. There does not exist an omnipotent, omniscient, wholly good being.

What are we to say about this argument for atheism, an argument based on the profusion of one sort of evil in our world? The argument is valid; therefore, if we have rational grounds for accepting its premises, to that extent we have rational grounds for accepting atheism. Do we, however, have rational grounds for accepting the premises of this argument?

Let's begin with the second premise. Let s_1 be an instance of intense human or animal suffering which an omniscient, wholly good being could prevent. We will also suppose that things are such that s_1 will occur unless prevented by the omniscient, wholly good (OG) being. We might be interested in determining what would be a *sufficient* condition of OG failing to prevent s_1. But, for our purpose here, we need only try to state a *necessary* condition for OG failing to prevent s_1. That condition, so it seems to me, is this:

Either (i) there is some greater good, G, such that G is obtainable by OG only if OG permits s_1[3],

or (ii) there is some greater good, G, such that G is obtainable by OG only if OG permits either s_1 or some evil equally bad or worse,

or (iii) s_1 is such that it is preventable by OG only if OG permits some evil equally bad or worse.

It is important to recognize that (iii) is not included in (i). For losing a good greater than s_1 is not the same as permitting an evil greater than s_1. And this because the *absence* of a good state of affairs need not itself be an evil state of affairs. It is also important to recognize that s_1 might be such that it is preventable by OG *without* losing G (so condition (i) is not satisfied) but also such that if OG did prevent it, G would be loss *unless* OG permitted some evil equal to or worse than s_1. If this were so, it does not seem correct to require that OG prevent s_1. Thus, condition (ii) takes into account an important possibility not encompassed in condition (i).

Is it true that if an omniscient, wholly good being permits the occurrence of some intense suffering it could have prevented, then either (i) or (ii) or (iii) obtains? It seems to me that it is true. But if it is true then so is premise (2) of the argument for atheism.

52

For that premise merely states in more compact form what we have suggested must be true if an omniscient, wholly good being fails to prevent some intense suffering it could prevent. Premise (2) says that an omniscient, wholly good being would prevent the occurrence of any intense suffering it could, unless it could not do so without thereby losing some greater good or permitting some evil equally bad or worse. This premise (or something not too distant from it) is, I think, held in common by many atheists and nontheists. Of course, there may be disagreement about whether something is good, and whether, if it is good, one would be morally justified in permitting some intense suffering to occur in order to obtain it. Someone might hold, for example, that no good is great enough to justify permitting an innocent child to suffer terribly.[4] Again, someone might hold that the mere fact that a given good outweighs some suffering and would be loss if the suffering were prevented, is not a morally sufficient reason for permitting the suffering. But to hold either of these views is not to deny (2). For (2) claims only that *if* an omniscient, wholly good being permits intense suffering *then* either there is some greater good that would have been loss, or some equally bad or worse evil that would have occurred, had the intense suffering been prevented. (2) does not purport to describe what might be a *sufficient* condition for an omniscient, wholly good being to permit intense suffering, only what is a *necessary* condition. So stated, (2) seems to express a belief that accords with our basic moral principles, principles shared by both theists and nontheists. If we are to fault the argument for atheism, therefore, it seems we must find some fault with its first premise.

Suppose in some distant forest lightning strikes a dead tree, resulting in a forest fire. In the fire a fawn is trapped, horribly burned, and lies in terrible agony for several days before death relieves its suffering. So far as we can see, the fawn's intense suffering is pointless. For there does not appear to be any greater good such that the prevention of the fawn's suffering would require either the loss of that good or the occurrence of an evil equally bad or worse. Nor does there seem to be any equally bad or worse evil so connected to the fawn's suffering that it would have had to occur had the fawn's suffering been prevented. Could an omnipotent, omniscient being have prevented the fawn's apparently pointless suffering? The answer is obvious, as even the theist will insist. An omnipotent, omniscient being could have easily prevented the fawn from being horribly burned, or, given the burning, could have spared the fawn the intense suffering by quickly ending its life, rather than allowing the fawn to lie in terrible agony for several days. Since the fawn's intense suffering was preventable and, so far as we can see, pointless, doesn't it appear that premise (1) of the argument is true, that there do exist instances of intense suffering which an omnipotent, omniscient being could have prevented without thereby losing some greater good or permitting some evil equally bad or worse.

It must be acknowledged that the case of the fawn's apparently pointless suffering does not *prove* that (1) is true. For even though we cannot see how the fawn's suffering is required to obtain some greater good (or to prevent some equally bad or worse evil), it hardly follows that it is not so required. After all, we are often surprised by how things we thought to be unconnected turn out to be intimately connected. Perhaps, for all we know, there is some familiar good outweighing the fawn's suffering to which that suffering is connected in a way we do not see. Furthermore, there may well be unfamiliar goods, goods we haven't dreamed of, to which the fawn's suffering is inextricably connected. Indeed, it would seem to require something like omniscience on our part before we could lay claim to *knowing* that there is no greater good connected to the fawn's suffering in such a manner than an omnipotent, omniscient being could not have achieved that good without permitting that suffering or some evil equally bad or worse. So the case of the fawn's suffering surely does not enable us to *establish* the truth of (1).

The truth is that we are not in a position to prove that (1) is true. We cannot know with certainty that instances of suffering of the sort described in (1) do occur in our world. But it is one thing to *know* or *prove* that (1) is true and quite another thing to have *rational grounds* for believing (1) to be true. We are often in the position where in the light of our experience and knowledge it is rational to believe that a certain statement is true, even though we are not in a position to prove or to know with certainty that the statement is true. In the light of our past experience and knowledge it is, for example, very reasonable to believe that neither Goldwater nor McGovern will ever be elected President, but we are scarcely in the position of knowing with certainty that neither will ever be elected President. So, too, with (1), although we cannot know with certainty that it is true, it perhaps can be rationally supported, shown to be a rational belief.

Consider again the case of the fawn's suffering. Is it reasonable to believe that there is some greater good so intimately connected to that suffering that even an omnipotent, omniscient being could not have obtained that good without permitting that suffering or some evil at least as bad? It certainly does not appear reasonable to believe this. Nor does it seem reasonable to believe that there is some evil at least as bad as the fawn's suffering such that an omnipotent being simply could not have prevented it without permitting the fawn's suffering. But even if it should somehow be reasonable to believe either of these things of the fawn's suffering, we must then ask whether it is reasonable to believe either of these things of *all* the instances of seemingly pointless human and animal suffering that occur daily in our world. And surely the answer to this more general question must be no. It seems quite unlikely that *all* the instances of intense suffering occurring daily in our world are intimately related to the occurrence of greater goods or the prevention of evils at least as bad; and even more unlikely, should they somehow all be so related, than an omnipotent, omniscient being could not have achieved at least some of those goods (or prevented some of those evils) without permitting the instances of intense suffering that are supposedly related to them. In the light of our experience and knowledge of the variety and scale of human and animal suffering in our world, the idea that none of this suffering could have been prevented by an omnipotent being without thereby losing a greater good or permitting an evil at least as bad seems an extraordinary absurd idea, quite beyond our belief. It seems then that although we cannot *prove* that (1) is true, it is, nevertheless, altogether *reasonable* to believe that (1) is true, that (1) is a *rational* belief.[5]

Returning now to our argument for atheism, we've seen that the second premise expresses a basic belief common to many theists and nontheists. We've also seen that our experience and knowledge of the variety and profusion of suffering in our world provides *rational support* for the first premise. Seeing that the conclusion, "There does not exist an omnipotent, omniscient, wholly good being" follows from these two premises, it does seem that we have *rational support* for atheism, that it is reasonable for us to believe that the theistic God does not exist.

II

Can theism be rationally defended against the argument for atheism we have just examined? If it can, how might the theist best respond to that argument? Since the argument from (1) and (2) to (3) is valid, and since the theist, no less than the nontheist, is more than likely committed to (2), it's clear that the theist can reject this atheistic argument only by rejecting its first premise, the premise that states that there are instances of intense suffering which an omnipotent, omniscient being could have prevented without thereby losing some greater good or permitting some evil equally bad or worse. How, then, can the theist best respond to this premise and the considerations advanced in its support?

There are basically three responses a theist can make. First, he might argue not that (1) is false or probably false, but only that the reasoning given in support of it is in some way *defective*. He may do this either by arguing that the reasons given in support of (1) are *in themselves* insufficient to justify accepting (1), or by arguing that there are other things we know which, when taken in conjunction with these reasons, do not justify us in accepting (1). I suppose some theists would be content with this rather modest response to the basic argument for atheism.

But given the validity of the basic argument and the theist's likely acceptance of (2), he is thereby committed to the view that (1) is false, not just that we have no good reasons for accepting (1) as true. The second two responses are aimed at showing that it is reasonable to believe that (1) is false. Since the theist is committed to this view I shall focus the discussion on these two attempts, attempts which we can distinguish as "the direct attack" and "the indirect attack."

By a direct attack, I mean an attempt to reject (1) by pointing out goods, for example, to which suffering may well be connected, goods which an omnipotent, omniscient being could not achieve without permitting suffering. It is doubtful, however, that the direct attack can succeed. The theist may point out that some suffering leads to moral and spiritual development impossible without suffering. But it's reasonably clear that suffering often occurs in a degree far beyond what is required for character development. The theist may say that some suffering results from free choices of human beings and might be preventable only by preventing some measure of human freedom. But, again, it's clear that much intense suffering occurs not as a result of human free choices. The general difficulty with this direct attack on premise (1) is twofold. First, it cannot succeed, for the theist does not know what greater goods might be served, or evils prevented, by each instance of intense human or animal suffering. Second, the theist's own religious tradition usually maintains that in this life it is not given to us to know God's purpose in allowing particular instances of suffering. Hence, the direct attack against premise (1) cannot succeed and violates basic beliefs associated with theism.

The best procedure for the theist to follow in rejecting premise (1) is the indirect procedure. This procedure I shall call "the G. E. Moore shift," so-called in honor of the twentieth century philosopher, G. E. Moore, who used it to great effect in dealing with the arguments of the skeptics. Skeptical philosophers such as David Hume have advanced ingenious arguments to prove that no one can know of the existence of any material object. The premises of their arguments employ plausible principles, principles which many philosophers have tried to reject directly, but only with questionable success. Moore's procedure was altogether different. Instead of arguing directly against the premises of the skeptic's arguments, he simply noted that the premises implied, for example, that he (Moore) did not know of the existence of a pencil. Moore then proceeded indirectly against the skeptic's premises by arguing:

I do know that this pencil exists.
If the skeptic's principles are correct I cannot know of the existence of this pencil.

∴ The skeptic's principles (at least one) must be incorrect.

Moore then noted that his argument is just as valid as the skeptic's, that both of their arguments contain the premise "If the skeptic's principles are correct Moore cannot know of the existence of this pencil," and concluded that the only way to choose between the two arguments (Moore's and the skeptic's) is by deciding which of the first premises it is more rational to believe—Moore's premise "I do know that this pencil exists" or the skeptic's premise asserting that his skeptical principles are correct. Moore concluded that his own first premise was the more rational of the two.[6]

Before we see how the theist may apply the G. E. Moore shift to the basic argument for atheism, we should note the general strategy of the shift. We're given an argument: p, q, therefore, r. Instead of arguing directly against p, another argument is constructed—not-r, q, therefore, not-p—which begins with the denial of the conclusion of the first argument, keeps its second premise, and ends with the denial of the first premise as its conclusion. Compare, for example, these two:

I. p II. not-r
   q q
   ——   ——
   r not-p

It is a truth of logic that If I is valid II must be valid as well. Since the arguments are the same so far as the second premise is concerned, any choice between them must concern their respective first premises. To argue against the first premise (*p*) by constructing the counter argument II is to employ the G. E. Moore shift.

Applying the G. E. Moore shift against the first premise of the basic argument for atheism, the theist can argue as follows:

not-3. There exists an omnipotent, omniscient, wholly good being.

2. An omniscient, wholly good being would prevent the occurrence of any intense suffering it could, unless it could not do so without thereby losing some greater good or permitting some evil equally bad or worse.

therefore,

not-1. It is not the case that there exist instances of intense suffering which an omnipotent, omniscient being could have prevented without thereby losing some greater good or permitting some evil equally bad or worse.

We now have two arguments: the basic argument for atheism from (1) and (2) to (3), and the theist's best response, the argument from (not-3) and (2) to (not-1). What the theist then says about (1) is that he has rational grounds for believing in the existence of the theistic God (not-3), accepts (2) as true, and sees that (not-1) follows from (not-3) and (2). He concludes, therefore, that he has rational grounds for rejecting (1). Having rational grounds for rejecting (1), the theist concludes that the basic argument for atheism is mistaken.

III

We've had a look at a forceful argument for atheism and what seems to be the theist's best response to that argument. If one is persuaded by the argument for atheism, as I find myself to be, how might one best view the position of the theist. Of course, he will view the theist as having a false belief, just as the theist will view the atheist as having a false belief. But what position should the atheist take concerning the *rationality* of the theist's belief? There are three major positions an atheist might take, positions which we may think of as some varieties of atheism. First, the atheist may believe that no one is rationally justified in believing that the theistic God exists. Let us call this position "unfriendly atheism." Second, the atheist may hold no belief concerning whether any theist is or isn't rationally justified in believing that the theistic God exists. Let us call this view "indifferent atheism." Finally, the atheist may believe that some theists are rationally justified in believing that the theistic God exists. This view we shall call "friendly atheism." In this final part of the paper I propose to discuss and defend the position of friendly atheism.

If no one can be rationally justified in believing a false proposition then friendly atheism is a paradoxical, if not incoherent position. But surely the truth of a belief is not a necessary condition of someone's being rationally justified in having that belief. So in holding that someone is rationally justified in believing that the theistic God exists, the friendly atheist is not committed to thinking that the theist has a true belief. What he is committed to is that the theist has rational grounds for his belief, a belief the atheist rejects and is convinced he is rationally justified in rejecting. But is this possible? Can someone, like our friendly atheist, hold a belief, be convinced that he is rationally justified in holding that belief, and yet believe that someone else is equally justified in believing the opposite? Surely this is possible. Suppose your friends see you off on a flight to Hawaii. Hours after take-off they learn that your plane has gone down at sea. After a twenty-four hour search, no survivors have been found. Under these circumstances they are rationally justified in believing that you have perished. But it is hardly rational for you to believe this, as you bob up and down in your life vest, wondering why the search planes have failed to spot you. Indeed, to amuse yourself while awaiting your fate, you might very well reflect on the fact that your friends are rationally justified in believing that you are now dead, a proposition you disbelieve and are rationally justified in disbelieving. So, too, perhaps an atheist may be rationally justified in his atheistic belief and yet hold that some theists are rationally justified in believing just the opposite of what he believes.

60

What sort of grounds might a theist have for believing that God exists. Well, he might endeavor to justify his belief by appealing to one or more of the traditional arguments: Ontological, Cosmological, Teleological, Moral, etc. Second, he might appeal to certain aspects of religious experience, perhaps even his own religious experience. Third, he might try to justify theism as a plausible theory in terms of which we can account for a variety of phenomena. Although an atheist must hold that the theistic God does not exist, can he not also believe, and be justified in so believing, that some of these "justifications of theism" do actually rationally justify some theists in their belief that there exists a supremely good, omnipotent, omniscient being? It seems to me that he can.

If we think of the long history of theistic belief and the special situations in which people are sometimes placed, it is perhaps as absurd to think that no one was ever rationally justified in believing that the theistic God exists as it is to think that no one was ever justified in believing that human being would never walk on the moon. But in suggesting that friendly atheism is preferable to unfriendly atheism, I don't mean to rest the case on what some human beings might reasonably have believed in the eleventh or thirteenth century. The more interesting question is whether some people in modern society, people who are aware of the usual grounds for belief and disbelief and are acquainted to some degree with modern science, are yet rationally justified in accepting theism. Friendly atheism is a significant position only if it answers this question in the affirmative.

It is not difficult for an atheist to be friendly when he has reason to believe that the theist could not reasonably be expected to be acquainted with the grounds for disbelief that he (the atheist) possesses. For then the atheist may take the view that some theists are rationally justified in holding to theism, but would not be so were they to be acquainted with the grounds for disbelief—those grounds being sufficient to tip the scale in favor of atheism when balanced against the reasons the theist has in support of his belief.

Friendly atheism becomes paradoxical, however, when the atheist contemplates believing that the theist has all the grounds for atheism that he, the atheist, has, and yet is rationally justified in maintaining his theistic belief. But even so excessively friendly a view as this perhaps can be held by the atheist if he also has some reason to think that the grounds for theism are not as telling as the theist is justified in taking them to be.[7]

In this paper I've presented what I take to be a strong argument for atheism, pointed out what I think is the theist's best response to that argument, distinguished three positions an atheist might take concerning the rationality of theistic belief, and made some remarks in defense of the position called "friendly atheism." I'm aware that the central points of the paper are not likely to be warmly received by many philosophers. Philosophers who are atheists tend to be tough minded—holding that there are no good reasons for supposing that theism is true. And theists tend either to reject the view that the existence of evil provides rational grounds for atheism or to hold that religious belief has nothing to do with reason and evidence at all. But such is the way of philosophy.[8]

Notes

1   Some philosophers have contended that the existence of evil is *logically inconsistent* with the existence of the theistic God. No one, I think, has succeeded in establishing such an extravagant claim. Indeed, granted incompatibilism, there is a fairly compelling argument for the view that the existence of evil is logically consistent with the existence of the theistic God. (For a lucid statement of this argument see Alvin Plantinga, *God, Freedom, and Evil* (New York, 1974), pp. 29–59.) There remains, however, what we may call the *evidential* form—as opposed to the *logical* form—of the problem of evil: the view that the variety and profusion of evil in our world, although perhaps not logically inconsistent with the existence of the theistic God, provides, nevertheless, *rational support* for atheism. In this paper I shall be concerned solely with the evidential form of the problem, the form of the problem which, I think, presents a rather severe difficulty for theism.

2   If there is some good, G, greater than any evil, (I) will be false for the trivial reason that no matter what evil, E, we pick the conjunctive good state of affairs consisting of G and E will outweigh E and be such that an omnipotent being could not obtain it without permitting E. (See Alvin Plantinga, *God and Other Minds* [Ithaca, 1967], p. 167.) To avoid this objection we may insert "unreplaceable" into our premises (I) and (2) between "some" and "greater."

62

If E isn't required for G, and G is better than G plus E, then the good conjunctive state of affairs composed of G and E would be *replaceable* by the greater good of G alone. For the sake of simplicity, however, I will ignore this complication both in the formulation and discussion of premises (1) and (2).

3   Three clarifying points need to be made in connection with (i). First, by "good" I don't mean to exclude the fulfillment of certain moral principles. Perhaps preventing s_1 would preclude certain actions prescribed by the principles of justice. I shall allow that the satisfaction of certain principles of justice may be a good that outweighs the evil of s_1. Second, even though (i) may suggest it, I don't mean to limit the good in question to something that would *follow in time* the occurrence of s_1. And, finally, we should perhaps not fault OG if the good G, that would be loss were s_1 prevented, is not actually greater than s_1, but merely such that allowing s_1 and G, as opposed to preventing s_1, and thereby losing G, would not alter the balance between good and evil. For reasons of simplicity, I have left this point out in stating (i), with the result that (i) is perhaps a bit stronger than it should be.

4   See Ivan's speech in Book V, Chapter IV of *The Brothers Karamazov*.

5   One might object that the conclusion of this paragraph is stronger than the reasons given warrant. For it is one thing to argue that it is unreasonable to think that (1) is false and another thing to conclude that we are therefore justified in accepting (1) as true. There are propositions such that believing them is much more reasonable than disbelieving them, and yet are such that *withholding judgment* about them is more reasonable than believing them. To take an example of Chisholm's : it is more reasonable to believe that the Pope will be in Rome (on some arbitrarily picked future date) than to believe that he won't; but it is perhaps more reasonable to suspend judgment on the question of the Pope's whereabouts on that particular date, than to believe that he will be in Rome. Thus, it might be objected, that while we've shown that believing (1) is more reasonable than disbelieving (1), we haven't shown that believing (1) is more reasonable than withholding belief. My answer to this objection is that there are things we know which render (1) probable to the degree that it is more reasonable to believe (1) than to suspend judgment on (1). What are these things we know? First, I think, is the fact that there is an enormous variety and profusion of intense human and animal suffering in our world. Second, is the fact that much of this suffering seems quite unrelated to any greater goods (or the absence of equal or greater evils) that might justify it. And, finally, there is the fact that such suffering as is related to greater goods (or the absence of equal or greater evils) does not, in many cases, seem so intimately related as to require its permission by an omnipotent being bent on securing those goods (the absence of those evils). These facts, I am claiming, make it more reasonable to accept (1) than to withhold judgment on (1).

6   See, for example, the two chapters on Hume in G. E. Moore, *Some Main Problems of Philosophy* (London, 1953).

7   Suppose that I add a long sum of numbers three times and get result x. I inform you of this so that you have pretty much the same evidence I have for

the claim that the sum of the numbers is x. You then use your calculator twice over and arrive at result y. You, then, are justified in believing that the sum of the numbers is *not* x. However, knowing that your calculator has been damaged and is therefore unreliable, and that you have no reason to think that it is damaged, I may reasonably believe not only that the sum of the numbers is x, but also that you are justified in believing that the sum is not x. Here is a case, then, where you have all of my evidence for p, and yet I can reasonably believe that you are justified in believing not-p—for I have reason to believe that your grounds for not-p are not as telling as you are justified in taking them to be.

8   I am indebted to my colleagues at Purdue University, particularly to Ted Ulrich and Lilly Russow, and to philosophers at The University of Nebraska, Indiana State University, and The University of Wisconsin at Milwaukee for helpful criticisms of earlier versions of this paper.

The Ethics of Belief

William K. Clifford

A shipowner was about to send to sea an emigrant-ship. He knew that she was old, and not over-well built at the first; that she had seen many seas and climes, and often had needed repairs. Doubts had been suggested to him that possibly she was not seaworthy. These doubts preyed upon his mind, and made him unhappy; he thought that perhaps he ought to have her thoroughly overhauled and refitted, even though this should put him to great expense. Before the ship sailed, however, he succeeded in overcoming these melancholy reflections. He said to himself that she had gone safely through so many voyages and weathered so many storms that it was idle to suppose she would not come safely home from this trip also. He would put his trust in Providence, which could hardly fail to protect all these unhappy families that were leaving their fatherland to seek for better times elsewhere. He would dismiss from his mind all ungenerous suspicions about the honesty of builders and contractors. In such ways he acquired a sincere and comfortable conviction that his vessel was thoroughly safe and seaworthy; he watched her departure with a light heart, and benevolent wishes for the success of the exiles in their strange new home that was to be; and he got his insurance-money when she went down in mid-ocean and told no tales.

What shall we say of him? Surely this, that he was verily guilty of the death of those men. It is admitted that he did sincerely believe in the soundness of his ship; but the sincerity of his conviction can in no wise help him, because *he had no right to believe on such evidence as was before him*. He had acquired his belief not by honestly earning it in patient investigation, but by stifling his doubts. And although in the end he may have felt so sure about it that he could not think otherwise, yet inasmuch as he had knowingly and willingly worked himself into that frame of mind, he must be held responsible for it.

Let us alter the case a little, and suppose that the ship was not unsound after all; that she made her voyage safely, and many others after it. Will that diminish the guilt of her owner? Not one jot. When an action is once done, it is right or wrong for ever; no accidental failure of its good or evil fruits can possibly alter that. The man would not have been innocent, he would only have been not found out. The question of right or wrong has to do with the origin of his belief, not the matter of it; not what it was, but how he got it; not whether it turned out to be true or false, but whether he had a right to believe on such evidence as was before him.

There was once an island in which some of the inhabitants professed a religion teaching neither the doctrine of original sin nor that of eternal punishment. A suspicion got abroad that the professors of this religion had made use of unfair means to get their doctrines taught to children. They were accused of wresting the laws of their country in such a way as to remove children from the care of their natural and legal guardians; and even of stealing them away and keeping them concealed from their friends and relations. A certain number of men formed themselves into a society for the purpose of agitating the public about this matter. They published grave accusations against individual citizens of the highest position and character; and did all in their power to injure these citizens in the exercise of their professions. So great was the noise they made, that a Commission was appointed to investigate the facts; but after the Commission had carefully inquired into all the evidence that could be got, it appeared that the accused were innocent. Not only had they been accused on insufficient evidence, but the evidence of their innocence was such as the agitators might easily have obtained, if they had attempted a fair inquiry. After these disclosures the inhabitants of that country looked upon the members of the agitating society, not only as persons whose judgment was to be distrusted, but also as no longer to be counted honourable men. For although they had sincerely and conscientiously believed in the charges they had made, yet *they had no right to believe on such evidence as was before them*. Their sincere convictions, instead of being honestly earned by patient inquiring, were stolen by listening to the voice of prejudice and passion.

Let us vary this case also, and suppose, other things remaining as before, that a still more accurate investigation proved the accused to have been really guilty. Would this make any difference in the guilt of the accusers? Clearly not; the question is not whether their belief was true or false, but whether they entertained it on wrong grounds. They would no doubt say, "Now you see that we were right after all; next time perhaps you will believe us." And they might be believed, but they would not thereby become honourable men. They would not be innocent, they would only be not found out. Every one of them, if he chose to examine himself *in foro conscientiae*, would know that he had acquired and nourished a belief, when he had no right to believe on such evidence as was before him; and therein he would know that he had done a wrong thing.

It may be said, however, that in both of these supposed cases it is not the belief which is judged to be wrong, but the action following upon it. The shipowner might say, "I am perfectly certain that my ship is sound, but still I feel it my duty to have her examined, before trusting the lives of so many people to her." And it might be said to the agitator, "However convinced you were of the justice of your cause and the truth of your convictions, you ought not to have made a public attack upon any man's character until you had examined the evidence on both sides with the utmost patience and care."

In the first place, let us admit that, so far as it goes, this view of the case is right and necessary; right, because even when a man's belief is so fixed that he cannot think otherwise, he still has a choice in regard to the action suggested by it, and so cannot escape the duty of investigating on the ground of the strength of his convictions; and necessary, because those who are not yet capable of controlling their feelings and thoughts must have a plain rule dealing with overt acts.

But this being premised as necessary, it becomes clear that it is not sufficient, and that our previous judgment is required to supplement it. For it is not possible so to sever the belief from the action it suggests as to condemn the one without condemning the other. No man holding a strong belief on one side of a question, or even wishing to hold a belief on one side, can investigate it with such fairness and completeness as if he were really in doubt and unbiased; so that the existence of a belief not founded on fair inquiry unfits a man for the performance of this necessary duty.

Nor is that truly a belief at all which has not some influence upon the actions of him who holds it. He who truly believes that which prompts him to an action has looked upon the action to lust after it, he has committed it already in his heart. If a belief is not realized immediately in open deeds, it is stored up for the guidance of the future. It goes to make a part of that aggregate of beliefs which is the link between sensation and action at every moment of all our lives, and which is so organized and compacted together that no part of it can be isolated from the rest, but every new addition modifies the structure of the whole. No real belief, however trifling and fragmentary it may seem, is ever truly insignificant; it prepares us to receive more of its like, confirms those which resembled it before, and weakens others; and so gradually it lays a stealthy train in our inmost thoughts, which may some day explode into overt action, and leave its stamp upon our character for ever.

And no one man's belief is in any case a private matter which concerns himself alone. Our lives are guided by that general conception of the course of things which has been created by society for social purposes. Our words, our phrases, our forms and processes and modes of thought, are common property, fashioned and perfected from age to age; an heirloom which every succeeding generation inherits as a precious deposit and a sacred trust to be handed on to the next one, not unchanged but enlarged and purified, with some clear marks of its proper handiwork. Into this, for good or ill, is woven every belief of every man who has speech of his fellows. An awful privilege, and an awful responsibility, that we should help to create the world in which posterity will live.

In the two supposed cases which have been considered, it has been judged wrong to believe on insufficient evidence, or to nourish belief by suppressing doubts and avoiding investigation. The reason of this judgment is not far to seek: it is that in both these cases the belief held by one man was of great importance to other men. But forasmuch as no belief held by one man, however seemingly trivial the belief, and however obscure the believer, is ever actually insignificant or without its effect on the fate of mankind, we have no choice but to extend our judgment to all cases of belief whatever. Belief, that sacred faculty which prompts the decisions of our will, and knits into harmonious working all the compacted energies of our being, is ours not for ourselves, but for humanity. It is rightly used on truths which have been established by long experience and waiting toil, and which have stood in the fierce light of free and fearless questioning. Then it helps to bind men together, and to strengthen and direct their common action. It is desecrated when given to unproved and unquestioned statements, for the solace and private pleasure of the believer; to add a tinsel splendour to the plain straight road of our life and display a bright mirage beyond it; or even to drown the common sorrows of our kind by a self-deception which allows them not only to cast down, but also to degrade us. Whoso would deserve well of his fellows in this matter will guard the purity of his belief with a very fanaticism of jealous care, lest at any time it should rest on an unworthy object, and catch a stain which can never be wiped away.

It is not only the leader of men, statesman, philosopher, or poet, that owes this bounden duty to mankind. Every rustic who delivers in the village ale-house his slow, infrequent sentences, may help to kill or keep alive the fatal superstitions which clog his race. Every hard-worked wife of an artisan may transmit to her children beliefs which shall knit society together, or rend it in pieces. No simplicity of mind, no obscurity of station, can escape the universal duty of questioning all that we believe.

It is true that this duty is a hard one, and the doubt which comes out of it is often a very bitter thing. It leaves us bare and powerless where we thought that we were safe and strong. To know all about anything is to know how to deal with it under all circumstances. We feel much happier and more secure when we think we know precisely what to do, no matter what happens, than when we have lost our way and do not know where to turn. And if we have supposed ourselves to know all about anything, and to be capable of doing what is fit in regard to it, we naturally do not like to find that we are really ignorant and powerless, that we have to begin again at the beginning, and try to learn what the thing is and how it is to be dealt with—if indeed anything can be learnt about it. It is the sense of power attached to a sense of knowledge that makes men desirous of believing, and afraid of doubting.

This sense of power is the highest and best of pleasures when the belief on which it is founded is a true belief, and has been fairly earned by investigation. For then we may justly feel that it is common property, and hold good for others as well as for ourselves. Then we may be glad, not that *I* have learned secrets by which I am safer and stronger, but that *we men* have got mastery over more of the world; and we shall be strong, not for ourselves, but in the name of Man and in his strength. But if the belief has been accepted on insufficient evidence, the pleasure is a stolen one. Not only does it deceive ourselves by giving us a sense of power which we do not really possess, but it is sinful, because it is stolen in defiance of our duty to mankind. That duty is to guard ourselves from such beliefs as from a pestilence, which may shortly master our own body and then spread to the rest of the town. What would be thought of one who, for the sake of a sweet fruit, should deliberately run the risk of bringing a plague upon his family and his neighbours?

And, as in other such cases, it is not the risk only which has to be considered; for a bad action is always bad at the time when it is done, no matter what happens afterwards. Every time we let ourselves believe for unworthy reasons, we weaken our powers of self-control, of doubting, of judicially and fairly weighing evidence. We all suffer severely enough from the maintenance and support of false beliefs and the fatally wrong actions which they lead to, and the evil born when one such belief is entertained is great and wide. But a greater and wider evil arises when the credulous character is maintained and supported, when a habit of believing for unworthy reasons is fostered and made permanent. If I steal money from any person, there may be no harm done by the mere transfer of possession; he may not feel the loss, or it may prevent him from using the money badly. But I cannot help doing this great wrong towards Man, that I make myself dishonest. What hurts society is not that it should lose its property, but that it should become a den of thieves; for then it must cease to be society. This is why we ought not to do evil that good may come; for at any rate this great evil has come, that we have done evil and are made wicked thereby. In like manner, if I let myself believe anything on insufficient evidence, there may be no great harm done by the mere belief; it may be true after all, or I may never have occasion to exhibit it in outward acts. But I cannot help doing this great wrong towards Man, that I make myself credulous. The danger to society is not merely that it should believe wrong things, though that is great enough; but that it should become credulous, and lose the habit of testing things and inquiring into them; for then it must sink back into savagery.

The harm which is done by credulity in a man is not confined to the fostering of a credulous character in others, and consequent support of false beliefs. Habitual want of care about what I believe leads to habitual want of care in others about the truth of what is told to me. Men speak the truth to one another when each reveres the truth in his own mind and in the other's mind; but how shall my friend revere the truth in my mind when I myself am careless about it, when I believe things because I want to believe them, and because they are comforting and pleasant? Will he not learn to cry, "Peace," to me, when there is no peace? By such a course I shall surround myself with a thick atmosphere of falsehood and fraud, and in that I must live. It may matter little to me, in my cloud-castle of sweet illusions and darling lies; but it matters much to Man that I have made my neighbours ready to deceive. The credulous man is father to the liar and the cheat; he lives in the bosom of this his family, and it is no marvel if he should become even as they are. So closely are our duties knit together, that whoso shall keep the whole law, and yet offend in one point, he is guilty of all.

68

To sum up: it is wrong always, everywhere, and for anyone, to believe anything upon insufficient evidence.

If a man, holding a belief which he was taught in childhood or persuaded of afterwards, keeps down and pushes away any doubts which arise about it in his mind, purposely avoids the reading of books and the company of men that call in question or discuss it, and regards as impious those questions which cannot easily be asked without disturbing it—the life of that man is one long sin against mankind.

If this judgment seems harsh when applied to those simple souls who have never known better, who have been brought up from the cradle with a horror of doubt, and taught that their eternal welfare depends on *what* they believe, then it leads to the very serious question, *Who hath made Israel to sin?*

It may be permitted me to fortify this judgment with the sentence of Milton—

> A man may be a heretic in the truth; and if he believe things only because his pastor says so, or the assembly so determine, without knowing other reason, though his belief be true, yet the very truth he holds becomes his heresy.

And with this famous aphorism of Coleridge—

> He who begins by loving Christianity better than Truth, will proceed by loving his own sect or Church better than Christianity, and end in loving himself better than all.

Inquiry into the evidence of a doctrine is not to be made once for all, and then taken as finally settled. It is never lawful to stifle a doubt; for either it can be honestly answered by means of the inquiry already made, or else it proves that the inquiry was not complete.

"But," says one, "I am a busy man; I have no time for the long course of study which would be necessary to make me in any degree a competent judge of certain questions, or even able to understand the nature of the arguments." Then he should have no time to believe.

From W. K. Clifford, *Lectures and Essays* (1879).

Is Belief in God Properly Basic?

Alvin Plantinga

Many philosophers have urged the *evidentialist* objection to theistic belief; they have argued that belief in God is irrational or unreasonable or not rationally acceptable or intellectually irresponsible or noetically substandard, because, as they say, there is insufficient evidence for it.[1] Many other philosophers and theologians—in particular, those in the great tradition of natural theology—have claimed that belief in God is intellectually acceptable, but only because the fact is there is sufficient evidence for it. These two groups unite in holding that theistic belief is rationally acceptable only if there is sufficient evidence for it. More exactly, they hold that a person is rational or reasonable in accepting theistic belief only if she has sufficient evidence for it—only if, that is, she knows or rationally believes some *other* propositions which support the one in question, and believes the latter on the basis of the former. In [4] I argued that the evidentialist objection is rooted in *classical foundationalism*, an enormously popular picture or total way of looking at faith, knowledge, justified belief, rationality and allied topics. This picture has been widely accepted ever since the days of Plato and Aristotle; its near relatives, perhaps, remain the dominant ways of thinking about these topics. We may think of the classical foundationalist as beginning with the observation that some of one's beliefs may be *based upon* others; it may be that there are a pair of propositions A and B such that I believe A *on the basis of* B. Although this relation isn't easy to characterize in a revealing and non-trivial fashion, it is nonetheless familiar. I believe that the word 'umbrageous' is spelled u-m-b-r-a-g-e-o-u-s: this belief is based on another belief of mine: the belief that that's how the dictionary says it's spelled. I believe that $72 \times 71 = 5112$. This belief is based upon several other beliefs I hold: that $1 \times 72 = 72$; $7 \times 2 = 14$; $7 \times 7 = 49$; $49 + 1 = 50$; and others. Some of my beliefs, however, I accept but don't accept on the basis of any other beliefs. Call these beliefs *basic*. I believe that $2 + 1 = 3$, for example, and don't believe it on the basis of other propositions. I also believe that I am seated at my desk, and that there is a mild pain in my right knee. These too are basic to me; I don't believe them on the basis of any other propositions. According to the classical foundationalist, some propositions are *properly* or *rightly* basic for a person and some are not. Those that are not, are rationally accepted only on the basis of *evidence*, where the evidence must trace back, ultimately, to what is properly basic. The existence of God, furthermore, is not among the propositions that are properly basic; hence a person is rational in accepting theistic belief only if he has evidence for it.

Now many Reformed thinkers and theologians[2] have rejected *natural theology* (thought of as the attempt to provide proofs or arguments for the existence of God). They have held not merely that the proffered arguments are unsuccessful, but that the whole enterprise is in some way radically misguided. In [5], I argue that the reformed rejection of natural theology is best construed as an inchoate and unfocused rejection of classical foundationalism. What these Reformed thinkers really mean to hold, I think, is that belief in God need not be based on argument or evidence from other propositions at all. They mean to hold that the believer is entirely within his intellectual rights in believing as he does even if he doesn't know of any good theistic argument (deductive or inductive), even if he doesn't believe that there is any such argument, and even if in fact no such argument exists. They hold that it is perfectly rational to accept belief in God without accepting it on the basis of any other beliefs or propositions at all. In a word, they hold that *belief in God is properly basic*. In this paper I shall try to develop and defend this position.

But first we must achieve a deeper understanding of the evidentialist objection. It is important to see that this contention is a *normative* contention. The evidentialist objector holds that one who accepts theistic belief is in some way irrational or noetically substandard. Here 'rational' and 'irrational' are to be taken as normative or evaluative terms; according to the objector, the theist fails to measure up to a standard he ought to confrom to. There is a right way and a wrong way with respect to belief as with respect to actions; we have duties, responsibilities, obligations with respect to the former just as with respect to the latter. So Professor Blanshard:

> ... everywhere and always belief has an ethical aspect. There is such a thing as a general ethics of the intellect. The main principle of that ethic I hold to be the same inside and outside religion. This principle is simple and sweeping: Equate your assent to the evidence. [1] p. 401.

This "ethics of the intellect" can be construed variously; many fascinating issues—issues we must here forebear to enter—arise when we try to state more exactly the various options the evidentialist may mean to adopt. Initially it looks as if he holds that there is a duty or obligation of some sort not to accept without evidence such propositions as that God exists—a duty flouted by the theist who has no evidence. If he has no evidence, then it is his duty to cease believing. But there is an oft remarked difficulty: one's beliefs, for the most part, are not directly under one's control. Most of those who believe in God could not divest themselves of that belief just by trying to do so, just as they could not in that way rid themselves of the belief that the world has existed for a very long time. So perhaps the relevant obligation is not that of divesting myself of theistic belief if I have no evidence, (that is beyond my power) but to try to cultivate the sorts of intellectual habits that will tend (we hope) to issue in my accepting as basic only propositions that are properly basic.

Perhaps this obligation is to be thought of *teleologically:* it is a moral obligation arising out of a connection between certain intrinsic goods and evils and the way in which our beliefs are formed and held. (This seems to be W. K. Clifford's way of construing the matter.) Perhaps it is to be thought of *aretetically:* there are valuable noetic or intellectual states (whether intrinsically or extrinsically valuable); there are also corresponding intellectual virtues, habits of acting so as to promote and enhance those valuable states. Among one's obligations, then, is the duty to try to fostor and cultivate these virtues in oneself or others. Or perhaps it is to be thought of *deontologically:* this obligation attaches to us just by virtue of our having the sort of noetic equipment human beings do in fact display; it does not arise out of a connection with valuable states of affairs. Such an obligation, furthermore, could be a special sort of moral obligation; on the other hand, perhaps it is a *sui generis* non-moral obligation.

Still further, perhaps the evidentialist need not speak of duty or obligation here at all. Consider someone who believes that Venus is smaller than Mercury, not because he has evidence of any sort, but because he finds it amusing to hold a belief no one else does—or consider someone who holds this belief on the basis of some outrageously bad argument. Perhaps there isn't any obligation he has failed to meet. Nevertheless his intellectual condition is deficient in some way; or perhaps alternatively there is a commonly achieved excellence he fails to display. And the evidentialist objection to theistic belief, then, might be understood, as the claim, not that the theist without evidence has failed to meet an obligation, but that he suffers from a certain sort of intellectual deficiency (so that the proper attitude toward him would be sympathy rather than censure).

These are some of the ways, then, in which the evidentialist objection could be developed; and of course there are still other possibilities. For ease of exposition, let us take the claim deontologically; what I shall say will apply *mutatis mutandis* if we take it one of the other ways. The evidentialist objection, therefore, presupposes some view as to what sorts of propositions are correctly, or rightly, or justifiably taken as basic; it presupposes a view as to what is *properly* basic. And the minimally relevant claim for the evidentialist objector is that belief in God is *not* properly basic. Typically this objection has been rooted in some form of *classical foundationalism*, according to which a proposition *p* is properly basic for a person *S* if and only if *p* is either self-evident or incorrigible for *S* (modern foundationalism) or either self-evident or 'evident to the senses' for *S* (ancient and medival foundationalism). In [4] I argued that both forms of foundationalism are self referentially incoherent and must therefore be rejected.

Insofar as the evidentialist objection is rooted in classical foundationalism, it is poorly rooted indeed: and so far as I know, no one has developed and articulated any other reason for supposing that belief in God is not properly basic. Of course it doesn't follow that it *is* properly basic; perhaps the class of properly basic propositions is broader than classical foundationalists think, but still not broad enough to admit belief in God. But why think so? What might be the objections to the Reformed view that belief in God is properly basic?

I've heard it argued that if I have no evidence for the existence of God, then if I accept that proposition, my belief will be groundless, or gratuitous, or arbitrary. I think this is an error; let me explain.

Suppose we consider perceptual beliefs, memory beliefs, and beliefs which ascribe mental states to other persons: such beliefs as

    (1)   I see a tree,

    (2)   I had breakfast this morning,

and

    (3)   That person is angry.

Although beliefs of this sort are typically and properly taken as basic, it would be a mistake to describe them as *groundless*. Upon having experience of a certain sort, I believe that I am perceiving a tree. In the typical case I do not hold this belief on the basis of other beliefs; it is nonetheless not groundless. My having that characteristic sort of experience—to use Professor Chisholm's language, my being appeared treely to—plays a crucial role in the formation and justification of that belief. We might say this experience, together, perhaps, with other circumstances, is what *justifies* me in holding it; this is the *ground* of my justification, and, by extension, the ground of the belief itself.

If I see someone displaying typical pain behavior, I take it that he or she is in pain. Again, I don't take the displayed behavior as *evidence* for that belief; I don't infer that belief from others I hold; I don't accept it on the basis of other beliefs. Still, my perceiving the pain behavior plays a unique role in the formation and justification of that belief; as in the previous case, it forms the ground of my justification for the belief in question. The same holds for memory beliefs. I seem to remember having breakfast this morning; that is, I have an inclination to believe the proposition that I had breakfast, along with a certain past-tinged experience that is familiar to all but hard to describe. Perhaps we should say that I am appeared to pastly; but perhaps this insufficiently distinguishes the experience in question from that accompanying beliefs about the past not grounded in my own memory. The phenomonology of memory is a rich and unexplored realm; here I have no time to explore it. In this case as in the others, however, there is a justifying circumstance present, a condition that forms the ground of my justification for accepting the memory belief in question.

In each of these cases, a belief is taken as basic, and in each case properly taken as basic. In each case there is some circumstance or condition that confers justification; there is a circumstance that serves as the *ground* of justification. So in each case there will be some true proposition of the sort

    (4)   In condition C, S is justified in taking p as basic.

Of course C will vary with p. For a perceptual judgment such as

    (5)   I see a rose colored wall before me,

C will include my being appeared to in a certain fashion. No doubt C will include more. If I'm appeared to in the familiar fashion but know that I'm wearing rose colored glasses, or that I am suffering from a disease that causes me to be thus appeared to, no matter what the color of the nearby objects, then I'm not justified in taking (5) as basic. Similarly for memory. Suppose I know that my memory is unreliable; it often plays me tricks. In particular, when I seem to remember having breakfast, then, more often than not, I *haven't* had breakfast. Under these conditions I am not justified in taking it as basic that I had breakfast, even though I seem to remember that I did.

So being appropriately appeared to, in the perceptual case, is not sufficient for justification; some further condition—a condition hard to state in detail—is clearly necessary. The central point, here, however, is that a belief is properly basic only in certain conditions; these conditions are, we might say, the ground of its justification and, by extension, the ground of the belief itself. In this sense, basic beliefs are not, or are not necessarily, *groundless* beliefs.

Now similar things may be said about belief in God. When the Reformers claim that this belief is properly basic, they do not mean to say, of course, that there are no justifying circumstances for it, or that it is in that sense groundless or gratuitious. Quite the contrary. Calvin holds that God "reveals and daily discloses himself to the whole workmanship of the universe," and the divine art "reveals itself in the innumerable and yet distinct and well ordered variety of the heavenly host." God has so created us that we have a tendency or disposition to see his hand in the world about us. More precisely, there is in us a disposition to believe propositions of the sort *this flower was created by God* or *this vast and intricate universe was created by God* when we contemplate the flower or behold the starry heavens or think about the vast reaches of the universe.

Calvin recognizes, at least implicitly, that other sorts of conditions may trigger this disposition. Upon reading the Bible, one may be impressed with a deep sense that God is speaking to him. Upon having done what I know is cheap, or wrong, or wicked I may feel guilty in God's sight and form the belief *God disapproves of what I've done*. Upon confession and repentence, I may feel forgiven, forming the belief *God forgives me for what I've done*. A person in grave danger may turn to God, asking for his protection and help; and of course he or she then forms the belief that God is indeed able to hear and help if he sees fit. When life is sweet and satisfying, a spontaneous sense of gratitude may well up within the soul; someone in this condition may thank and praise the Lord for his goodness, and will of course form the accompanying belief that indeed the Lord is to be thanked and praised.

There are therefore many conditions and circumstances that call forth belief in God: guilt, gratitude, danger, a sense of God's presense, a sense that he speaks, perception of various parts of the universe. A complete job would explore the phenomenology of all these conditions and of more besides. This is a large and important topic; but here I can only point to the existence of these conditions.

Of course none of the beliefs I mentioned a moment ago is the simple belief that God exists. What we have instead are such beliefs as

(6) God is speaking to me,
(7) God has created all this,

(8) God disapproves of what I have done,

(9) God forgives me,

and

(10) God is to be thanked and praised.

These propositions are properly basic in the right circumstances. But it is quite consistent with this to suppose that the proposition *there is such a person as God* is neither properly basic nor taken as basic by those who believe in God. Perhaps what they take as basic are such propositions as (6)-(10), believing in the existence of God on the basis of propositions such as those. From this point of view, it isn't exactly right to say that it is belief in God that is properly basic; more exactly, what are properly basic are such propositions as (6)-(10), each of which self-evidently entails that God exists. It isn't the relatively high level and general proposition *God exists* that is properly basic, but instead propositions detailing some of his attributes or actions.

Suppose we return to the analogy between belief in God and belief in the existence of perceptual objects, other persons, and the past. Here too it is relatively specific and concrete propositions rather than their more general and abstract colleagues that are properly basic. Perhaps such items are

(11) There are trees,

(12) There are other persons,

and

(13) The world has existed for more than 5 minutes,

are not in fact properly basic; it is instead such propositions as

(14) I see a tree,

(15) that person is pleased,

and

(16) I had breakfast more than an hour ago,

that deserve that accolade. Of course propositions of the latter sort immediately and self-evidently entail propositions of the former sort; and perhaps there is thus no harm in speaking of the former as properly basic, even though so to speak is to speak a bit loosely.

The same must be said about belief in God. We may say, speaking loosely, that belief in God is properly basic; strictly speaking, however, it is probably not that proposition but such propositions as (6)-(10) that enjoy that status. But the main point, here, is that belief in God or (6)-(10), are properly basic; to say so, however, is not to deny that there are justifying conditions for these beliefs, or conditions that confer justification on one who accepts them as basic. They are therefore not groundless or gratuitous.

A second objection I've often heard: if belief in God is properly basic, why can't *just any* belief be properly basic? Couldn't we say the same for any bizarre abberation we can think of? What about voodoo or astrology? What about the belief that the Great Pumpkin returns every Halloween? Could I properly take *that* as basic? And if I can't, why can I properly take belief in God as basic? Suppose I believe that if I flap my arms with sufficient vigor, I can take off and fly about the room; could I defend myself against the charge of irrationality by claiming this belief is basic? If we say that belief in God is properly basic, won't we be committed to holding that just anything, or nearly anything, can properly be taken as basic, thus throwing wide the gates to irrationalism and superstitution?

Certainly not. What might lead one to think the Reformed epistemologist is in this kind of trouble? The fact that he rejects the criteria for proper basicality purveyed by classical foundationalism? But why should *that* be thought to commit him to such tolerance of irrationality? Consider an analogy. In the palmy days of positivism, the positivists went about confidently wielding their verifiability criterion and declaring meaningless much that was obviously meaningful. Now suppose someone rejected a formulation of that criterion—the one to be found in the second edition of A. J. Ayer's *Language, Truth and Logic*, for example. Would that mean she was committed to holding that

(17)   Twas brillig; and the slithy toves did gyre and gym-
       ble in the wabe

contrary to appearances, makes good sense? Of course not. But then the same goes for the Reformed epistemologist; the fact that he rejects the Classical Foundationalist's criterion of proper basicality does not mean that he is committed to supposing just anything is properly basic.

But what then is the problem? Is it that the Reformed epistemologist not only rejects those criteria for proper basicality, but seems in no hurry to produce what he takes to be a better substitute? If he has no such criterion, how can he fairly reject belief in the Great Pumpkin as properly basic?

This objection betrays an important misconception. How do we rightly arrive at or develop criteria for meaningfulness, or justified belief, or proper basicality? Where do they come from? Must one have such a criterion before one can sensibly make any judgments—positive or negative—about proper basicality? Surely not. Suppose I don't know of a satisfactory substitute for the criteria proposed by classical foundationalism; I am nevertheless entirely within my rights in holding that certain propositions are not properly basic in certain conditions. Some propositions seem self-evident when in fact they are not; that is the lesson of some of the Russell paradoxes. Nevertheless it would be irrational to take as basic the denial of a proposition that seems self-evident to you. Similarly, suppose it seems to you that you see a tree; you would then be irrational in taking as basic the proposition that you don't see a tree, or that there aren't any trees. In the same way, even if I don't know of some illuminating criterion of meaning, I can quite properly declare (17) meaningless.

And this raises an important question—one Roderick Chisholm has taught us to ask. What is the status of criteria for knowledge, or proper basicality, or justified belief? Typically, these are universal statements. The modern foundationalist's criterion for proper basicality, for example, is doubly universal:

(18)   For any proposition *A* and person *S*, *A* is properly
        basic for *S* if and only if *A* is incorrigible for *S* or
        self-evident to *S*.

But how could one know a thing like that? What are its credentials?
Clearly enough, (18) isn't self-evident or just obviously true. But if it
isn't, how does one arrive at it? What sorts of arguments would be
appropriate? Of course a foundationalist might find (18) so appealing,
he simply takes it to be true, neither offering argument for it, nor
accepting it on the basis of other things he believes. If he does so,
however, his noetic structure will be self-referentially incoherent. (18)
itself is neither self-evident nor incorrigible; hence in accepting (18) as
basic, the modern foundationalist violates the condition of proper
basicality he himself lays down in accepting it. On the other hand,
perhaps the foundationalist will try to produce some argument for it
from premises that are self-evident or incorrigible: it is exceedingly
hard to see, however, what such an argument might be like. And until
he has produced such arguments, what shall the rest of us do—we who
do not find (18) at all obvious or compelling? How could he use (18) to
show us that belief in God, for example, is not properly basic? Why
should we believe (18), or pay it any attention?

The fact is, I think, that neither (18) nor any other revealing
necessary and sufficient condition for proper basicality follows from
clearly self-evident premises by clearly acceptable arguments. And
hence the proper way to arrive at such a criterion is, broadly speaking,
inductive. We must assemble examples of beliefs and conditions such
that the former are obviously properly basic in the latter, and examples
of beliefs and conditions such that the former are obviously *not*
properly basic in the latter. We must then frame hypotheses as to the
necessary and sufficient conditions of proper basicality and test these
hypothesis by reference to those examples. Under the right conditions,
for example, it is clearly rational to believe that you see a human person
before you: a being who has thoughts and feelings, who knows and
believes things, who makes decisions and acts. It is clear, furthermore,
that you are under no obligation to reason to this belief from others you
hold; under those conditions that belief is properly basic for you. But
then (18) must be mistaken; the belief in question, under those circumstances, is properly basic, though neither self-evident nor incorrigible for you. Similarly, you may seem to remember that you had
breakfast this morning, and perhaps you know of no reason to suppose
your memory is playing you tricks. If so, you are entirely justified in
taking that belief as basic. Of course it isn't properly basic on the criteria
offered by classical offered by classical foundationalists; but that fact
counts not against you but against those criteria.

Accordingly, criteria for proper basicality must be reached from
below rather than above; they should not be presented as *ex Cathedra*,
but argued to and tested by a relevant set of examples. But there is no
reason to assume, in advance, that everyone will agree on the examples.
The Christian will of course suppose that belief in God is entirely
proper and rational; if he doesn't accept this belief on the basis of other
propositions, he will conclude that it is basic for him and quite properly

so. Followers of Bertrand Russell and Madelyn Murray O'Hare may disagree, but how is that relevant? Must my criteria, or those of the Christian community, conform to their examples? Surely not. The Christian community is responsible to *its* set of examples, not to theirs.

Accordingly, the Reformed epistemologist can properly hold that belief in the Great Pumpkin is not properly basic, even though he holds that belief in God is properly basic and even if he has no full fledged criterion of proper basicality. Of course he is committed to supposing that there is a relevant *difference* between belief in God and belief in the Great Pumpkin, if he holds that the former but not the latter is properly basic. But this should prove no great embarrassment; there are plenty of candidates. These candidates are to be found in the neighborhood of the conditions I mentioned in the last section that justify and ground belief in God. Thus, for example, the Reformed epistemologist may concur with Calvin in holding that God has implanted in us a natural tendency to see his hand in the world around us; the same cannot be said for the Great Pumpkin. there being no Great Pumpkin and no natural tendency to accept beliefs about the Great Pumpkin.

By way of conclusion then: being self-evident, or incorrigible, or evident to the senses is not a necessary condition of proper basicality. Furthermore, one who holds that belief in God *is* properly basic is not thereby committed to the idea that belief in God is groundless or gratuitous or without justifying circumstances. And even if he lacks a general criterion of proper basicality, he is not obliged to suppose that just any or nearly any belief—belief in the Great Pumpkin, for example —is properly basic. Like everyone should, he begins with examples; and he may take belief in the Great Pumpkin as a paradigm of irrational basic belief.

REFERENCES

[1] Blanshard, Brand, *Reason and Belief* (London: Allen & Unwin, 1974).
[2] Clifford, W. K., "The Ethics of Belief" in *Lectures and Essays* (London: Macmillan, 1879).
[3] Flew, A. G. N., *The Presumption of Atheism* (London: Pemberton Publishing Co., 1976).
[4] Plantinga, A., "Is Belief in God Rational?" in *Rationality and Religious Belief*, ed. C. Delaney (Notre Dame: University of Notre Dame Press, 1979).
[5] ———, "The Reformed Objection to Natural Theology," *Proceedings of the American Catholic Philosophical Association*, 1980.
[6] Russell, Bertrand, "Why I am not a Christian," in *Why I am Not a Christian* (New York: Simon & Schuster, 1957).
[7] Scrivin, Michael, *Primary Philosophy* (New York: McGraw-Hill, 1966).

NOTES

[1]See, for example [1], pp. 400 ff, [2], pp. 345 ff, [3], p. 22, [6], pp. 3 ff. and [7], pp. 87 ff. In [4] I consider and reject the evidentialist objection to theistic belief.

[2]A Reformed thinker or theologian is one whose intellectual sympathies lie with the Protestant tradition going back to John Calvin (not someone who was formerly a theologian and has since seen the light).

What Sorts of Religion Are There?

Keith Yandell

Different religions offer differing diagnoses and cures. Given that criterion, there are a good many religions. The diagnosis that a particular religion articulates asserts that every human person has a basic nonphysical illness so deep that, unless it is cured, one's potential is unfulfilled and one's nature cripplingly flawed. Then a cure is proffered. The diagnosis and cure assume (or, if you prefer, entail) the essential structure of a religion's view of what there is, at least insofar as what there is has religious importance.

Not only are there different religions; there are different *sorts* of religion. The notion of a *sort* or kind of religion is not a paradigm of clarity. Perhaps this criterion will lend it some clarity:

Criterion 1: Religion A is of a *different sort* from Religion B if one can have the problem that A diagnoses without having the problem that B diagnoses, one can have the problem that B diagnoses without having the problem that A diagnoses, the cure that A proffers would not cure the disease that B diagnoses, and the cure that B proffers would not cure the disease that A diagnoses.

A different criterion that nonetheless will yield results that at least largely overlap those we get from applying Criterion 1 is:

Criterion 2: Religion A is of a *different sort* from Religion B if what must exist if A's diagnosis and cure are correct can exist without what must exist if B's diagnosis and cure are correct, and conversely.

A stronger version goes:

Criterion 3: Religion A is of a *different sort* from Religion B if what must exist if A's diagnosis and cure are correct cannot co-exist with what must exist if B's diagnosis and cure are correct, and conversely.

To offer an even partial answer as to what sorts of religion there are, examples are crucial. Consider, then, four traditions that are generally accepted as being religious: Christianity, Advaita Vedanta Hinduism, Jainism, and Theravada Buddhism. Christendom contains an incredible variety of perspectives. Hinduism, even if it is not the invention of nineteenth-century British scholars, is at least as diverse as Christendom. Buddhism is also a collection of quite diverse traditions and even Jainism has its complications. Nonetheless, there is such a thing as *orthodox* Christianity ("orthodox" with a small "o"), and an absolutist variety of Hinduism, Advaita Vedanta, whose greatest figure is Shankara. Indian Buddhism splits into Mahayana or "Great Vehicle" as well as Hinayana or "Small Vehicle;" our present concern is with Hinayana or Theravada Buddhism, the "Tradition of the Elders." Jainism, by contrast, is doctrinally uniform. A description of each of these four traditions in terms that would be accepted by its own adherents[2] will tell us a good deal about what sorts of religion there are. Each tradition represents a distinct sort of religion.

Monotheism

Christianity

Christianity, of course, is a variety of monotheism. It shares with Judaism the exhortation to "Hear, O Israel, the Lord is one God." Like Judaism and Islam, it holds that an omnipotent, omniscient, and morally perfect God created the world and is providential over it. God depends for existence on nothing else, and everything else that exists depends on God for its existence. The created world is real, not illusory, and that it exists is a good, not an evil, state of affairs. Human beings are created in God's image, and thus have some degree of knowledge, power, and (potential) goodness. This has two consequences. One is that every person, as a person, has (in Immanuel Kant's terms) dignity and not price – if you like, has irreplaceable worth by virtue of being in God's image. Persons having inherent worth as creatures made in God's image is different from their being inherently morally good; whether a person becomes morally good or not depends on his or her choices. We might put the point this way: *being created in God's image* comprises a *metaphysical* goodness that is a gift provided in the very circumstance of being created; *being morally virtuous* constitutes *moral* goodness and it is not involved in the very act of being created. The other consequence is that the basis of morality lies in realizing one's nature by imitating the behavior biblically ascribed to God, insofar as this is humanly possible. God is holy, so we are to be holy. God unselfishly loves, so we ought to love unselfishly. Human individuality is real, not illusory, and it is good not evil, that individuals exist. God loves all persons in the sense of willing their ultimate good and acting for it. Central to being made in God's image is having the capacity for loving others and oneself in the sense of willing their and our ultimate good and acting for it. Love in this sense is primarily volitional, not primarily emotional. God is providential in the sense of governing the course of history and moving it toward the Kingdom of God, so that time is real and the historical process is real and one-directional (not cyclical). It is a good, not an evil, that there are temporal and historical events. God is holy both in the sense of being unique, alone worthy of being worshipped, and of being morally pure or righteous. Thus worship is not a preliminary religious experience to be later transcended; its appropriateness is built into the nature of the distinction between Creator and creature, which is not a dissolvable distinction. As God is righteous, God judges sin. Sin is freely performed action that violates God's moral law; sin also is a defect of our nature due to our living in a world in which sinful actions proliferate. Sin prevents one's realizing his or her nature as made in God's image. Since God loves all persons, God hates what harms persons, and hence hates sin. Intolerance of sin is not opposed to, but follows from, the nature of divine love. Thus human sin and guilt are real, not illusory, and it is better that persons act freely and exercise moral agency than that they be made unable to sin. The basic religious problem is sin, and the deepest religious need is for forgiveness. Forgiveness is provided by God's grace or unmerited favor; it is not earned by human effort. God has acted in history at real times and in real places to reveal information that otherwise we would not have had and to act on our behalf. Central religious doctrines make *essential* reference to certain persons and events. Religious knowledge, at least in part, is gained through revelation rather than through reflection, meditation, self-abasement, or the like.

Much or all of this applies as well to Judaism and Islam, at least in their more orthodox varieties. What is distinct about Christianity, not surprisingly, is the life, death, and resurrection of Christ. In the Apostle Paul's summary of the basic Christian Gospel, he tells his audience: "I delivered unto you what I also received, that Christ died for our sins according to the Scriptures, and was buried, and rose again from the dead, according to the Scriptures." That Christ lived sinlessly, that Christ died "the Just for the Unjust in order to bring us to God," that "Christ, who knew no sin, was made to be sin for us," that "Christ bore our sins in his own body on the tree," and that Christ bodily rose from the dead, are claims central to – indeed, they *are* – the Christian Gospel, the content of the Christian message.

Transition

Vedanta, Jainism, and Theravada Buddhism at root are Indian religions. Each has its own sacred texts. Advaita Vedanta and Theravada Buddhism rather considerably qualify what is meant by reincarnation and karma, but they begin with these as assumptions. There is a story that, in its Jain version, goes as follows:

> A traveller was journeying through a dense forest when he encountered a mad elephant which charged him with upraised trunk. As he turned to flee, a terrible demoness with a naked sword in her hand appeared before him and barred his path. There was a great tree near the track, and he ran up to it, hoping to find safety in its branches, but he could find no foothold in its smooth trunk. His only refuge was an old well, covered with grass and weeds, at the foot of the tree, and into this he leapt. As he fell, he managed to catch hold of a clump of reeds which grew from the wall, and there he hung, midway between the mouth of the well and its bottom. Looking down, he saw that the bottom did not contain water, but was surrounded by snakes, which hissed at him as he hung above them. In their midst was a mighty python, its mouth agape, waiting to catch him when he fell. Raising his head again, he saw two mice, one white and the other black, busily eating away at the roots. Meanwhile, the

wild elephant ran up to the well and, enraged at losing its victim, began charging at the trunk of the tree. Thus he dislodged a honeycomb which hung from a branch above the well, and it fell upon the man hanging there so precariously. Angry bees swarmed round his head and tormented him with their stings. But one drop of honey fell on his brow, rolled down to his face, and reached his lips. Immediately, he forgot his peril and thought of nothing more than of obtaining another drop of honey.

Reincarnation and karma

Common to Hinduism, Jainism, and Theravada Buddhism are two familiar assumptions. Each accepts as a basic framework the doctrines of *reincarnation* (that each person is beginninglessly born and dies and is reborn and redies, and that this will occur endlessly short of one's achieving enlightenment) and *karma* (that one's right actions will be rewarded and one's wrong actions will be punished, without exception, save as this is qualified in some varieties of Vedanta by a doctrine of divine grace). Thus for each of these perspectives a religion should tell you how to 'escape the wheel' or stop the otherwise endless sequence of births and deaths.

From the perspective of a reincarnation/karma view, there might seem to be a highly attractive alternative open to us all. By living morally decent lives, according to this perspective, we can guarantee that we are reborn in pleasant circumstances; there is no necessary end to this process. Thus by living according to a decent moral code, we can look forward to an unending travel program under positive circumstances. Why isn't this a recommended alternative?

One reason is that on the relevant perspective one cannot, in this lifetime, make a decision that is irrevocably effective over one's future lifetimes; perhaps in the very next lifetime one will opt for drunken stupors and drug trips over endeavor for enlightenment. But there is also a deeper reason.

A Hindu text reads as follows:

> In this ill-smelling body, which is a conglomerate of bone, skin, muscle, marrow, flesh, semen, blood, mucus, tears, rheum, feces, urine, wind, bile, and phlegm, what is the good of enjoyment of desires? . . . In this body, which is afflicted with desire, anger, covetousness, delusion, fear, despondency, envy, separation from the desirable, union with the undesirable, hunger, thirst, senility, disease, sorrow, and the like, what is the good of the enjoyment of desires? . . . we see that this whole world is decaying . . . In this sort of cycle of existence, what is the good of the enjoyment of desires, when after a man has fed on them there is seen repeatedly his return here to earth? . . . in this cycle of existence I am a frog in a waterless well.

A Theravada text[11] says:

What then is the Holy Truth of Ill? Birth is ill, decay is ill, sickness is ill, death is ill. To be disjoined from what one likes means suffering. Not to get what one wants also that means suffering. In short, all grasping at any of the five Skandas [the elements of personality] involves suffering.

Being a frog in countless waterless wells, or suffering in endless cosmic variety, in these views, only prolongs a problem to which religion should provide a solution. An everlasting series of reincarnations would be the analogue to hell. Life is viewed as inherently unsatisfactory or unsatisfying – one scholar uses "unsatisfactoriness" rather than "suffering" in dealing with the sort of Buddhist text just quoted. Hinduism, Jainism, and Theravada Buddhism, then, each offers an escape from the Wheel of reincarnations.

The point of the story of the traveller in the forest now becomes clear. Most people are like the traveller. We focus our attention on "the things of this world" as the traveller focuses simply on the sweet taste of the honey. But the honey gives no solution to his deep, real problem. So most of us pay no attention to our deep religious problem. "The things of this world" provide no solution to that problem, whether we live grandly or barely survive. This is the point of the story. On that point, at least, religious traditions typically agree.

Advaita Vedanta

Advaita Vedanta is one of three main schools of Vedantic Hinduism; the other two are monotheistic. Popular Advaita Vedanta tends to polytheistic or monotheistic practices. Nonetheless, Advaita Vedanta takes monotheism to belong to *the realm of appearance* rather than to *the realm of reality*. There are two major ways of trying to explain what this distinction amounts to. One way treats the appearance/reality distinction epistemologically or relative to human knowledge, and speaks of *levels of truth*. Another way treats the appearance versus reality distinction metaphysically or in terms of what exists independent of human thought, and speaks of *levels of being*. The levels of being view goes something like this.

Suppose that something A depends for its existence on B, and B does not depend for its existence on anything else. Then one might (somewhat misleadingly) say that B has more reality than A, although strictly what is true is that B's existence is more secure than A's. Suppose, further, that B has more power, and knowledge, and goodness than A, or is more complex than A, or the like – suppose that B's properties are in some way more glorious than A's. Then one might say that B is "more real" than A in the sense of being more valuable than A, more worth imitating than A, or the like. It seems less open to misunderstanding to say all of this in terms of the greater existential security and the higher value that attaches to B, but insofar as what was intended was consistent, these sorts of things seem to be what philosophers who have talked about "degrees of existence" have had in mind. But this – the levels of being line – cannot be the way to understand Shankara. For if appearance depends on Reality, then appearance and Reality are such that appearance bears a genuine and non-illusory or non-apparent relationship to Reality; both appearance and Reality exist, and the former depends on the latter. On Shankara's view, Reality can bear no such relationship to anything. Further, the properties of Reality can be more glorious than appearance's properties only if Reality has more glorious properties than those of appearance, and so on this view Reality has properties. But according to Shankara, Reality is *nirguna* or qualityless. So the levels of being line will not do as an exposition of Advaita Vedanta.

There remains the levels of truth line. Some elementary points regarding this are: (1) strictly, truth has no degrees; as a property of propositions, which seems what is here relevant, it is either present or not; (2) no doubt "more true" can be given some use, and if one is very careful no doubt this will cause no confusion; then we need to ask exactly what this sense is: compare "more perfect;" (3) if two propositions are contradictory then one must be true and the other false.

Now on a levels of truth view, the truth about Reality is one level of truth and the truth about appearance is another level of truth. Reality is qualityless Brahman. Thus when Brahman is described as being, consciousness, and bliss — *sat, cit, ananda* — this (if Brahman is really qualityless) is but to deny that Brahman has the properties of being non-existent, unconscious, and miserable. The truth about Reality, on Shankara's view, is that Brahman exists, and for any property, Brahman lacks it. This is a bit sparse, but it is the truth at the level of reality. The other level concerns appearance. There is something funny about the phrase "the truth about appearance" when used in this context. The reason for this is simple: strictly speaking, appearance does not exist. *That* is the truth about it. Perhaps, then, appearance is simply the way Reality looks to the unenlightened. But the unenlightened are *part* of appearance. Thus *they* do not exist, and so cannot be appeared to. The levels of truth view is that Reality appears to be one way and is another; there are perceptual experiences but they are all unreliable or misleading and there are perceivers but they are misled. But then these misleading experiences and misled perceivers must be real. But strictly they do not exist; they are not merely less glorious than the Real, but altogether non-existent. It is thus not easy to see how the lower level of truth is to be conceived. On it, appearance is as hard to make out as Reality.

Having spent some time in indicating some of the complexity involved in interpreting Advaita Vedanta, and given some indication of the sort of features that lead to objections by such non-Advaitic figures as Ramanuja and Madhva, let me turn to offering a brief and fairly straightforward description of this tradition. There is an ultimate and independent reality that is apersonal. To say that God is infinite is not, as in monotheistic contexts, to say that God is omnipotent, omniscient, and morally perfect. Rather, it is to say that everything is divine. For monotheism, "infinite" is an adjective, and to speak of "the Infinite" is to raise the question "The Infinite *what?*" For Advaita Vedanta, "the Infinite" is a noun referring to Brahman. Persons seem to be enduring mental substances, and the objects of sensory perception seem to be enduring physical substances. This indeed is how they are to be viewed unless we turn to the level of Reality. Then the truth is that each Atman or enduring self is identical to Brahman; "Thou art that." The basic religious problem is ignorance — taking appearance to be Reality. Escape from this ignorance requires that one attain *moksha*, an esoteric experience in which it is alleged that no subject/conscious/object or subject/object distinction can be made. Personal identity obviously is not retained in one's solving one's religious problem; indeed, strictly, personal identity is viewed as always illusory and you cannot retain what you never had. Achieving *moksha* is due to one's efforts; salvation is essentially a do-it-yourself project for Advaita Vedanta, as it is for Jainism and Theravada Buddhism. An Advaita Vedanta text tells us that "the man who has once comprehended Brahman to be the [real] self does not belong to this transmigratory world . . . There prevails the false notion that the Lord [i.e. Brahman] and the transmigrating soul are different." The description of Advaita Vedanta offered here is, in effect, an explanation of what this passage means according to an Advaitic interpretation.

Jainism

Jainism is a particularly interesting religion in that it holds to the immortality of the soul without being monotheistic. It holds that the self or person or *jiva* is an enduring mental substance that is inherently immortal. Human persons *appear to be* enduring mental substances because they *are* enduring mental substances, just as physical objects appear to be enduring physical substances because they are. A Jaina text says straightforwardly that "modifications cannot exist without an abiding or eternal something – a permanent substance." But persons seem to have limitations that they do not have, and by attaining an esoteric state of enlightenment – *kevala* – one can see that these limitations are illusory. Thus in the *Jaina Sutras* one reads that when the Venerable Ascetic Mahavira had become enlightened, he was

> omniscient and comprehending all objects; he knew and saw all conditions of the world, of gods, men, and demons: whence they come, whither they go, whether they are born as men or animals . . . or become gods or hell-beings . . . the ideas, the thoughts of their minds, the food, doings, desires, the open and secret deeds of all living beings in the whole world; he the Arhat, for whom there is no secret, knew and saw all conditions of all living beings in the world, what they thought, spoke, or did at any moment.

Occasionally it is claimed that one who reaches *kevala* even learns that he or she is omnipotent; at any rate, one learns that one is omniscient and dependent for one's existence on nothing external to oneself. The same *Sutras* say of the soul that "since it possesses no corporeal form, it is eternal." This is not a variety of monotheism; there is no reference to God or (as in monotheistic Hinduism) to Brahman with qualities. Nor does it posit an identity between the soul and qualityless Brahman. Another Jaina text says that

Liberation is the freedom from all karmic matter, owing to the non-existence of the cause of bondage and to the shedding of the *karmas*. After the soul is released, there remain perfect right-belief, perfect right-knowledge, and the state of having accomplished all.

Thus personal identity is retained in enlightenment; a mental substance that once existed under severe epistemic and other constraints is freed from those constraints.

Buddhism

Theravada Buddhism

A Buddhist text says that

Nagasena [or any other personal proper name] is but a way of counting, term, appellation, convenient designation, mere name for the hair of my head, hair of my body . . . brain of the head, form, sensation, perception, the predispositions and consciousness. But in the absolute sense there is no ego.

An individual person is a set of elements, each momentary and transitory, and everything else is made up of momentary, transitive states as well. There is no *atman* or *jiva* or enduring self – no enduring mental substance – nor is there an unchanging ultimate Brahman. Thus one reads that

Misery only doth exist, none miserable. No doer is there; naught save the deed is found. Nirvana is, but not the man who seeks this. That path exists, but not the man who seeks this. That path exists, but not the traveller on it.

We are told that as

the word "chariot" is but a name for pole, axle, wheels, chariot-body, and banner staff . . . [the proper name] "Nagasena" is but a . . . mere name for the hair of my head, brain of the head, form, sensation, perception, the predispositions, and consciousness. But in the absolute sense there is no ego to be found.

In a this-life experience that prefigures final nirvana the enlightened one learns this truth concerning impermanence. Final nirvana is the cessation of even this transitory self with consequent release from all desire. Nirvana alone is changeless.

Comparison

It may aid comprehension if we compare and contrast our Indian traditions. For Advaita Vedanta, there is a distinction between the apparent self and the real; one cannot escape transmigration without knowing the nature of this distinction — namely, that the real self is identical with qualityless Brahman. For Jainism, there is a distinction between the way the self appears regarding knowledge and dependence and the way the self is regarding knowledge and dependence; we are omniscient and independent, and one cannot escape transmigration without knowing this. For Theravada, we tend to believe that there is an enduring ego or self, and there is none; one cannot escape transmigration without knowing this. In each case, the religious problem we all face is said to be ignorance of our own nature. Each religious tradition has its own account of the truth about what our nature is. Correspondingly, each has its own cure, namely the recognition of and appropriate reaction to the truth about ourselves.

The criteria applied

According to Christianity, our sickness is that we have sinned against God and the cure is that God provide forgiveness and restoration. According to Advaita Vedanta, the sickness is our ignorance of our being identical with Brahman and the cure is gaining this knowledge. According to Jainism, the sickness is that we think we are ignorant and dependent and the cure is learning that we are omniscient and existentially independent. According to Theravada Buddhism, our sickness is that we take ourselves to be enduring substances and the cure is learning that we are only transitory states. While brief, lacking subtlety and detail, these remarks are also accurate.

We can summarize the diagnoses and cures as follows:

- Christianity: sinners, divine forgiveness and restoration;
- Advaita Vedanta: ignorance of Brahman, knowledge of Brahman;
- Jainism: assumed ignorance and dependence, knowledge of independence and omniscience;
- Theravada Buddhism: assumed status as enduring substances, knowledge of transitory states.

Earlier, three criteria were offered of what it might mean to speak about different *sorts* of religions. The first of these was:

Criterion 1: Religion A is of a *different sort* from Religion B if one can have the problem that A diagnoses without having the problem that B diagnoses, one can have the problem that B diagnoses without having the problem that A diagnoses, the cure that A proffers would not cure the disease that B diagnoses, and the cure that B proffers would not cure the disease that A diagnoses.

Assuming that it is logically possible that any one of these diagnoses be correct, and logically possible that any one of these cures works regarding its target disease, it is obviously possible to have any of the alleged diseases – sin, ignorance of Brahman, assumed dependence and ignorance, assumed enduring substance and actual transitory states – without having any of the others. Further, no one cure would work for any of the sicknesses save the one with which it is correlated by the religious tradition that suggests it. So, by Criterion 1, we have four distinct sorts of religions.

The second criterion was:

Criterion 2: Religion A is of a *different sort* from Religion B if what must exist if A's diagnosis and cure is correct can exist without what must exist if B's diagnosis and cure are correct, and conversely.

What must exist if the diagnoses and cures are correct can be represented as follows:

- Christianity: God, persons created by God;
- Advaita Vedanta: only qualityless Brahman;
- Jainism: independently existing persons;
- Theravada Buddhism:[11] only transitory states.

Assuming that each account of what there must be if the diagnoses and cures are correct is possibly true, it is obvious that each could exist without the others existing.

The third criterion was:

Criterion 3: Religion A is of a *different sort* from Religion B if what must exist if A's diagnosis and cure are correct cannot co-exist with what must exist if B's diagnosis and cure are correct, and conversely.

Plainly, in the context of its overall religious tradition, each account of what there is has this feature: if it is true, the others are not.

Given the discussion just concluded, it is clear that Christianity, Advaita Vedanta, Theravada Buddhism, and Jainism are, given any of these criteria, different sorts of religions. One may like, dislike, or be indifferent to this fact; but it is a fact. These are neither all the religions nor all the sorts of religion that there are. But we have made progress in laying out data relevant to philosophical reflections about religion.

Religious Pluralism

Keith Yandell

Religious plurality and religious pluralism

Religious plurality is simply a fact. There are religious traditions that differ deeply in terms of their doctrines, practices, institutions, scriptures, experiences, and hopes. Our concern is with religious pluralism – RP for short. RP is one interpretation of religious plurality. It comes in several varieties, among which one is in danger of becoming canonical. The nearly canonical version says that all nice religious traditions are "equally valid." Its longest expression is in Professor John Hick's 1989 *An Interpretation of Religion*. The expression that makes the strongest effort to answer criticisms is Professor Hick's 1995 *A Christian Theology of Religions*. We will focus on the 1995 expression, assessing RP as one finds it there.

The content of religious pluralism

At least much of the core of RP is captured by these claims.

1 Each religion asks generically the same question: how do we get from our present lack to a better future?
2 Each world religion is a response to the same thing.
3 Each world religion has its own phenomenal reality.
4 Since each world religion has its own phenomenal reality, the claims of one world religion do not conflict with those of another world religion.
5 Responding to this phenomenal reality is, so far as we can tell, equally effective in each world religion.
6 Each world religion is equally valid.
7 The sentences that apparently express the doctrines of the great world religions actually are mythological in the sense of telling a story which elicits behavior.
8 The mythology is true if the behavior is good.
9 The reason for accepting religious pluralism is that it is the best explanation of central facts about religious plurality.

The general idea of RP goes like this. One begins by engaging in an act of abstraction. Particular diagnoses and cures are replaced by a vague question. Then appeal is made to the notion of phenomenal reality. The language of "phenomenal versus noumenal" is derived from the philosophy of Immanuel Kant. Its relevance to religious pluralism is that all the things that all religions think exist turn out to exist only phenomenally, not noumenally. Each religious phenomenal being is peculiar to one religious tradition. Each religious tradition makes claims about its own phenomenal being. Response to one phenomenal being in one religious tradition seems to produce people who are roughly as nice as response to another phenomenal being in another religious tradition.[10] Since this is so, one religious tradition is about equally effective in producing niceness as another. We can express this by saying that each is "equally valid." If we use "true" here we should mean "effective in producing nice people." We remove religious traditions further from considerations of truth if we claim that while they appear to make claims about what there is, religious traditions are myths or extended metaphors whose function is to elicit behavior. The reason for accepting this is that it better explains religious plurality than anything else.

Some religion-relevant consequences of RP

Here are some religion-relevant consequences of RP. First, each religious tradition is said to deal with phenomenal realities. According to RP, Jahweh and the Father and Allah and Brahman and Jivas and the Buddha-nature are all phenomenal realities. A phenomenal reality is something to which human cognitive capacities and the Real contribute. It is something that RP says arises when a human being responds to the Real in religious experience. It is how the Real appears to someone. Remove all human beings and you remove all phenomenal reality. One not immersed in the evasionary language of RP would simply say: phenomenal beings do not exist. After all, ghosts and leprechauns are describable as responses to something external to the one who claims to experience them. At best, the things that religious traditions think exist are like colors on the standard view in Modern Philosophy: they exist only in the sense that perceivers of colorless objects are affected by those objects. On this view, colors are subjective, mind-dependent contents of perceptual experiences that do not represent qualities in the things that cause them. RP, then, claims that Jahweh, the Father, Allah, etc. have an existence that depends on our minds and experiences. Put without evasion, RP has this to say to religious traditions: what you believe in simply does not exist. So far, it agrees with naturalism.

This comes out in another way when RP claims that religious traditions are really extended metaphors or myths that are, not true or false, but useful. I deny that there are roses if I say that there are no roses. I also deny that there are roses if I say that all talk of roses is an extended metaphor or a myth which is useful if it produces a certain sort of behavior. The same goes for parallel claims regarding God or nirvana.

Second, if RP is true, then no one has any of the problems that any religious tradition says they have. The one religious problem is that we are not morally nice. The one solution to that is to respond to something in such a way as to become nice. If things the traditions believe in do not exist, then the problems they think need solution do not actually plague anyone.

Third, evangelism is anathema to RP. Any member of any religious tradition who tries to convert someone is guilty of "treason against the peace and diversity of the human family."[11] Evangelism for RP of course comes under no such condemnation.

It is hardly obvious that, whatever the intent, one actually shows great respect for all religions by holding a view that denies that anything they think exists does exist and denying that what they take to be deep problems are problems at all. The same goes for holding a view that proposes replacing them by different claims that do not claim that any of the things they believe in exist or any of the problems they take seriously exist either. Further, RP itself looks suspiciously like an attempt at a new world religion which gives us a diagnosis of what it takes our deep problem to be really, though it has yet to propose a cure of its own.

There remains, then, the philosophical question to which everything said here thus far is preparatory: what reason, if any, is there to accept or reject RP?

A critical discussion of RP: Part one

It is on the face of it implausible to think that all religious experience is experience of the same thing. Neither the content nor the structure of such experience indicates that this suggestion is anything better than fanciful.[12] Thus there is a considerable hurdle over which RP must jump in order to have any initial promise. But set this aside.

Human concepts

What should be said about RP depends on which of various emphases one has in mind. RP makes various claims about restrictions on what one may properly say about Real. More than one account is given of these restrictions.

One account speaks of "human concepts."[13] A human concept is not a concept that applies to humans, but one that humans use. RP uses this claim, or one much like it, to deny that such concepts as *self-conscious being* and *non-self-conscious being* apply to the Real. The claim again comes in two steps:

(HC1) A human concept is any concept humans use.
(HC2) No human concept applies to the Real.

These two claims constitute what might be called Maximally Restrictive RP. In this mood one finds RP denying that even "exists" and "does not exist" can apply to the Real. RP denies that number concepts apply to the Real[14] though it also claims that there is only one item appropriately designated "the Real." The result is that Maximally Restrictive RP is self-destructing. It says about the Real that nothing can be so said.

RP also insists that the Real is transcendent, a condition of our existence and our highest good,[16] and that to which religion and religious experience are responses.[17] But of course these too are human concepts, and the same filter that stops concepts used by actual religious traditions would also stop them in RP were RP not to cheat on its own behalf. But on Maximally Restrictive RP it is also a mistake to ascribe transcendence, being a condition of our existence and wellbeing, and a contributor to religious experience to the Real.

Another account of the restrictions on what may properly be said about the Real is that only properties that are "generated" by logic alone may be ascribed to the Real. I take the notion to be this. Logic holds in all possible worlds. It applies to anything there possibly is, and hence to everything there actually is. To deny this is to embrace a self-contradictory claim. So far, so good.

The sorts of property logic "generates" are those properties that something must have if it is to be anything at all.[19] "Properties" here covers qualities and relations. Examples of such properties are *having properties, having only consistent properties, being self-identical, not being identical to anything different* and the like.[20] A letter home from a college student saying "I've met the most wonderful person — she *has properties* and *has only consistent properties*" will not communicate much about the student's new love interest. Mediumly Restrictive RP says that the only properties we can properly ascribe to the Real are properties that logic "generates."

The point is worth laboring. It has two parts as follows.

1   A property P is generated by logic if and only if *logic applies to X entails X has P*.
2   The only properties that can properly be ascribed to the Real are properties generated by logic.

This supposedly trivial admission has devastating consequences for RP.

Why the point is not trivial

First, note the properties that RP ascribes to the Real. It is transcendent.[21] There being the Real is a condition of our existence.[22] There being the Real is a condition of our wellbeing.[23] The Real is what all religious experience is a response to.[24] Talk of "the Real" with its various historical associations with features often spoken of with reference to God should not mislead us here. The Real is not personal, not conscious, and not God.

Second, note that none of these properties is generated by logic. It goes against a fundamental rule of Mediumly Restrictive RP to apply them to the Real. According to this RP doctrine, these properties cannot be ascribed to the Real. In case the point isn't clear, if RP is true, the Real cannot be said to be transcendent, a condition of our existence or our wellbeing, or what religious experience responds to. To ascribe such properties to the Real is to cheat at the RP game. No amount of talk about triviality alters the fact that this is so.

Third, note that if none of these properties – *being transcendent, being a condition of our existence, being a condition of our wellbeing, being what religious experience is a response to* – can be ascribed to the Real, then the explanation that RP offers of religious plurality is impermissible. That explanation, stated consistently with RP, is this:

(RPE) There is something to which only such properties as *having properties, having only consistent properties,* and other logically generable properties can be ascribed, which is transcendent, a condition of our existence and wellbeing, and is what religious experience responds to.

Which entails:

(RPE*) There is something to which only logically generable properties may properly be ascribed and to which properties that are not logically generable may properly be ascribed.

Now (RPE*) is self-contradictory. Anything that entails a self-contradiction is itself self-contradictory. So (RPE) is self-contradictory. Self-contradictions are necessarily false. So (RPE) is necessarily false. But (RPE) is the very core of RP. So RP is necessarily false. It commits intellectual suicide of the worst sort. It has no possibly true explanation of religious plurality. Explanations that are not even possibly true are not genuine explanations. So it has no genuine explanation of religious plurality – none whatever.

We might ask if there is another way to restrict RP. This brings us to Minimally Restricted RP which says that properties to be ascribed to the Real so long as they are *either* properties generable from logic alone *or* what we might call *happy* properties – short for "properties an RP supporter could without inconsistency be happy to ascribe to the Real."[26] Then we need something like this:

(H) A property is *happy* if and only if it is (i) not generable from logic, (ii) the Real's having it is not incompatible with any doctrine that any religion accepts, (iii) there is no reason to think that the Real lacks this property, and (iv) the Real having this property would give content to the idea that there being such a thing as the Real might explain something RP is supposed to explain.

Whatever charm this idea has is at least matched by its vacuity. The Real being intelligent is one candidate for being a happy property. There are religious doctrines with which ascribing it to the Real are incompatible. So it will go for example after example. The implicit assumption of RP (in some passages, at least) is that we won't find any happy properties. This seems very plausible indeed. In fact, the existence of Advaita Vedanta and the absolutist brand of Mahayana Buddhism guarantee this result. Causal or dependence relations between what Advaita Vedanta or absolutist Mahayana Buddhism takes to exist and human persons are denied. RP's own attempt to be consistent with everything leads it to internal inconsistency. Any talk of the Real being

93

what we respond to in religious experience, being transcendent in relation to our immanence as things that do exist, or being a condition of our existence and of our highest good distinguishes between us and ultimate reality in a way that Advaita Vedanta and absolutist Mahayana Buddhism (to take but two examples) deny. So Minimally Restrictive RP fails as well.

The importance to RP of (RPE)

According to RP, the Real is not anything described within any of the religious traditions – not Jahweh, the Father, Allah, the Buddha or the Buddha-nature, Brahman, Atman, Jiva, or whatever. It is supposed to be what is experienced as all these things, and more. Of course, *being experienced as Jahweh, the Father, Allah, the Buddha or the Buddha-nature, Brahman, Atman, Jiva, etc.* is also not a property – neither a quality nor a relation – generated by logic alone. Any such ascription to the Real – another ascription essential to RP – is bogus on RP terms.

This suggests the possibility that perhaps RP should simply drop the claim that only properties generated by logic can apply to the Real. After all, RP makes a career of violating the rule that only properties generated by logic may be ascribed to the Real. So one who accepts RP might as well abandon in theory what it habitually violates in practice. This suggestion ignores the crucial role that the claim that only properties that are generated by logic may properly be ascribed to the Real plays in RP. Professor Hick is aware of that role.

The gist of the reasoning behind the various RP restrictions is that if one does not limit RP-approved descriptions of the Real to properties generated by logic alone, one has no basis in RP for not doing one or the other of two RP-forbidden things:

1   One might ascribe to the Real either only the properties ascribed to Jahweh by Judaism, or to the Father by Christianity, or to Allah by Islam, or to the Buddha-nature by Mahayana Buddhism, etc. and then allow other ascriptions only if they are compatible with the favored ascription (this would treat one religion as true, the others as importantly false) or
2   One might try to ascribe to the Real all of the properties ascribed to Jahweh by Judaism, the Father by Christianity, Allah by Islam, the Buddha-nature by Mahayana Buddhism, etc. with the result that the Real allegedly has a lot of logically inconsistent properties (this would treat all religions as true).

Even with the few examples given, and especially if one considers the long list of alternatives not mentioned, two things should be clear:

1   The only-one-religion-is-true line will require that much of very many religious traditions is false.
2   The all-religions-are-true line will yield one massive contradiction – indeed, a whole intellectual museum of contradictions.

The all-religions-are-true line is self-contradictory. The only-one-religion-is-true line is not self-contradictory, but it is anathema to RP. Reject the view that only properties generated from logic alone can be properly ascribed to the Real, and one has either the all-religions-are-true line or the only-one-religion-is-true line. So rejection of the view that only properties generated from logic can be properly ascribed to the Real leads to self-contradiction or to what RP finds despicable. So that view is one RP is reluctant to reject. Dropping it is as attractive to RP as beekeeping in swimwear is to those allergic to stings.

To put things bluntly, it is by appeal to the idea that the Real is both what religious experience is a response to and can be said to have no property not generable from logic alone that RP shifts religious traditions from being *either true or false, and largely incompatible* to *being useful, and non-competitive.* Drop either of those claims, and the shift is without basis in RP.

A critical discussion of RP:
Part two

Various other attempts might be made to state a non-self-destructive and non-self-contradictory version of the restriction that RP so desperately needs. For example, one might consider two views about properties as follows.

Natures or essences

Consider the doctrine of *property universalism* which holds this:

(PU)   For any item X and property Q, necessarily either X has Q or X does not have Q.

Contrast it to *restricted property universalism* which holds:

(RPU)   For any item X and property Q, necessarily either X has Q or X does not have Q, unless X has a nature N such that *X has N* entails *X is not the sort of thing to have Q or not to have Q.*

Property universalism is a nice simple doctrine. It entails that, for any property Q, the Real – if there is any such thing – either has Q or lacks Q. Restricted property universalism entails the same claim minus those properties the Real cannot by its nature have. But according to RP one cannot ascribe *having a nature* to the Real.[27] So RP cannot appeal to restricted property universalism. If RP accepts unrestricted property realism, then for almost every property one can think of, it is *false* that the Real has that property. The importance of this entailment will become evident shortly.

In each of these ways – rejection of "human concepts" as applying to the Real, the denial that simple mathematics applies to the Real, the claim that only properties generable from logic apply to the Real, the denial of any nature ascribable to the Real – RP emphasizes its doctrine

of the alleged inaccessibility of the Real to concepts. This simply under-
lines its own inconsistency in ascribing transcendence, necessity to
existence and wellbeing, and contributing to religious experience[28] to the
Real.

Maximally indeterminate beings

I suspect that talk of "the Real" gives RP the appearance of having more
substance that it can possess on its own terms. Consider such properties as
having a property and *having only consistent properties*. They are maximally indeterminate. Consider such properties as *being exactly an inch
long* and *weighing one gram*. These are maximally determinate. In
between are such properties as *being in space, being material, having
length, having weight*. These are neither maximally determinate nor
maximally indeterminate. Consider what we might call Maximally
Indeterminate RP according to which the Real is maximally indeterminate
in the sense that only maximally indeterminate properties can properly be
ascribed to it. Given the history of philosophy, the term "the Real" has
certain connotations. RP takes full advantage of these connotations in
offering its theory. The Real, for example, is itself uncaused. The Real can
cause other things. The Real has ultimate value. Highly positive itself, it
has highly positive effects. There is a problem here. The problem is due to
two facts:

1. According to Maximally Indeterminate RP, we can ascribe to the Real
   only maximally indeterminate properties.
2. Nothing to which we can ascribe only maximally indeterminate properties can consistently be conceived of as uncaused, cause of anything,
   of positive worth, or having positive effects.

The reason is simple: none of *being uncaused, being a cause, having
positive worth, having positive effects* is a maximally indeterminate
property. Given this simple pair of facts, devastating consequences follow
for Maximally Indeterminate RP.

In order not to be led into conceptual sleight of hand, let's drop
talk of "the Real" and replace it by an expression that is less lovely
but free from traditional associations. Let's talk about a *maximally
indeterminate being* – for short, a MIB. An MIB is not a being that
has only maximally indeterminate properties. There cannot be anything like that. Anything has maximally indeterminate properties
only by virtue of having more determinate properties, and at bottom
fully determinate properties. Instead, an MIB is a being to whom for
some reason we can only ascribe maximally indeterminate properties.
If we ascribe even one property that is not maximally indeterminate
to an MIB, we anger the MIB police who come out and dip us in
colored dye. But even an MIB actually has fully determinate
properties. There are some things that are just flagrantly obvious about
an MIB.

To begin with, here are two facts about the properties that RP ascribes
to the Real in order to have any explanation to offer or hypothesis to
consider.

Fact 1: None of *being uncaused, being a cause, having positive worth, having positive effects* is a maximally indeterminate property. They are highly abstract, but they are not maximally indeterminate.

Fact 2: None of *being uncaused, being a cause, having positive worth, having positive effects* is a logical property – a property that logicians in their role as logicians ascribe to things.

It is obvious that by RP rules:

1 No MIB can be said to be uncaused, a cause, something of positive value, or something having positive effects.

It is obvious that:

2 Nothing that cannot be said to be a cause can be said to be a cause of religious experience.

It follows that:

3 No MIB can be said to be a cause of religious experience.

The same thing holds if we try to talk of "being what we respond to in religious experience" or the like. The idea such talk expresses is that the Real contributes something to religious experience and we contribute something to religious experience. But no MIB can be said to be something we respond to or something that is a co-contributor to experiences.

It is obvious that:

4 There is nothing that can be said about an MIB by virtue of which it is a cause of moral virtue in us.
5 There is nothing that can be said about an MIB that would make any response to it more appropriate to it as an MIB than any other.
6 There is as much to be said in favor of moral neutrality or moral viciousness being an appropriate response to an MIB as there is to moral virtuousness being an appropriate response to it.

An MIB cannot be said to have any relationship to any sort of moral character in any thing. So when we find RP saying that the Real is what lies beyond all religious experience, or what all religious experience is a response to, or the like, what it says is logically inconsistent with its doctrine of what can be said about the Real. No MIB can do what RP desperately needs it to do. This is important in understanding religious pluralism, since RP also desperately needs that the Real be an MIB in order for religious pluralism not to be plainly false. Here are some of the defusing strategies:

1 Talk about myth, not doctrine.
2 Use the word "true" to mean something other than "true."
3 Given 1 and 2, let a true myth be one that tends to produce behavior you approve of.

But such strategies do nothing to provide RP with content.

A critical discussion of RP: Part three

Besides the inconsistency, another basic problem arises. Suppose one posits that there being something X will explain there being something else Y. This is a candidate for being an explanation only if X is said to have some property such that X having that property would explain there being Y. Here are two specifications of this general point that use the "generable from logic alone" vocabulary introduced by RP:

1 If no properties beyond those generated by logic alone are properly ascribable to the Real, then it is no more reasonable or appropriate to think of the Real as transcendent than as not transcendent.
2 If no properties beyond those generated by logic are ascribable to the Real, no experience is better thought of as a response to (or as contributed to by) the Real than any other.

Further, RP allows no moral properties to be ascribed to the Real. But then:

3 If no moral properties are ascribable to the Real, then there being the Real no better explains moral niceness than it does moral degradation.

Presumably on RP no causal powers or properties are ascribable to the Real. But then:

4 If no causal properties are ascribable to the Real, then there being the Real no better explains our existence than it would the existence of a world without us or there being no world at all.

and:

5 There is no reason to think of only religious experience as a response to the Real; eating a Big Mac or kicking a can is *as* reasonably thought of as an experience of the Real.
6 Wishing one were torturing one's enemies, enjoying mugging a help-less victim, or happily kicking a dog is *as* reasonably viewed as an experience that is a response to (or as contributed to by) the Real. None of them is *at all* reasonably thought of in such terms, since no property that is properly ascribable to the Real would make it reason-able to make any such suggestion about response or contribution.

So there are two points here: (i) there is no such thing as an experience reasonably thought of as a response to, or as contributed to by, the Real; (ii) there is no reason at all to suppose that only nice religious and moral experiences are such responses or are contributed to by the Real.

The second basic point can be put again in two stages:

1   If one cannot in principle ascribe any property to X by virtue of which X can explain Y, then positing X as an explanation of Y is entirely vacuous – it offers a sham explanation.
2   RP cannot ascribe to the Real any property by virtue of which positing it might explain anything whatever.

But then RP is explanatorily vacuous. When it comes to unpack its cognitive content, its briefcase is empty.

One might offer this suggestion: when RP posits the Real, it is to be seen as itself a metaphor. It has no literal meaning and it is to be judged in terms of whether it is useful. Does encountering the RP-myth make people nicer? But then RP will offer no explanations of anything. It will not be an alternative to the one-religion-is-right line, the all-religions-are-right line, or any other actual account of religious plurality.

The Philosophy of Religious Pluralism

John Hick

The lamps are different, but the Light is the same.
(Jalalu'l-Din Rumi [13th century])

The need for such an hypothesis. I have argued that it is rational on the part of those who experience religiously to believe and to live on this basis. And I have further argued that, in so believing, they are making an affirmation about the nature of reality which will, if it is substantially true, be developed, corrected and enlarged in the course of future experience. They are thus making genuine assertions and are making them on appropriate and acceptable grounds. If there were only one religious tradition, so that all religious experience and belief had the same intentional object, an epistemology of religion could come to rest at this point. But in fact there are a number of different such traditions and families of traditions witnessing to many different personal deities and nonpersonal ultimates.

To recall the theistic range first, the history of religions sets before us innumerable gods, differently named and often with different characteristics.... What are we to say, from a religious point of view, about all these gods? Do we say that they exist? And what would it be for a named god, say Balder, with his distinctive characteristics, to exist? In any straightforward sense it would at least seem to involve there being a consciousness, answering to this name, in addition to all the millions of human consciousnesses. Are we then to say that for each name in our directory of gods there is an additional consciousness, with the further attributes specified in the description of that particular deity? In most cases this would be theoretically possible since in most cases the gods are explicitly or implicitly finite beings whose powers and spheres of operation are at least approximately known; and many of them could coexist without contradiction. On the other hand the gods of the monotheistic faiths are thought of in each case as the one and only God, so that it is impossible for there to be more than one instantiation of this concept. It is thus not feasible to say that all the named gods, and particularly not all the most important ones, exist—at any rate not in any simple and straightforward sense.

Further, in addition to the witness of theistic religion to this multiplicity of personal deities there are yet other major forms of thought and experience which point to non-personal ultimates: Brahman, the Dharmakaya, Nirvana, Sunyata, the Tao.... But if the ultimate Reality is the blissful, universal consciousness of Brahman, which at the core of our own being we all are, how can it also be the emptiness, non-being, void of Sunyata? And again, how could it also be the Tao, as the principle of cosmic order, and again, the Dharmakaya or the eternal Buddha-nature? And if it is any of these, how can it be a personal deity? Surely these reported ultimates, personal and non-personal, are mutually exclusive. Must not any final reality either be personal, with the nonpersonal aspect of divinity being secondary, or be impersonal, with the worship of personal deities represent-

100

ing a lower level of religious consciousness, destined to be left behind in the state of final enlightenment?

The naturalistic response is to see all these systems of belief as factually false although perhaps as expressing the archetypal daydreams of the human mind whereby it has distracted itself from the harsh problems of life. From this point of view the luxuriant variety and the mutual incompatibility of these conceptions of the ultimate, and of the modes of experience which they inform, demonstrates that they are "such stuff as dreams are made on." However ... it is entirely reasonable for the religious person, experiencing life in relation to the transcendent—whether encountered beyond oneself or in the depths of one's own being—, to believe in the reality of that which is thus, apparently, experienced. Having reached that conclusion one cannot dismiss the realm of religious experience and belief as illusory, even though its internal plurality and diversity must preclude any simple and straightforward account of it.

Nor can we reasonably claim that our own form of religious experience, together with that of the tradition of which we are a part, is veridical whilst the others are not. We can of course claim this; and indeed virtually every religious tradition has done so, regarding alternative forms of religion either as false or as confused and inferior versions of itself. But the kind of rational justification ... for treating one's own form of religious experience as a cognitive response—though always a complexly conditioned one—to a divine reality must (as we have already noted) apply equally to the religious experience of others. In acknowledging this we are obeying the intellectual Golden Rule of granting to others a premise on which we rely ourselves. Persons living within other traditions, then, are equally justified in trusting their own distinctive religious experience and in forming their beliefs on the basis of it. For the only reason for treating one's tradition differently from others is the very human, but not very cogent, reason that it is one's own!...

Having, then, rejected ... the sceptical view that religious experience is *in toto* delusory, and the dogmatic view that it is all delusory except that of one's own tradition, I propose to explore the third possibility that the great post-axial faiths constitute different ways of experiencing, conceiving and living in relation to an ultimate divine Reality which transcends all our varied visions of it.

The real in itself and as humanly experienced. In discussing ... problems of terminology I opted—partly as a matter of personal linguistic taste—for "the Real" (in preference to "the Ultimate," "Ultimate Reality," "the One" or whatever) as a term by which to refer to the postulated ground of the different forms of religious experience. We now have to distinguish between the Real *an sich* [in itself] and the Real as variously experienced-and-thought by different human communities. In each of the great traditions a distinction has been drawn, though with varying degrees of emphasis, between the Real (thought of as God, Brahman, the Dharmakaya ...) in itself and the Real as manifested within the intellectual and experiential purview of that tradition....

In one form or another such a distinction is required by the thought that God, Brahman, the Dharmakaya, is unlimited and therefore may not be equated without remainder with anything that can be humanly experienced and defined. Unlimitedness, or infinity, is a negative concept, the denial of limitation. That this denial must be made of the Ultimate is a basic assumption of all the great traditions. It is a natural and reasonable assumption: for an ultimate that is limited in some mode

101

would be limited by something other than itself, and this would entail its non-ultimacy. And with the assumption of the unlimitedness of God, Brahman, the Dharmakaya, goes the equally natural and reasonable assumption that the Ultimate, in its unlimitedness exceeds all positive characterisations in human thought and language....

Using this distinction between the Real *an sich* and the Real as humanly thought-and-experienced I want to explore the pluralistic hypothesis that the great world faiths embody different perceptions and conceptions of, and correspondingly different responses to, the Real from within the major variant ways of being human; and that within each of them the transformation of human existence from self-centredness to Reality-centredness is taking place. These traditions are accordingly to be regarded as alternative soteriological "spaces" within which, or "ways" along which, men and women can find salvation/liberation/ultimate fulfilment.

Kant's epistemological model. In developing this thesis our chief philosophical resource will be one of Kant's most basic epistemological insights, namely that the mind actively interprets sensory information in terms of concepts, so that the environment as we consciously perceive and inhabit it is our familiar three-dimensional world of objects interacting in space.

... Kant's later much more detailed development of the theme is particularly helpful because he went on to distinguish explicitly between an entity as it is in itself and as it appears in perception. For the realisation that the world, as we consciously perceive it, is partly our own construction leads directly to a differentiation between the world *an sich* unperceived by anyone, and the world as it appears to, that is as it is perceived by, us.[1] The distinction plays a major part in Kant's thought. He points out that since the properties of something as experienced "depend upon the mode of intuition of the subject, this object as appearance is to be distinguished from itself as object in itself" (*Crit. Pure Reason*, B69 1958, 88). And so Kant distinguished between noumenon and phenomenon, or between a *Ding an sich* [thing in itself] and that thing as it appears to human consciousness.... In this strand of Kant's thought—not the only strand, but the one which I am seeking to press into service in the epistemology of religion—the noumenal world exists independently of our perception of it and the phenomenal world is that same world as it appears to our human consciousness. The world as it appears is thus entirely real.... Analogously, I want to say that the noumenal Real is experienced and thought by different human mentalities, forming and formed by different religious traditions, as the range of gods and absolutes which the phenomenology of religion reports. And these divine *personae* and metaphysical *impersonae*, as I shall call them, are not illusory but are empirically, that is experientially, real as authentic manifestations of the Real.

... In the religious case there are two fundamental circumstances: first, the postulated presence of the Real to the human life of which it is the ground; and second, the cognitive structure of our consciousness, with its capacity to respond to the meaning or character of our environment, including its religious meaning or character. In terms of information theory, we are speaking of the transmission of information from a transcendent source to the human mind/brain and its transformation by the mind/brain into conscious experience.... The "presence" of the Real consists in the availability, from a transcendent source, of information that the human mind/brain is capable of transforming into what we call religious experience. And, as in the case of our awareness of the physical world, the environing divine reality is brought to consciousness in terms of certain basic concepts or categories. These are, first, the concept of God, or of the Real as personal, which presides over the various theistic forms of religious experience; and second, the concept of the Absolute, or of the Real as non-personal, which presides over its various non-theistic forms.[2]

... On this view our various religious languages—Buddhist, Christian, Muslim, Hindu ... —each refer to a divine phenomenon or configuration of divine phenomena. When we speak of a personal God, with moral attributes and purposes, or when we speak of the non-personal Absolute, Brahman, or of the Dharmakaya, we are speaking of the Real as humanly experienced: that is, as phenomenon.

The Relation between the Real *an sich* **and its** *personae* **and** *impersonae.* It follows from this distinction between the Real as it is in itself and as it is thought and experienced through our religious concepts that we cannot apply to the Real *an sich* the characteristics encountered in its *personae* and *impersonae.* Thus it cannot be said to be one or many, person or thing, substance or process, good or evil, purposive or non-purposive. None of the concrete descriptions that apply within the realm of human experience can apply literally to the unexperiencable ground of that realm. For whereas the phenomenal world is structured by our own conceptual frameworks, its noumenal ground is not. We cannot even speak of this as a thing or an entity .... However we can make certain purely formal statements about the postulated Real in itself. The most famous instance in western religious discourse of such a formal statement is Anselm's definition of God as that than which no greater can be conceived. This formula refers to the ultimate divine reality without attributing to it any concrete characteristics. And in this purely formal mode we can say of the postulated Real *an sich* that it is the noumenal ground of the encountered gods and experienced absolutes witnessed to by the religious traditions.

There are at least two thought-models in terms of which we can conceive of the relationship between the Real *an sich* and its *personae* and *impersonae.* One is that of noumenon and phenomena, which enables us to say that the noumenal Real is such as to be authentically experienced as a range of both theistic and non-theistic phenomena. On this basis we cannot, as we have seen, say that the Real *an sich* has the characteristics displayed by its manifestations, such as (in the case of the heavenly Father) love and justice or (in the case of Brahman) consciousness and bliss. But it is nevertheless the noumenal ground of these characteristics. In so far as the heavenly Father and Brahman are two authentic manifestations of the Real, the love and justice of the one and the consciousness and bliss of the other are aspects of the Real as manifested within human experience. As the noumenal ground of these and other modes of experience, and yet transcending all of them, the Real is so rich in content that it can only be finitely experienced in the various partial and inadequate ways which the history of religions describes.

The other model is the more familiar one in western thought of analogical predication, classically expounded by Aquinas. According to him we can say that God is, for example, good—not in the sense in which we say of a human being that he or she is good, nor on the other hand in a totally unrelated sense, but in the sense that there is in the divine nature a quality that is limitlessly superior and yet at the same time analogous to human goodness. But Aquinas was emphatic that we cannot know what the divine super-analogue of goodness is like: "we cannot grasp what God is, but only what He is not and how other things are related to Him" (*Summa contra Gentiles,* 1:30:4—Pegis 1955, 141). Further, the divine attributes which are distinguished in human thought and given such names as love, justice, knowledge, power, are identical in God. For "God ... as considered in Himself, is altogether one and simple, yet our intellect knows Him according to diverse conceptions because it cannot see Him as He is in Himself."[3] When we take these two doctrines together and apply them to the Real we see that, whilst there is a noumenal ground for the phenomenal divine attributes, this does not enable us to trace each attribute separately upwards into the Godhead or the Real. They represent the Real as both reflected and refracted within human thought and experience. But nevertheless the Real is the ultimate ground or source of those qualities which characterise each divine *personae* and *impersonae* insofar as these are authentic phenomenal manifestations of the Real.

This relationship between the ultimate noumenon and its multiple phenomenal appearances, or between the limitless transcendent reality and our many partial human images of it, makes possible mythological speech about the Real. I define a myth as a story or statement which is not literally true but which tends to evoke an appropriate dispositional attitude to its subject-matter. Thus the truth of a myth is a practical truthfulness: a true myth is one which rightly relates us to a reality about which we cannot speak in non-mythological terms. For we exist inescapably in relation to the Real, and in all that we do and undergo we are inevitably having to do with it in and through our neighbours and our world. Our attitudes and actions are accordingly appropriate or inappropriate not only in relation to our physical and social environments but also in relation to our ultimate environment. And true religious myths are accordingly those that evoke in us attitudes and modes of behaviour which are appropriate to our situation in relation to the Real....

But what is it for human attitudes, behaviours, patterns of life to be appropriate or inappropriate within this ultimate situation? It is for the *persona* or *impersona* in relation to which we live to be an authentic manifestation of the Real and for our practical response to be appropriate to that manifestation. To the extent that a *persona* or *impersona* is in soteriological alignment with the Real, an appropriate response to that deity or absolute is an appropriate response to the Real. It need not however be the only such response for other phenomenal manifestations of the Real within other human traditions evoke other responses which may be equally appropriate.... [T]he "truthfulness" of each tradition is shown by its soteriological effectiveness. But what the traditions severally regard as ultimates are different and therefore cannot be all truly ultimate. They can however be different manifestations of the truly Ultimate within different streams of human thought-and-experience—hence the postulation of the Real *an sich* as the simplest way of accounting for the data....

But if the Real in itself is experienced, why postulate such an unknown and unknowable *Ding an sich*? The answer is that the divine noumenon is a necessary postulate of the pluralistic religious life of humanity. For within each tradition we regard as real the object of our worship or contemplation. If, as I have already argued, it is also proper to regard as real the objects of worship or contemplation within the other traditions, we are led to postulate the Real *an sich* as the presupposition of the veridical character of this range of forms of religious experience. Without this postulate we should be left with a plurality of *personae* and *impersonae* each of which is claimed to be the Ultimate, but no one of which alone can be. We should have either to regard all the reported experiences as illusory or else return

104

to the confessional position in which we affirm the authenticity of our own stream of religious experience whilst dismissing as illusory those occurring within other traditions. But for those to whom neither of these options seems realistic the pluralistic affirmation becomes inevitable, and with it the postulation of the Real *an sich* which is variously experienced and thought as the range of divine phenomena described by the history of religion....

Notes

1. And also as it may appear to creatures with different cognitive equipment from our own. Kant was conscious that he was investigating the specifically *human* forms and categories of perception (*Critique of Pure Reason*, B59).
2. The term "Absolute" seems to be the best that we have, even though it is not ideal for the purpose, being more naturally applied to some non-personal manifestations of the Real than to others. It is more naturally applicable, e.g., to Brahman than to Nirvana...
3. *Summa Theologica*, part I, Q. 13, art. 12—Pegis, Anton C. (ed.), *Basic Writings of St. Thomas Aquinas* (New York: Random House, 1945), I:133.

Pluralism:
A Defense of Religious Exclusivism

Alvin Plantinga

When I was a graduate student at Yale, the philosophy department prided itself on diversity: and it was indeed diverse. There were idealists, pragmatists, phenomenologists, existentialists, Whiteheadians, historians of philosophy, a token positivist, and what could only be described as observers of the passing intellectual scene. In some ways, this was indeed something to take pride in; a student could behold and encounter real live representatives of many of the main traditions in philosophy. It also had an unintended and unhappy side effect, however. If anyone raised a philosophical question inside, but particularly outside, class, the typical response would be a catalog of some of the various different answers the world has seen: there is the Aristotelian answer, the existentialist answer, the Cartesian answer, Heidegger's answer, perhaps the Buddhist answer, and so on. But the question 'what is the truth about this matter?' was often greeted with disdain as unduly naive. There are all these different answers, all endorsed by people of great intellectual power and great dedication to philosophy; for every argument *for* one of these positions, there is another *against* it; would it not be excessively naive, or perhaps arbitrary, to suppose that one of these is in fact *true*, the others being false? Or, if there really is a truth of the matter, so that one of them is true and conflicting ones false, wouldn't it be merely arbitrary, in the face of this embarrassment of riches, to *endorse* one of them as the truth, consigning the others to falsehood? How could you possibly know which was true?

Some urge a similar attitude with respect to the impressive variety of religions the world displays. There are theistic religions but also at least some nontheistic religions (or perhaps nontheistic strands of religion) among the enormous variety of religions going under the names 'Hinduism' and 'Buddhism'; among the theistic religions, there are strands of Hinduism and Buddhism and American Indian religion as well as Islam, Judaism, and Christianity; and all these differ significantly from one another. Isn't it somehow arbitrary, or irrational, or unjustified, or unwarranted, or even oppressive and imperialistic to endorse one of these as opposed to all the others? According to Jean Bodin, "each is refuted by all";[1] must we not agree? It is in this neighborhood that the so-called problem of pluralism arises. Of course, many concerns and problems can come under this rubric; the specific problem I mean to discuss can be thought of as follows. To put it in an internal and personal way, I find myself with religious beliefs, and religious beliefs that I realize aren't shared by nearly everyone else. For example, I believe both

(1)   The world was created by God, an almighty, all-knowing, and per-
       fectly good personal being (one that holds beliefs; has aims, plans,
       and intentions; and can act to accomplish these aims)

and

(2)   Human beings require salvation, and God has provided a unique
       way of salvation through the incarnation, life, sacrificial death, and
       resurrection of his divine son.

Now there are many who do not believe these things. First, there are
those who agree with me on (1) but not (2): there are non-Christian
theistic religions. Second, there are those who don't accept either (1)
or (2) but nonetheless do believe that there is something beyond the
natural world, a something such that human well-being and salvation
depend upon standing in a right relation to it. And third, in the West
and since the Enlightenment, anyway, there are people—*naturalists*, we
may call them—who don't believe any of these three things. And my
problem is this: when I become really aware of these other ways of
looking at the world, these other ways of responding religiously to the
world, what must or should I do? What is the right sort of attitude to
take? What sort of impact should this awareness have on the beliefs I
hold and the strength with which I hold them? My question is this:
how should I think about the great religious diversity the world in fact
displays? Can I sensibly remain an adherent of just one of these religions, rejecting the others? And here I am thinking specifically of *beliefs*. Of course, there is a great deal more to any religion or religious
practice than just belief, and I don't for a moment mean to deny it.
But belief is a crucially important part of most religions; it is a crucially
important part of *my* religion; and the question I mean to ask here is
what the awareness of religious diversity means or should mean for my
religious beliefs.
    Some speak here of a *new* awareness of religious diversity, and speak
of this new awareness as constituting (for us in the West) a crisis, a
revolution, an intellectual development of the same magnitude as the
Copernican revolution of the sixteenth century and the alleged discovery of evolution and our animal origins in the nineteenth.[2] No doubt
there is at least some truth to this. Of course, the fact is all along many
Western Christians and Jews have known that there are other religions
and that not nearly everyone shares *their* religion.[3] The ancient Israel-
ites—some of the prophets, say—were clearly aware of Canaanitish
religion; and the apostle Paul said that he preached "Christ crucified,
a stumbling block to Jews and folly to the Greeks" (I Cor. 1:23). Other
early Christians, the Christian martyrs, say, must have suspected that
not everyone believed as they did. The church fathers, in offering de-
fenses of Christianity, were certainly apprised of this fact; Origen, indeed, wrote an eight-volume reply to Celsus, who urged an argument
similar to those put forward by contemporary pluralists. Aquinas,
again, was clearly aware of those to whom he addressed the *Summa
contra gentiles,* and the fact that there are non-Christian religions would
have come as no surprise to the Jesuit missionaries of the sixteenth

and seventeenth centuries or to the Methodist missionaries of the nineteenth. In more recent times, when I was a child, *The Banner*, the official publication of the Christian Reformed Church, contained a small column for children; it was written by 'Uncle Dick', who exhorted us to save our nickels and send them to our Indian cousins at the Navaho mission in New Mexico. Both we and our elders knew that the Navahos had or had had a religion different from Christianity, and part of the point of sending the nickels was to try to rectify that situation.

Still, in recent years probably more of us Western Christians have become aware of the world's religious diversity; we have probably learned more about people of other religious persuasions, and we have come to see more clearly that they display what looks like real piety, devoutness, and spirituality. What is new, perhaps, is a more widespread sympathy for other religions, a tendency to see them as more valuable, as containing more by way of truth, and a new feeling of solidarity with their practitioners.

There are several possible reactions to awareness of religious diversity. One is to continue to believe what you have all along believed; you learn about this diversity but continue to believe, that is, take to be true, such propositions as (1) and (2) above, consequently taking to be false any beliefs, religious or otherwise, that are incompatible with (1) and (2). Following current practice, I call this *exclusivism;* the exclusivist holds that the tenets or some of the tenets of *one* religion—Christianity, let's say—are in fact true; he adds, naturally enough, that any propositions, including other religious beliefs, that are incompatible with those tenets are false. Now there is a fairly widespread belief that there is something seriously wrong with exclusivism. It is irrational, or egotistical and unjustified,[4] or intellectually arrogant,[5] or elitist,[6] or a manifestation of harmful pride,[7] or even oppressive and imperialistic.[8] The claim is that exclusivism as such is or involves a vice of some sort: it is wrong or deplorable; and it is this claim I want to examine. I propose to argue that exclusivism need not involve either epistemic or moral failure and that furthermore something like it is wholly unavoidable, given our human condition.

These objections are not to the *truth* of (1) or (2) or any other proposition someone might accept in this exclusivist way (although, of course, objections of that sort are also put forward); they are instead directed to the *propriety* or *rightness* of exclusivism. And there are initially two different kinds of indictments of exclusivism: broadly moral or ethical indictments and broadly intellectual or epistemic indictments. These overlap in interesting ways, as we shall see below. But initially, anyway, we can take some of the complaints about exclusivism as *intellectual* criticisms: it is *irrational* or *unjustified* to think in an exclusivistic way. And the other large body of complaint is moral: there is something *morally* suspect about exclusivism: it is arbitrary, or intellectually arrogant, or imperialistic. As Joseph Runzo suggests, exclusivism is "neither tolerable nor any longer intellectually honest in the context of our contemporary knowledge of other faiths."[9] I want to consider both kinds of claims or criticisms; I propose to argue that the exclusivist is not as such necessarily guilty of any of these charges.

108

Moral Objections to Exclusivism

I first turn to the moral complaints: that the exclusivist is intellectually arrogant, or egotistical, or self-servingly arbitrary, or dishonest, or imperialistic, or oppressive. But first three qualifications. An exclusivist, like anyone else, will probably be guilty of some or all of these things to at least some degree, perhaps particularly the first two; the question is, however, whether she is guilty of these things just by virtue of being an exclusivist. Second, I shall use the term 'exclusivism' in such a way that you don't count as an exclusivist unless you are rather fully aware of other faiths, have had their existence and their claims called to your attention with some force and perhaps fairly frequently, and have to some degree reflected on the problem of pluralism, asking yourself such questions as whether it is or could be really true that the Lord has revealed himself and his programs to us Christians, say, in a way in which he hasn't revealed himself to those of other faiths. Thus my grandmother, for example, would not have counted as an exclusivist. She had, of course, *heard* of the heathen, as she called them, but the idea that perhaps Christians could learn from them, and learn from them with respect to religious matters, had not so much as entered her head; and the fact that it *hadn't* entered her head, I take it, was not a matter of moral dereliction on her part. The same would go for a Buddhist or Hindu peasant. These people are not, I think, plausibly charged with arrogance or other moral flaws in believing as they do.

Third, suppose I am an exclusivist with respect to (1), for example, but nonculpably believe, like Thomas Aquinas, say, that I have a knockdown, drag-out argument, a demonstration or conclusive proof of the proposition that there is such a person as God; and suppose I think further (and nonculpably) that if those who don't believe (1) were to be apprised of this argument (and had the ability and training necessary to grasp it, and were to think about the argument fairly and reflectively), they too would come to believe (1). Then I could hardly be charged with these moral faults. My condition would be like that of Gödel, let's say, upon having recognized that he had a proof for the incompleteness of arithmetic. True, many of his colleagues and peers didn't believe that arithmetic was incomplete, and some believed that it *was* complete; but presumably Gödel wasn't arbitrary or egotistical in believing that arithmetic is in fact incomplete. Furthermore, he would not have been at fault had he nonculpably but *mistakenly* believed that he had found such a proof. Accordingly, I shall use the term 'exclusivist' in such a way that you don't count as an exclusivist if you nonculpably think you know of a demonstration or conclusive argument for the beliefs with respect to which you are an exclusivist, or even if you nonculpably think you know of an argument that would convince all or most intelligent and honest people of the truth of that proposition. So an exclusivist, as I use the term, not only believes something like (1) or (2) and thinks false any proposition incompatible with it; she also meets a further condition C that is hard to state precisely and in detail (and in fact any attempt to do so would involve a long and at present irrelevant discussion of ceteris paribus clauses). Suffice it to say that C includes (1) being rather fully aware of other religions, (2) knowing that there is much that at the least looks like genuine piety and devoutness in them, and (3) believing that you know of no arguments that would necessarily convince all or most honest and intelligent dissenters of your own religious allegiances.

Given these qualifications, then, why should we think that an exclusivist is properly charged with these moral faults? I shall deal first and most briefly with charges of oppression and imperialism: I think we must say that they are on the face of it wholly implausible. I daresay there are some among you who reject some of the things I believe; I do not believe that you are thereby oppressing me, even if you do not believe you have an argument that would convince me. It is conceivable that exclusivism might in some way *contribute to* oppression, but it isn't in itself oppressive.

The important moral charge is that there is a sort of self-serving arbitrariness, an arrogance or egotism, in accepting such propositions as (1) or (2) under condition C; exclusivism is guilty of some serious moral fault or flaw. According to Wilfred Cantwell Smith, "except at the cost of insensitivity or delinquency, it is morally not possible actually to go out into the world and say to devout, intelligent, fellow human beings: '. . . we believe that we know God and we are right; you believe that you know God, and you are totally wrong'."[10]

So what can the exclusivist have to say for herself? Well, it must be conceded immediately that if she believes (1) or (2), then she must also believe that those who believe something incompatible with them are mistaken and believe what is false. That's no more than simple logic. Furthermore, she must also believe that those who do not believe as she does—those who believe neither (1) nor (2), whether or not they believe their negations—*fail* to believe something that is true, deep, and important, and that she *does* believe. She must therefore see herself as *privileged* with respect to those others—those others of both kinds. There is something of great value, she must think, that *she* has and *they* lack. They are ignorant of something—something of great importance—of which she has knowledge. But does this make her properly subject to the above censure?

I think the answer must be no. Or if the answer is yes, then I think we have here a genuine moral dilemma; for in our earthly life here below, as my Sunday School teacher used to say, there is no real alternative; there is no reflective attitude that is not open to the same strictures. These charges of arrogance are a philosophical tar baby: get close enough to them to use them against the exclusivist, and you are likely to find them stuck fast to yourself. How so? Well, as an exclusivist, I realize I can't convince others that they should believe as I do, but I nonetheless continue to believe as I do: and the charge is that I am as a result arrogant or egotistical, arbitrarily preferring my way of doing things to other ways.[11] But what are my alternatives with respect to a proposition like (1)? There seem to be three choices.[12] I can continue to hold it; I can withhold it, in Roderick Chisholm's sense, believing neither it nor its denial; and I can accept its denial. Consider the third way, a way taken by those pluralists who, like John Hick, hold that such propositions as (1) and (2) and their colleagues from other faiths are literally false although in some way still valid responses to the Real.

110

This seems to me to be no advance at all with respect to the arrogance or egotism problem; this is not a way out. For if I do this, I will then be in the very same condition as I am now: I will believe many propositions others don't believe and will be in condition C with respect to those propositions. For I will then believe the denials of (1) and (2) (as well as the denials of many other propositions explicitly accepted by those of other faiths). Many others, of course, do not believe the denials of (1) and (2), and in fact believe (1) and (2). Further, I will not know of any arguments that can be counted on to persuade those who do believe (1) or (2) (or propositions accepted by the adherents of other religions). I am therefore in the condition of believing propositions that many others do not believe and furthermore am in condition C. If, in the case of those who believe (1) and (2), that is sufficient for intellectual arrogance or egotism, the same goes for those who believe their denials.

So consider the second option: I can instead *withhold* the proposition in question. I can say to myself; "the right course here, given that I can't or couldn't convince these others of what *I* believe, is to believe neither these propositions nor their denials." The pluralist objector to exclusivism can say that the right course under condition C, is to *abstain* from believing the offending proposition and also abstain from believing its denial; call him, therefore, 'the abstemious pluralist'. But does he thus really avoid the condition that, on the part of the exclusivist, leads to the charges of egotism and arrogance? Think, for a moment, about disagreement. Disagreement, fundamentally, is a matter of adopting conflicting propositional attitudes with respect to a given proposition. In the simplest and most familiar case, I disagree with you if there is some proposition p such that I believe p and you believe -p. But that's just the simplest case: there are also others. The one that is at present of interest is this: I believe p and you withhold it, fail to believe it. Call the first kind of disagreement 'contradicting'; call the second 'dissenting'.

My claim is that if contradicting others (under the condition C spelled out above) is arrogant and egotistical, so is dissenting (under that same condition). For suppose you believe some proposition p but I don't: perhaps you believe it is wrong to discriminate against people simply on the grounds of race, but I, recognizing that there are many people who disagree with you, do not believe this proposition. I don't disbelieve it either, of course, but in the circumstances I think the right thing to do is to abstain from belief. Then am I not implicitly condemning your attitude, your *believing* the proposition, as somehow improper—naive, perhaps, or unjustified, or in some other way less than optimal? I am implicitly saying that my attitude is the superior one; I think my course of action here is the right one and yours somehow wrong, inadequate, improper, in the circumstances at best second-rate. Also, I realize that there is no questions, here, of *showing* you that your attitude is wrong or improper or naive; so am I not guilty of intellectual arrogance? Of a sort of egotism, thinking I know better than you, arrogating to myself a privileged status with respect to you? The problem for the exclusivist was that she was obliged to think she possessed a truth missed by many others; the problem for the abstemious pluralist is that he is obliged to think he possesses a virtue others don't, or acts rightly where others don't. If, in conditions C, one is arrogant by way of believing a proposition others don't, isn't one equally, under those reflective conditions, arrogant by way of withholding a proposition others don't?

Perhaps you will respond by saying that the abstemious pluralist gets into trouble, falls into arrogance, by way of implicitly saying or believing that his way of proceeding is *better* or *wiser* than other ways pursued by other people, and perhaps he can escape by abstaining from *that* view as well. Can't he escape the problem by refraining from believing that racial bigotry is wrong, and also refraining from holding the view that it is *better*, under the conditions that obtain, to withhold that proposition than to assert and believe it? Well, yes, he can; then he has no *reason* for his abstention; he doesn't believe that abstention is better or more appropriate; he simply does abstain. Does this get him off the egotistical hook? Perhaps. But then, of course, he can't, in consistency, also hold that there is something wrong with *not* abstaining, with coming right out and *believing* that bigotry is wrong; he loses his objection to the exclusivist. Accordingly, this way out is not available for the abstemious pluralist who accuses the exclusivist of arrogance and egotism.

Indeed, I think we can show that the abstemious pluralist who brings charges of intellectual arrogance against exclusivism is hoist with his own petard, holds a position that in a certain way is self-referentially inconsistent in the circumstances. For he believes

(3)   If S knows that others don't believe p and that he is in condition C with respect to p, then S should not believe p;

this or something like it is the ground of the charges he brings against the exclusivist. But, the abstemious pluralist realizes that many do not accept (3); and I suppose he also realizes that it is unlikely that he can find arguments for (3) that will convince them; hence he knows that he is in condition C. Given his acceptance of (3), therefore, the right course for him is to abstain from believing (3). Under the conditions that do in fact obtain—namely, his knowledge that others don't accept it and that condition C obtains—he can't properly accept it.

I am therefore inclined to think that one can't, in the circumstances, properly hold (3) or any other proposition that will do the job. One can't find here some principle on the basis of which to hold that the exclusivist is doing the wrong thing, suffers from some moral fault— that is, one can't find such a principle that doesn't, as we might put it, fall victim to itself.

So the abstemious pluralist is hoist with his own petard; but even apart from this dialectical argument (which in any event some will think unduly cute), aren't the charges unconvincing and implausible? I must concede that there are a variety of ways in which I can be and have been intellectually arrogant and egotistic; I have certainly fallen into this vice in the past and no doubt am not free of it now. But am I really arrogant and egotistic just by virtue of believing what I know others don't believe, where I can't show them that I am right? Suppose I think the matter over, consider the objections as carefully as I can,

112

realize that I am finite and furthermore a sinner, certainly no better than those with whom I disagree, and indeed inferior both morally and intellectually to many who do not believe what I do; but suppose it *still* seems clear to me that the proposition in question is true: can I really be behaving immorally in continuing to believe it? I am dead sure that it is wrong to try to advance my career by telling lies about my colleagues; I realize there are those who disagree; I also realize that in all likelihood there is no way I can find to show them that they are wrong; nonetheless, I think they *are* wrong. If I think this after careful reflection—if I consider the claims of those who disagree as sympathetically as I can, if I try level best to ascertain the truth here— and it *still* seems to me sleazy, wrong, and despicable to lie about my colleagues to advance my career, could I really be doing something immoral in continuing to believe as before? I can't see how. If, after careful reflection and thought, you find yourself convinced that the right propositional attitude to take to (1) and (2) in the face of the facts of religious pluralism is abstention from belief, how could you properly be taxed with egotism, either for so believing or for so abstaining? Even if you knew others did not agree with you? So I can't see how the moral charge against exclusivism can be sustained.

Epistemic Objections to Exclusivism

I turn now to *epistemic* objections to exclusivism. There are many different specifically epistemic virtues, and a corresponding plethora of epistemic vices; the ones with which the exclusivist is most frequently charged, however, are *irrationality* and *lack of justification* in holding his exclusivist beliefs. The claim is that as an exclusivist, he holds unjustified beliefs and/or irrational beliefs. Better, *he* is unjustified or irrational in holding these beliefs. I shall therefore consider those two claims, and I shall argue that the exclusivistic views need not be either unjustified or irrational. I shall then turn to the question whether his beliefs could have *warrant*: that property, whatever precisely it is, that distinguishes knowledge from mere true belief, and whether they could have enough warrant for knowledge.

Justification

The pluralist objector sometimes claims that to hold exclusivist views, in condition C, is *unjustified—epistemically* unjustified. Is this true? And what does he mean when he makes this claim? As even a brief glance at the contemporary epistemological literature shows, justification is a protean and multifarious notion.[13] There are, I think, substantially two possibilities as to what he means. The central core of the notion, its beating heart, the paradigmatic center to which most of the myriad contemporary variations are related by way of analogical extension and family resemblance, is the notion of *being within one's intellectual rights*, having violated no intellectual or cognitive duties or obligations in the formation and sustenance of the belief in question. This is the palimpsest, going back to Descartes and especially Locke, that underlies the multitudinous battery of contemporary inscriptions. There is no space to argue that point here; but chances are when the pluralist objector to exclusivism claims that the latter is unjustified, it is some notion lying in this neighborhood that he has in mind. (And, here we should note the very close connection between the moral objections to exclusivism and the objection that exclusivism is epistemically unjustified.)

The duties involved, naturally enough, would be specifically *epistemic* duties: perhaps a duty to proportion degree of belief to (propositional) evidence from what is *certain*, that is, self-evident or incorrigible, as with Locke, or perhaps to try one's best to get into and stay in the right relation to the truth, as with Roderick Chisholm,[14] the leading contemporary champion of the justificationist tradition with respect to knowledge. But at present there is widespread (and, as I see it, correct) agreement that there is no duty of the Lockean kind. Perhaps there is one of the Chisholmian kind;[15] but isn't the exclusivist conforming to that duty if, after the sort of careful, indeed prayerful, consideration I mentioned in the response to the moral objection, it still seems to him strongly that (1), say, is true and he accordingly still believes it? It is therefore hard to see that the exclusivist is necessarily unjustified in this way.

The second possibility for understanding the charge—the charge that exclusivism is epistemically unjustified—has to do with the oft-repeated claim that exclusivism is intellectually *arbitrary*. Perhaps the idea is that there is an intellectual duty to treat similar cases similarly; the exclusivist violates this duty by arbitrarily choosing to believe (for the moment going along with the fiction that we *choose* beliefs of this sort) (1) and (2) in the face of the plurality of conflicting religious beliefs the world presents. But suppose there is such a duty. Clearly, you do not violate it if you nonculpably think the beliefs in question are *not* on a par. And, as an exclusivist, I *do* think (nonculpably, I hope) that they are not on a par: I think (1) and (2) *true* and those incompatible with either of them *false*.

The rejoinder, of course, will be that it is not *alethic* parity (their having the same truth value) that is at issue: it is *epistemic* parity that counts. What kind of epistemic parity? What would be relevant here, I should think, would be *internal* or internalist epistemic parity: parity with respect to what is internally available to the believer. What is internally available to the believer includes, for example, detectable relationships between the belief in question and other beliefs you hold; so internal parity would include parity of propositional evidence. What is internally available to the believer also includes the *phenomenology* that goes with the beliefs in question: the *sensuous* phenomenology, but also the nonsensuous phenomenology involved, for example, in the belief's just having the feel of being *right*. But once more, then, (1) and (2) are not on an internal par, for the exclusivist, with beliefs that are incompatible with them. (1) and (2), after all, seem to me to be true; they have for me the phenomenology that accompanies that seeming. The same cannot be said for propositions incompatible with them. If, furthermore, John Calvin is right in thinking that there is such a thing as the Sensus Divinitatis and the Internal Testimony of the Holy Spirit, then perhaps (1) and (2) are produced in me by those belief-producing processes, and have for me the phenomenology that goes with them; the same is not true for propositions incompatible with them.

But then the next rejoinder: isn't it probably true that those who reject (1) and (2) in favor of other beliefs have propositional evidence for their beliefs that is on a par with mine for my beliefs; and isn't it also probably true that the same or similar phenomenology accompanies their beliefs as accompanies mine? So that those beliefs really are epistemically and internally on a par with (1) and (2), and the exclusivist is still treating like cases differently? I don't think so: I think there really are arguments available for (1), at least, that are not available for its competitors. And as for similar phenomenology, this is not easy to say; it is not easy to look into the breast of another; the secrets of the human heart are hard to fathom; it is hard indeed to discover this sort of thing even with respect to someone you know really well. But I am prepared to stipulate both sorts of parity. Let's agree for purposes of argument that these beliefs are on an epistemic par in the sense that those of a different religious tradition have the same sort of internally available markers—evidence, phenomenology, and the like— for their beliefs as I have for (1) and (2). What follows?

Return to the case of moral belief. King David took Bathsheba, made her pregnant, and then, after the failure of various stratagems to get her husband Uriah to think the baby was his, arranged for Uriah to be killed. The prophet Nathan came to David and told him a story about a rich man and a poor man. The rich man had many flocks and herds; the poor man had only a single ewe lamb, which grew up with his children, "ate at his table, drank from his cup, lay in his bosom, and was like a daughter to him." The rich man had unexpected guests. Instead of slaughtering one of his own sheep, he took the poor man's single ewe lamb, slaughtered it, and served it to his guests. David exploded in anger: "The man who did this deserves to die!" Then, in one of the most riveting passages in all the Bible, Nathan turns to David, stretches out his arm and points to him, and declares, "*You are that man!*" And David sees what he has done.

My interest here is in David's reaction to the story. I agree with David: such injustice is utterly and despicably wrong; there are really no words for it. I believe that such an action is wrong, and I believe that the proposition that it *isn't* wrong—either because really *nothing* is wrong, or because even if *some* things are wrong, *this* isn't—is false. As a matter of fact, there isn't a lot I believe more strongly. I recognize, however, that there are those who disagree with me; and once more, I doubt that I could find an argument to show them that I am right and they wrong. Further, for all I know, their conflicting beliefs have for them the same internally available epistemic markers, the same phenomenology, as mine have for me. Am I then being arbitrary, treating similar cases differently in continuing to hold, as I do, that in fact that kind of behavior *is* dreadfully wrong? I don't think so. Am I wrong in thinking racial bigotry despicable, even though I know there are others who disagree, and even if I think they have the same internal markers for their beliefs as I have for mine? I don't think so. I believe in Serious

Actualism, the view that no objects have properties in worlds in which they do not exist, not even nonexistence. Others do not believe this, and perhaps the internal markers of their dissenting views have for them the same quality as my views have for me. Am I being arbitrary in continuing to think as I do? I can't see how.

And the reason here is this: in each of these cases, the believer in question doesn't really think the beliefs in question *are* on a relevant epistemic par. She may agree that she and those who dissent are equally convinced of the truth of their belief, and even that they are internally on a par, that the internally available markers are similar, or relevantly similar. But she must still think that there is an important epistemic difference: she thinks that somehow the other person has *made a mistake,* or *has a blind spot,* or hasn't been wholly attentive, or hasn't received some grace she has, or is in some way epistemically less fortunate. And, of course, the pluralist critic is in no better case. He thinks the thing to do when there is internal epistemic parity is to withhold judgment; he knows there are others who don't think so, and for all he knows, that belief has internal parity with his; if he continues in that belief, therefore, he will be in the same condition as the exclusivist; and if he doesn't continue in this belief, he no longer has an objection to the exclusivist.

But couldn't I be wrong? Of course I could! But I don't avoid that risk by withholding all religious (or philosophical or moral) beliefs; I can go wrong that way as well as any other, treating all religions, or all philosophical thoughts, or all moral views, as on a par. Again, there is no safe haven here, no way to avoid risk. In particular, you won't reach safe haven by trying to take the same attitude toward all the historically available patterns of belief and withholding: for in so doing, you adopt a particular pattern of belief and withholding, one incompatible with some adopted by others. You pays your money and you takes your choice, realizing that you, like anyone else, can be desperately wrong. But what else can you do? You don't really have an alternative. And how can you do better than believe and withhold according to what, after serious and responsible consideration, seems to you to be the right pattern of belief and withholding?

Irrationality

I therefore can't see how it can be sensibly maintained that the exclusivist is unjustified in his exclusivistic views; but perhaps, as is sometimes claimed, he or his view is *irrational.* Irrationality, however, is many things to many people; so there is a prior question: what is it to be irrational? More exactly: precisely what quality is it that the objector is attributing to the exclusivist (in condition C) when the former says the latter's exclusivist beliefs are irrational? Since the charge is never developed at all fully, it isn't easy to say. So suppose we simply consider the main varieties of irrationality (or, if you prefer, the main senses of 'irrational') and ask whether any of them attach to the exclusivist just by virtue of being an exclusivist. I believe there are substantially five varieties of rationality, five distinct but analogically[16] connected senses of the term 'rational'; fortunately, not all of them require detailed consideration.

116

(1) *Aristotelian Rationality.* This is the sense in which man is a rational animal, one that has *ratio,* one that can look before and after, can hold beliefs, make inferences, and is capable of knowledge. This is perhaps the basic sense, the one of which the others are analogical extensions. It is also, presumably, irrelevant in the present context; at any rate, I hope the objector does not mean to hold that an exclusivist will by that token no longer be a rational animal.

(2) *The Deliverances of Reason.* To be rational in the Aristotelian sense is to possess reason: the power of thinking, believing, inferring, reasoning, knowing. Aristotelian rationality is thus *generic.* But there is an important more specific sense lurking in the neighborhood; this is the sense that goes with reason taken more narrowly, as the source of a priori knowledge and belief.[17] An important use of 'rational' analogically connected with the first has to do with reason taken in this more narrow way. It is by reason thus construed that we know *self-evident* beliefs—beliefs so obvious that you can't so much as grasp them without seeing that they couldn't be false. These are among the *deliverances of reason.* Of course, there are other beliefs—*38 x 39 = 1482*, for example—that are not self-evident but are a consequence of self-evident beliefs by way of arguments that are self-evidently valid; these too are among the deliverances of reason. So say that the deliverances of reason is the set of those propositions that are self-evident for us human beings, closed under self-evident consequence. This yields another sense of rationality: a belief is *rational* if it is among the deliverances of reason and *irrational* if it is contrary to the deliverances of reason. (A belief can therefore be neither rational nor irrational, in this sense.) This sense of 'rational' is an analogical extension of the fundamental sense, but it is itself extended by analogy to still other senses. Thus we can broaden the category of reason to include memory, experience, induction, probability, and whatever else goes into science; this is the sense of the term when reason is sometimes contrasted with faith. And we can also soften the requirement for self-evidence, recognizing both that self-evidence or a priori warrant is a matter of degree, and that there are many propositions that have a priori warrant but are not such that no one who understands them can fail to believe them.[18]

Is the exclusivist irrational in *these* senses? I think not; or at any rate the question whether he is isn't the question at issue. For his exclusivist beliefs are irrational in these senses only if there is a good argument from the deliverances of reason (taken broadly) to the denials of what he believes. I myself do not believe there are any such arguments. Presumably, the same goes for the pluralist objector; at any rate his objection is not that (1) and (2) are demonstrably false or even that there are good arguments against them from the deliverances of reason; his objection is instead that there is something wrong or subpar with believing them in condition C. This sense too, then, is irrelevant to our present concerns.

(3) *The Deontological Sense.* This sense of the term has to do with intellectual *requirement,* or *duty,* or *obligation:* a person's belief is irrational in this sense if in forming or holding it she violates such a duty. This is the sense of 'irrational' in which, according to many contemporary evidentialist objectors to theistic belief, those who believe in God without propositional evidence are irrational.[19] Irrationality in this sense is

117

a matter of failing to conform to intellectual or epistemic duties; and the analogical connection with the first, Aristotelian sense is that these duties are thought to be among the deliverances of reason (and hence among the deliverances of the power by virtue of which human beings are rational in the Aristotelian sense). But we have already considered whether the exclusivist is flouting duties; we need say no more about the matter here. As we saw, the exclusivist is not necessarily irrational in this sense either.

(4) *Zweckrationalität.* A common and very important notion of rationality is *means-end* rationality—what our Continental cousins, following Max Weber, sometimes call *Zweckrationalität,* the sort of rationality displayed by your actions if they are well calculated to achieve your goals. (Again, the analogical connection with the first sense is clear: the calculation in question requires the power by virtue of which we are rational in Aristotle's sense.) Clearly, there is a whole constellation of notions lurking in the nearby bushes: what would *in fact* contribute to your goals, what you *take* it would contribute to your goals, what you *would* take it would contribute to your goals if you were sufficiently acute, or knew enough, or weren't distracted by lust, greed, pride, ambition, and the like, what you would take it would contribute to your goals if you weren't thus distracted and were also to reflect sufficiently, and so on. This notion of rationality has assumed enormous importance in the last one hundred fifty years or so. (Among its laurels, for example, is the complete domination of the development of the discipline of economics.) Rationality thus construed is a matter of knowing how to get what you want; it is the cunning of reason. Is the exclusivist properly charged with irrationality in this sense? Does his believing in the way he does interfere with his attaining some of his goals, or is it a markedly inferior way of attaining those goals?

An initial caveat: it isn't clear that this notion of rationality applies to belief at all. It isn't clear that in *believing* something, I am acting to achieve some goal. If believing is an action at all, it is very far from being the paradigmatic kind of action taken to achieve some end; we don't have a choice as to whether to have beliefs, and we don't have a lot of choice with respect to which beliefs we have. But suppose we set this caveat aside and stipulate for purposes of argument that we have sufficient control over our beliefs for them to qualify as actions: would the exclusivist's beliefs then be irrational in this sense? Well, that depends upon what his goals *are*; if among his goals for religious belief is, for example, not believing anything not believed by someone else, then indeed it would be. But, of course, he needn't have *that* goal. If I do have an end or goal in holding such beliefs as (1) and (2), it would presumably be that of believing the truth on this exceedingly important matter, or perhaps that of trying to get in touch as adequately as possible with God, or more broadly with the deepest reality. And if (1) and (2) are *true,* believing them will be a way of doing exactly that. It is only if they are *not* true, then, that believing them could sensibly be thought to be irrational in this means-ends sense. Since the objector does not propose to take as a premise the proposition that (1) and (2) are false— he holds only that there is some flaw involved in *believing* them—this also is presumably not what he means.

(5) *Rationality as Sanity and Proper Function.* One in the grip of pathological confusion, or flight of ideas, or certain kinds of agnosia, or the manic phase of manic-depressive psychosis will often be said to be irrational; the episode may pass, after which he regains rationality. Here 'rationality' means absence of dysfunction, disorder, impairment, pathology with respect to rational faculties. So this variety of rationality is again analogically related to Aristotelian rationality; a person is rational in this sense when no malfunction obstructs her use of the faculties by virtue of the possession of which she is rational in the Aristotelian sense. Rationality as sanity does not require possession of particularly exalted rational faculties; it requires only normality (in the nonstatistical sense), or health, or proper function. This use of the term, naturally enough, is prominent in psychiatric discussions—Oliver Sacks's man who mistook his wife for a hat,[20] for example, was thus irrational.[21] This fifth and final sense of rationality is itself a family of analogically related senses. The fundamental sense here is that of sanity and proper function, but there are other closely related senses. Thus we may say that a belief (in certain circumstances) is irrational not because no sane person would hold it, but because no person who was sane and had also undergone a certain course of education would hold it, or because no person who was sane and furthermore was as intelligent as we and our friends would hold it; alternatively and more briefly, the idea is not merely that no one who was functioning properly in those circumstances would hold it but rather no one who was functioning *optimally,* as well or nearly as well as human beings ordinarily do (leaving aside the occasional great genius) would hold it. And this sense of rationality leads directly to the notion of *warrant*; I turn now to that notion; in treating it we also treat *ambulando* this fifth kind of irrationality.

Warrant

So the third version of the epistemic objection: that at any rate the exclusivist doesn't have warrant, or anyway *much* warrant (enough warrant for knowledge), for his exclusivistic views. Many pluralists—for example, Hick, Runzo, and Wilfred Cantwell Smith—unite in declaring that at any rate the exclusivist certainly can't *know* that his exclusivistic views are true.[22] But is this really true? I shall argue briefly that it is not. At any rate from the perspective of each of the major contemporary accounts of knowledge, it may very well be that the exclusivist knows (1) or (2) or both. First, consider the two main internalistic accounts of knowledge: the justified true belief account(s) and the coherentist account(s). As I have already argued, it seems clear that a theist, a believer in (1), could certainly be *justified* (in the primary sense) in believing as she does: she could be flouting no intellectual or cognitive duties or obligations. But then on the most straightforward justified true belief account of knowledge, she can also *know* that it is true—if, that is, it *can* be true. More exactly, what must be possible is that both the exclusivist is justified in believing (1) and/or (2) and they be true. Presumably, the pluralist does not mean to dispute this possibility.

For concreteness, consider the account of justification given by the classical Chisholm.[23] On this view, a belief has warrant for me to the

119

extent that accepting it is apt for the fulfillment of my epistemic duty, which (roughly speaking) is that of trying to get and remain in the right relation to the truth. But if after the most careful, thorough, thoughtful, open, and prayerful consideration, it still seems to me—perhaps more strongly than ever—that (1) and (2) are true, then clearly accepting them has great aptness for the fulfillment of that duty.[24]

A similarly brief argument can be given with respect to coherentism, the view that what constitutes warrant is coherence with some body of belief. We must distinguish two varieties of coherentism. On the one hand, it might be held that what is required is coherence with some or all of the other beliefs I actually hold; on the other, that what is required is coherence with my *verific* noetic structure (Keith Lehrer's term): the set of beliefs that remains when all the false ones are deleted or replaced by their contradictories. But surely a coherent set of beliefs could include both (1) and (2) together with the beliefs involved in being in condition C; what would be required, perhaps, would be that the set of beliefs contain some explanation of why it is that others do not believe as I do. And if (1) and (2) *are* true, then surely (and a fortiori) there can be coherent verific noetic structures that include them. Hence neither of these versions of coherentism rules out the possibility that the exclusivist in condition C could know (1) and/or (2).

And now consider the main externalist accounts. The most popular externalist account at present would be one or another version of *reliabilism*. And there is an oft-repeated pluralistic argument (an argument that goes back at least to John Stuart Mill's *On Liberty* and possibly all the way back to the third century) that seems to be designed to appeal to reliabilist intuitions. The conclusion of this argument is not always clear, but here is its premise, in John Hick's words:

> For it is evident that in some ninety-nine percent of cases the religion which an individual professes and to which he or she adheres depends upon the accidents of birth. Someone born to Buddhist parents in Thailand is very likely to be a Buddhist, someone born to Muslim parents in Saudi Arabia to be a Muslim, someone born to Christian parents in Mexico to be a Christian, and so on.[25]

As a matter of sociological fact, this may be right. Furthermore, it can certainly produce a sense of intellectual vertigo. But what is one to do with this fact, if fact it is, and what follows from it? Does it follow, for example, that I ought not to accept the religious views that I have been brought up to accept, or the ones that I find myself inclined to accept, or the ones that seem to me to be true? Or that the belief-producing processes that have produced those beliefs in me are unreliable? Surely not. Furthermore, self-referential problems once more loom; this argument is another philosophical tar baby.

For suppose we concede that if I had been born in Madagascar rather than Michigan, my beliefs would have been quite different.[26] (For one thing, I probably wouldn't believe that I was born in Michigan.) But, of course, the same goes for the pluralist. Pluralism isn't and hasn't been widely popular in the world at large; if the pluralist had been born in Madagascar, or medieval France, he probably wouldn't have been a pluralist. Does it follow that he shouldn't be a pluralist or that his pluralistic beliefs are produced in him by an unreliable belief-producing process? I doubt it. Suppose I hold

(4)   If S's religious or philosophical beliefs are such that if S had been born elsewhere and elsewhen, she wouldn't have held them, then those beliefs are produced by unreliable belief-producing mechanisms and hence have no warrant;

or something similar: then once more I will be hoist with my own petard. For in all probability, someone born in Mexico to Christian parents wouldn't believe (4) itself. No matter what philosophical and religious beliefs we hold and withhold (so it seems), there are places and times such that if we had been born there and then, then we would not have displayed the pattern of holding and withholding of religious and philosophical beliefs we *do* display. As I said, this can indeed be vertiginous; but what can we make of it? What can we infer from it about what has warrant and how we should conduct our intellectual lives? That's not easy to say. Can we infer *anything at all* about what has warrant or how we should conduct our intellectual lives? Not obviously.

To return to reliabilism, then: for simplicity, let's take the version of reliabilism according to which S knows p iff the belief that p is produced in S by a reliable belief-producing mechanism or process. I don't have the space, here, to go into this matter in sufficient detail: but it seems pretty clear that if (1) and (2) are true, then it *could be* that the beliefs that (1) and (2) be produced in me by a reliable belief-producing process. For either we are thinking of *concrete* belief-producing processes, like your memory or John's powers of a priori reasoning (*tokens* as opposed to types), or else we are thinking of *types* of belief-producing processes (type reliabilism). The problem with the latter is that there are an enormous number of *different* types of belief-producing processes for any given belief, some of which are reliable and some of which are not; the problem (and a horrifying problem it is[27]) is to say which of these is the type the reliability of which determines whether the belief in question has warrant. So the first (token reliabilism) is the better way of stating reliabilism. But then, clearly enough, if (1) or (2) *is* true, it could be produced in me by a reliable belief-producing process. Calvin's Sensus Divinitatis, for example, could be working in the exclusivist in such a way as reliably to produce the belief that (1); Calvin's Internal Testimony of the Holy Spirit could do the same for (2). If (1) and (2) are true, therefore, then from a reliabilist perspective there is no reason whatever to think that the exclusivist might not know that they are true.

There is another brand of externalism that seems to me to be closer to the truth than reliabilism: call it (faute de mieux) 'proper functionalism'. This view can be stated to a first approximation as follows: S knows p iff (1) the belief that p is produced in S by cognitive faculties that are functioning properly (working as they ought to work, suffering from no dysfunction), (2) the cognitive environment in which p is produced is appropriate for those faculties, (3) the purpose of the module

121

of the epistemic faculties producing the belief in question is to produce true beliefs (alternatively: the module of the design plan governing the production of p is aimed at the production of true beliefs), and (4) the objective probability of a belief's being true, given that it is produced under those conditions, is high.[28] All this needs explanation, of course; for present purposes, perhaps, we can collapse the account into the first condition. But then clearly it *could* be, if (1) and (2) are true, that they are produced in me by cognitive faculties functioning properly under condition C. For suppose (1) is true. Then it is surely possible that God has created us human beings with something like Calvin's Sensus Divinitatis, a belief-producing process that in a wide variety of circumstances functions properly to produce (1) or some very similar belief. Furthermore, it is also possible that in response to the human condition of sin and misery, God has provided for us human beings a means of salvation, which he has revealed in the Bible. Still further, perhaps he has arranged for us to come to believe what he means to teach there by way of the operation of something like the Internal Testimony of the Holy Spirit of which Calvin speaks. So on this view, too, if (1) and (2) are true, it is certainly possible that the exclusivist *know* that they are. We can be sure that the exclusivist's views lack warrant and are irrational in this sense, then, only if they are false; but the pluralist objector does not mean to claim that they *are* false; this version of the objection, therefore, also fails. The exclusivist isn't necessarily irrational, and indeed might *know* that (1) and (2) are true, if indeed they *are* true.

All this seems right. But don't the realities of religious pluralism count for anything at all? Is there nothing at all to the claims of the pluralists?[29] Could that really be right? Of course not. For many or most exclusivists, I think, an awareness of the enormous variety of human religious response serves as a *defeater* for such beliefs as (1) and (2)—an *undercutting* defeater, as opposed to a *rebutting* defeater. It calls into question, to some degree or other, the sources of one's belief in (1) or (2). It doesn't or needn't do so by way of an *argument*; and indeed, there isn't a very powerful argument from the proposition that many apparently devout people around the world dissent from (1) and (2) to the conclusion that (1) and (2) are false. Instead, it works more directly; it directly reduces the level of confidence or degree of belief in the proposition in question. From a Christian perspective, this situation of religious pluralism and our awareness of it is itself a manifestation of our miserable human condition; and it may deprive us of some of the comfort and peace the Lord has promised his followers. It can also deprive the exclusivist of the *knowledge* that (1) and (2) are true, even if they *are* true and he *believes* that they are. Since degree of warrant depends in part on degree of belief, it is possible, though not necessary, that knowledge of the facts of religious pluralism should reduce an exclusivist's degree of belief and hence of warrant for (1) and (2) in such a way as to deprive him of knowledge of (1) and (2). He might be such that if he *hadn't* known the facts of pluralism, then he would have known (1) and (2), but now that he *does* know those facts, he doesn't know (1) and (2). In this way he may come to know less by knowing more.

Things *could* go this way with the exclusivist. On the other hand, they *needn't* go this way. Consider once more the moral parallel. Perhaps you have always believed it deeply wrong for a counselor to use his position of trust to seduce a client. Perhaps you discover that others disagree; they think it more like a minor peccadillo, like running a red light when there's no traffic; and you realize that possibly these people have the same internal markers for their beliefs that you have for yours. You think the matter over more fully, imaginatively recreate and rehearse such situations, become more aware of just what is involved in such a situation (the breach of trust, the breaking of implied promises, the injustice and unfairness, the nasty irony of a situation in which someone comes to a counselor seeking help but receives only hurt) and come to believe even more firmly the belief that such an action is wrong—which belief, indeed, can in this way acquire more warrant for you. But something similar can happen in the case of religious beliefs. A fresh or heightened awareness of the facts of religious pluralism could bring about a reappraisal of one's religious life, a reawakening, a new or renewed and deepened grasp and apprehension of (1) and (2). From Calvin's perspective, it could serve as an occasion for a renewed and more powerful working of the belief-producing processes by which we come to apprehend (1) and (2). In that way knowledge of the facts of pluralism could initially serve as a defeater, but in the long run have precisely the opposite effect.

Notes

[1] *Colloquium Heptaplomeres de rerum sublimium arcanis abditis*, written by 1593 but first published in 1857. English translation by Marion Kuntz (Princeton: Princeton University Press, 1975). The quotation is from the Kuntz translation, p. 256.

[2] Thus Joseph Runzo: "Today, the impressive piety and evident rationality of the belief systems of other religious traditions inescapably confronts Christians with a crisis—and a potential revolution." "God, Commitment, and Other Faiths: Pluralism vs. Relativism," *Faith and Philosophy* 5 (October 1988), 343.

[3] As explained in detail in Robert Wilken, "Religious Pluralism and Early Christian Thought," so far unpublished. Wilken focuses on the third century; he explores Origen's response to Celsus and concludes that there are striking parallels between Origen's historical situation and ours. What is different today, I suspect, is not that Christianity has to confront other religions but that we now call this situation 'religious pluralism'.

[4] Thus Gary Gutting: "Applying these considerations to religious belief, we seem led to the conclusion that, because believers have many epistemic peers who do not share their belief in God . . . , they have no right to maintain their belief without a justification. If they do so, they are guilty of epistemological egoism." *Religious Belief and Religious Skepticism* (Notre Dame: University of Notre Dame Press, 1982), p. 90 (but see the following pages for an important qualification).

[5] "Here my submission is that on this front the traditional doctrinal position of the Church has in fact militated against its traditional moral position, and has in fact encouraged Christians to approach other men immorally. Christ has taught us humility, but we have approached them with arrogance. . . . This charge of arrogance is a serious one." Wilfred Cantwell Smith, *Religious Diversity* (New York: Harper and Row, 1976), p. 13.

[6] Runzo, "Ethically, Religious Exclusivism has the morally repugnant result of making those who have privileged knowledge, or who are intellectually astute, a religious elite, while penalizing those who happen to have no access to the putatively correct religious view, or who are incapable of advanced understanding." "God, Commitment, and Other Faiths," p. 348.

[7] "But natural pride, despite its positive contribution to human life, becomes harmful when it is elevated to the level of dogma and is built into the belief system of a religious community. This happens when its sense of its own validity and worth is expressed in doctrines implying an exclusive or a decisively superior access to the truth or the power to save." John Hick, "Religious Pluralism and Absolute Claims," in Leroy Rouner, ed. *Religious Pluralism* (Notre Dame: University of Notre Dame Press, 1984), p. 197.

[8] Thus John Cobb: "I agree with the liberal theists that even in Pannenberg's case, the quest for an absolute as a basis for understanding reflects the long tradition of Christian imperialism and triumphalism rather than the pluralistic spirit." "The Meaning of Pluralism for Christian Self-Understanding," in Rouner, *Religious Pluralism*, p. 171.

[9] "God, Commitment, and Other Faiths," p. 357.

[10] Smith, *Religious Diversity*, p. 14. A similar statement: "Nor can we reasonably claim that our own form of religious experience, together with that of the tradition of which we are a part, is veridical whilst others are not. We can of course claim this; and indeed virtually every religious tradition has done so, regarding alternative forms of religion either as false or as confused and inferior versions of itself. . . . Persons living within other traditions, then, are equally justified in trusting their own distinctive religious experience and in forming their beliefs on the basis of it. . . . let us avoid the implausibly arbitrary dogma that religious experience is all delusory with the single exception of the particular form enjoyed by the one who is speaking." John Hick, *An Interpretation of Religion* (New Haven, Yale University Press, 1989), p. 235.

[11] "The only reason for treating one's tradition differently from others is the very human but not very cogent reason that it is one's own!" Hick, *Interpretation of Religion*, p. 235.

[12] To speak of choice here suggests that I can simply choose which of these three attitudes to adopt; but is that at all realistic? Are my beliefs to that degree within my control? Here I shall set aside the question whether and to what degree my beliefs are subject to my control and within my power. Perhaps we have very little control over them; then the moral critic of exclusivism can't properly accuse the exclusivist of dereliction of moral duty, but he could still argue that the exclusivist's stance is unhappy, bad, a miserable state of affairs. Even if I can't help it that I am overbearing and conceited, my being that way is a bad state of affairs.

[13] See my "Justification in the Twentieth Century," *Philosophy and Phenomenological Research* 50, supplement (Fall 1990), 45 ff., and see chap. 1 of my *Warrant: The Current Debate* (New York: Oxford University Press, 1993).

[14] See the three editions of *Theory of Knowledge* referred to in note 23.

[15] Some people think there is, and also think that withholding belief, abstaining from belief, is always and automatically the safe course to take with respect to this duty, whenever any question arises as to what to believe and withhold. But that isn't so. One can go wrong by withholding as well as by believing: there is no safe haven here, not even abstention. If there is a duty of the Chisholmian kind, and if I, out of epistemic pride and excessive scrupulosity, succeed in training myself not to accept ordinary perceptual judgments in ordinary perceptual circumstances, I am not performing works of epistemic supererogation; I am epistemically culpable.

[16] In Aquinas's sense, so that analogy may include causality, proportionality, resemblance, and the like.

[17] But then (because of the Russell paradoxes) we can no longer take it that the deliverances of reason are closed under self-evident consequence. See my *Warrant and Proper Function* (New York: Oxford University Press, 1993), chap. 6.

[18] See my *Warrant and Proper Function*, chap. 6. Still another analogical extension: a *person* can be said to be irrational if he won't listen to or pay attention to the deliverances of reason. He may be blinded by lust, or inflamed by passion, or deceived by pride: he might then act contrary to reason—*act* irrationally but also *believe* irrationally. Thus Locke: "Let never so much probability land on one side of a covetous man's reasoning, and money on the other, it is easy to foresee which will outweigh. Tell a man, passionately in love, that he is jilted; bring a score of witnesses of the falsehood of his mistress, 'tis ten to one but three kind words of hers, shall invalidate all their testimonies. . . . and though men cannot always openly gain-say, or resist the force of manifest probabilities, that make against them; yet yield they not to the argument." *An Essay Concerning Human Understanding*, ed. A. D. Woozley (New York: World Publishing Co., 1963), bk. IV, sec. xx, p. 439.

[19] Among those who offer this objection to theistic belief are Brand Blanshard, *Reason and Belief* (London: Allen and Unwin, 1974), pp. 400 ff.; Antony Flew, *The Presumption of Atheism* (London: Pemberton, 1976), pp. 22 ff.; and Michael Scriven, *Primary Philosophy* (New York: McGraw-Hill, 1966), pp. 102 ff. See my "Reason and Belief in God," in Alvin Plantinga and Nicholas Wolterstorff, eds., *Faith and Rationality*: (Notre Dame: University of Notre Dame Press, 1983), pp. 17 ff.

[20] Oliver Sacks, *The Man Who Mistook His Wife for a Hat* (New York: Harper and Row, 1987).

[21] In this sense of the term, what is properly called an 'irrational impulse' may be perfectly rational: an irrational impulse is really one that goes contrary to the deliverances of reason; but undergoing such impulses need not be in any way dysfunctional or a result of the impairment of cognitive faculties. To go back to some of William James's examples, that I will survive my serious illness might be unlikely, given the statistics I know and my evidence generally; perhaps we are so constructed, however, that when our faculties function properly in extreme situations, we are more optimistic than the evidence warrants. This belief, then, is irrational in the sense that it goes contrary to the deliverances of reason; it is rational in the sense that it doesn't involve dysfunction.

[22] Hick, *An Interpretation of Religion*, p. 234; Runzo, "God, Commitment, and Other Faiths," p. 348; Smith, *Religious Diversity*, p. 16.

[23] See his *Perceiving: A Philosophical Study* (Ithaca: Cornell University Press, 1957), the three editions of *Theory of Knowledge* (New York: Prentice-Hall, 1st ed., 1966; 2d ed., 1977; 3d ed., 1989), and *The Foundations of Knowing* (Minneapolis: University of Minnesota Press, 1982); and see my "Chisholmian Internalism," in David Austin, ed., *Philosophical Analysis: A Defense by Example* (Dordrecht: D. Reidel, 1988), and chap. 2 of *Warrant: The Current Debate*.

[24] Of course, there are many variations on this internalist theme. Consider briefly the postclassical Chisholm (see his "The Place of Epistemic Justification," in Roberta Klein, ed., *Philosophical Topics* 14, no. 1 (1986), 85, and the intellectual autobiography in *Roderick M. Chisholm*, ed. Radu Bogdan [Dordrecht: D. Reidel, 1986], pp. 52 ff.), who bears a startling resemblance to Brentano. According to this view, justification is not *deontological* but *axiological*. To put it another way, warrant is not really a matter of justification, of fulfilling duty and obligation; it is instead a question whether a certain relation of fittingness holds between one's evidential base (very roughly, the totality of one's present experiences and other beliefs) and the belief in question. (This relationship's holding, of course, is a valuable state of affairs; hence the axiology.) Can the exclusivist have warrant from this perspective? Well, without more knowledge about what this relation is, it isn't easy to tell. But here at the least the postclassical Chisholmian pluralist would owe us an explanation why he thinks the exclusivist's beliefs could not stand in this relation to his evidence base.

[25] *Interpretation of Religion*, p. 2.

[26] Actually, this conditional as it stands is probably not true; the point must be stated with more care. Given my parents and their proclivities, if I had been born in Madagascar, it would probably have been because my parents were (Christian) missionaries there.

[27] See Richard Feldman, "Reliability and Justification," *The Monist* 68 (1986), 159–74, and chap. 9 of my *Warrant and Proper Function*.

[28] See chap. 10 of my *Warrant: The Current Debate* and the first two chapters of my *Warrant and Proper Function* for exposition and defense of this way of thinking about warrant.

[29] See William P. Alston, "Religious Diversity and Perceptual Knowledge of God," *Faith and Philosophy* 5 (October 1988), 433 ff.

Divine Knowledge and Human Freedom

Scott Davison

All of the major theistic religious traditions hold that God is omniscient, which means that God knows everything that can be known. And the vast majority of theists also hold that human beings act freely, at least sometimes. How can these two beliefs fit together? If God knows in advance everything that you are going to do, then how can you act freely? How can anything at all be up to you, if God already knows what the future holds? And if nobody ever acts freely, then how can people be properly praised or blamed for what they do?

In order to consider these questions carefully, it will be important to take a closer look at the nature of knowledge and the nature of freedom. Then it will be possible to consider the strengths and weaknesses of the main answers that people have suggested to these questions, and maybe even to make up our own minds about what to think. We will try to consider every possibility in order to keep our options open.

1. KNOWLEDGE

What does it mean to say that someone knows something? First of all, to know that something is the case, it must be *true*. For example, you can't know that the Washington Monument is full of circus peanuts because it isn't.

Second, you must have a *belief* about something before you can claim to know it. It is true that I buried my pet mouse in the back yard when I was a young child, but you could not have known that this was true until I told you so (because you did not have a belief about my pet mouse until I mentioned it).

So in order for people to know something, they must have a true belief concerning it. But that is not all. Just because you have a true belief, this does not necessarily mean that you have knowledge. There is such a thing as lucky true belief, which does not count as knowledge.

Suppose that my mischievous friend wants to lure me off campus for a surprise party, so he makes up a story and tells me that my dormitory room has been closed because of asbestos removal. Now imagine that by sheer coincidence, as I am walking off campus towards the surprise party, my dormitory room actually does become closed because of asbestos removal. At this point, I believe that my dormitory room is closed because of asbestos removal, and that is true, but I certainly don't have knowledge of it. My belief turned out to be true by accident.

What else is required, then, for knowledge, besides true belief? Philosophers who study Epistemology (the theory of knowledge and related topics) disagree quite a bit about how to answer this question, but they all agree that knowledge is belief that is *true in a non-accidental way*. In other words, if a person knows something, then it is not the case that this person's belief is true by accident, or that this person's belief could have turned out to be false just as easily as it turned out to be true. There must be some kind of appropriate connection between the person who has knowledge and the fact that is known, although it is hard to be more specific than that.

When we turn from knowledge in general to God's knowledge, we encounter some puzzles immediately. For instance, God is supposed to be omniscient, which means that God knows how many hairs you have on your head right now (for example). But how does God know this? In order for me to know how many hairs there are on your head, I would need to count them using my eyes or my fingers or something. But God has no eyes or fingers.

In fact, God has no physical body at all, since God is a nonphysical spirit. So God has no sense organs. How then does God know things about the physical world?

Theists have suggested different answers to this question. One popular answer is that the world is created in accordance with perfect exemplars or ideas in God's mind. Since God knows those exemplars or ideas perfectly, God knows the world by extension.

Another popular answer is that God is so deeply connected to the world through creation that God knows first hand everything that occurs in the physical world. Most theists throughout history have claimed that God not only created the world at the first moment of time, but also that at every moment of time, God sustains the world in being and contributes actively to every event that occurs in it. If God is this closely connected to the physical world, then perhaps God's knowledge of the world is direct and immediate, so that it doesn't require any sense organs at all.

Of course, this solution to the question about God's knowledge of the physical world raises a different question about God's power. If God has no body, as we mentioned earlier, then how does God create a physical world or sustain it in being? How could a spiritual being cause things to happen in a physical world?

Theists throughout history have just said that God is the kind of agent who can bring about effects in the physical world without being physical. Although human beings manage to bring about effects in the physical world only through the use of their bodies, God is different. (For more on this, see Swinburne 1979.) God's power is unlimited, human power is limited. Is this a satisfactory answer? Well, it's a bit mysterious, but theists have always been happy to admit that there are aspects of God's nature that will always remain mysterious to our limited minds. So this mystery may

GOD'S FOREKNOWLEDGE DOES NOT
RULE OUT FREEDOM * *St. Augustine*

Wherefore, although God foreknows our wills to be, it does not thereby follow that we do not will a thing by our will. You said about happiness that you could not become happy through yourself, and said it as if I would deny it. But I say, when you are going to be happy you are not going to be happy against your will, but wanting to be happy. When therefore, God foreknows your future happiness, it cannot come to pass otherwise than as He has foreknown it, else there is no foreknowledge; nevertheless we are not obliged to think what is most absurd and far removed from the truth, that you are going to be happy when you do not want to. Moreover, just as God's foreknowledge, which today is certain of your future happiness, does not take away your will for happiness when you shall have begun to be happy; so also a culpable will, if you are going to have one, will be none the less your own will because God foreknows that it is to be so . . .

For mark, I beg you, with what blindness it is said that if God has foreknown my future will, it is necessary that I will what He has foreknown, since naught can come to pass otherwise than as He has foreknown. But if it is necessary, it must be acknowledged that I will no longer by will, but by necessity. O strange unreason! How then could it not be otherwise than as God has foreknown, if that should not be a will which He foreknew would be a will? I pass over that equally monstrous thing which a little while ago I said was said by the same man: It is necessary that I so will—thus endeavoring to take away the will and to substitute necessity. For if it is necessary that He so will, how then does He will when there is no will? . . .

And so it comes about both that we do not deny God foreknows all that is to be, and that notwithstanding we may will what we will. For when He foreknows our will, it will be that very will that He foreknows. It will therefore, be a will, because His foreknowledge is of a will. Nor can it be a will if it is not in our power. Therefore, that power is not taken from me by His foreknowledge . . .

From *St. Augustine on Free Will*, trans. C. Sparrow University of Virginia Studies (1947).

not trouble those who are theists already, but those who are not theists might wonder whether or not they can accept this approach to understanding God's power or knowledge.

2. FREEDOM

What does it mean to say that an action is free? At this moment, you are reading this chapter. But you could have been doing something else instead, right? Although you decided to read this chapter right now, you might decide to do something else in the next moment. (If this chapter doesn't get interesting fast, I might lose you, right?) Apparently you are reading this chapter now freely. Can we say anything more about the qualities of a free action in general?

First of all, one necessary ingredient in free decisions is that they are not compelled by any outside forces. This point was made first by Aristotle (384–322 B.C.), a student of Plato and the tutor of Alexander the Great. Imagine that you and I are visiting a museum, and that I push you into a display of very old vases, causing you to knock them over in order to break your fall. In that case, your knocking over the vases is not a free action because it was forced by an outside source.

After that, though, philosophers begin to disagree sharply about what else is necessary in order for an action to be free. Some philosophers insist that in order for an action to be free, it must not be determined in advance, so that at the time of choice, it was possible to do one thing and also possible to do something else. These philosophers are called *incompatibilists* because they believe that acting freely is incompatible with being determined to act by anything else. For example, although it may seem to you that you are now reading this chapter freely, what if a psychiatrist told you that were compelled by guilt and anxiety to read this chapter now? What if this psychiatrist also identified some chemical imbalance in your brain, and said that all of these factors together made it impossible for you to do anything else besides read this chapter now? If this were to happen, an incompatibilist would insist that your action of reading this chapter right now was not free after all, since it was determined by the factors just mentioned.

By contrast, compatibilists claim that acting freely and being determined are compatible, that it is possible to perform a free action and to be determined to perform that very action at the same time. Suppose that the psychiatrist mentioned above offers a completely different explanation as to why you are reading this chapter right now. Instead of saying that you suffer from guilt, anxiety, and chemical imbalances, the psychiatrist says that you are a perfectly normal person, and that you are reading this chapter just because you want to do so. Furthermore, the psychiatrist adds that given your desire to read this chapter, together with the fact that you don't have a stronger desire to do anything else right now, together with the fact that nothing is preventing you from reading, it follows that you are determined to pursue your desire to read. In other words, you are determined to read by your own strong desire to read. Since you are determined by your own desires, though, and not by anything outside of yourself, compatibilists would insist that you are reading freely now. Even though no other option is open to you, given your psychological and physical condition at the moment, they insist that you are acting freely in this situation.

Philosophers disagree sharply about whether or not we should be incompatibilists or compatibilists. This debate is very, very old, and there is no indication that it will stop any time soon. Since we want to know about the relationship between God's knowledge and human freedom, and there are these very two different accounts of freedom, we will need to consider them separately in order to see how their differences make a difference.

3. COMPATIBILISM
AND GOD'S KNOWLEDGE

Let's consider first the compatibilist approach to freedom. Suppose that when a person performs an action freely, that action is determined at the same time. Earlier we supposed that your action of reading this chapter right now was free. Could God have known long ago that you were going to be reading this chapter right now, even if you are currently reading freely?

As long as we accept the compatibilist's approach to freedom, there seems to be no reason to deny that God could have known long ago that you would freely read now. After all, this reading of yours is also determined, according to compatibilists, so by knowing what would determine you to read now God could have concluded that you certainly would read now. (In fact, anyone at all who knew enough about the world a long time ago could have concluded that you certainly would read now, if compatibilism is true.)

In terms of our discussion concerning the nature of knowledge, God could have a true belief about what you would do in the future, a belief that was appropriately connected to the future fact (through what would determine it to occur), a belief that was not true by accident. So if we are compatibilists about freedom, we can accept complete divine foreknowledge without the threat of any contradiction. (For some theists who are already strongly committed to God's complete omniscience, this result has become a reason to accept compatibilism about freedom.)

However, it is important to recognize the fact that some philosophers think that the compatibilist approach to freedom is mistaken. They insist that in order to perform an action freely, there must be some alternative action open to an agent. If an action is determined, they say, then it cannot be free, and vice versa. These days, there are several common arguments that are often offered for this conclusion.

To get our terminology straight, let's suppose that an event is *determined* when its occurrence is implied by a description of the past history of the world plus the laws of nature. When I drop a pencil on the floor, for instance, a description of my dropping the pencil in these circumstances, together with the law of gravity, implies that the pencil will fall towards the floor. So the falling of the pencil is a determined event.

The first common argument against compatibilism begins with the claim that you have no choice now about how past events turned out. (This is what people mean when they say that the past cannot be changed.) Then it adds the claim that you have no choice now about which laws of nature hold. Finally, it suggests that if you have no choice about P and Q, and if P and Q together imply a third proposition R, then you have no choice about R, either. These three claims together lead to the conclusion that if an action is determined, then nobody has any choice about it, which seems to show that determined actions cannot be free. (This argument is defended in detail in

GOD'S FOREKNOWLEDGE RULES
OUT LIBERTARIAN FREEDOM * *Jonathan Edwards*

To suppose the future volitions of moral agents not to be necessary events; or, which is the same thing, events which it is not impossible but that they may not come to pass; and yet to suppose that God certainly foreknows them, and knows all things; is to suppose God's knowledge to be inconsistent with itself.

For to say, that God certainly, and without all conjecture, knows that a thing will infallibly be, which at the same time he knows to be so contingent, that it may possibly not be, is to suppose his knowledge inconsistent with itself; or that one thing he knows, is utterly inconsistent with another thing he knows. It is the same as to say, he now knows a proposition to be of certain infallible truth, which he knows to be of contingent uncertain truth. If a future volition is so without all Necessity, that nothing hinders but it may not be, then the proposition which asserts its future existence, is so uncertain, that nothing hinders, but that the truth of it may entirely fail.

And if God knows all things, he knows this proposition to be thus uncertain. And that is inconsistent with his knowing that it is infallibly true; and so inconsistent with his infallibly knowing that it is true. If the thing be indeed contingent, God views it so, and judges it to be contin-gent, if he views things as they are. If the event be not necessary, then it is possible it may never be: and if it be possible it may never be, God knows it may possibly never be; and that is to know that the proposition, which affirms its existence, may possibly not be true; and that is to know that the truth of it is uncertain; which surely is inconsistent with his knowing it as a certain truth.

If volitions are in themselves contingent events, without all Necessity, then it is no argument of perfection of knowledge in any being to determine peremptorily that they will be; but on the contrary, an argument of ignorance and mistake; because it would argue, that he supposes that proposition to be certain, which in its own nature, and all things considered, is uncertain and contingent. To say, in such a case, that God may have ways of knowing contingent events which we cannot conceive of, is ridiculous; as much so, as to say, that God may know contradictions to be true, for ought we know; or that he may know a thing to be certain, and at the same time know it not to be certain, though we cannot conceive how; because he has ways of knowing which we cannot comprehend.

From Jonathan Edwards, *Freedom of the Will* (1754).

Van Inwagen 1983 and criticized in Dennett 1985.) This argument has been the source of lots of controversy, but many philosophers find it persuasive as a reason for rejecting compatibilism.

The second common argument against compatibilism that is often offered by incompatibilists has to do with moral responsibility. It seems natural to say that if people freely perform actions, then they are morally responsible for doing so. But if all of our actions are determined, then how can anyone be held morally responsible for anything? If all of my actions are determined, then it will always be true to say that I could not have helped but do what I did; I could not do otherwise. And this suggests that I should be neither praised nor blamed for what I did. So if all of our actions are determined, then none of them are free, either. (A slightly different version of this argument is defended in Van Inwagen 1983, explored in Fischer 1986, and criticized in Dennett 1985.) Philosophers argue quite a bit about this argument too, but some of them find it to be a compelling reason for rejecting compatibilism.

The third common argument against compatibilism comes from a theistic perspective, and it concerns the problem of evil. Theists believe that God is all-powerful and perfectly loving, yet the world is full of creatures who perform evil actions. How can this be explained? Why isn't God responsible for the evil actions performed by these creatures?

The most common answer to this question is that these creatures are free to do as they please. It is good to have free creatures, even if they do bad things sometimes, and God cannot be blamed for the actions of free creatures because not even God could control free actions. (One version of this argument can be found in Plantinga 1974.) In fact, if God *could* control free actions, then God would be to blame for the evil actions of creatures. But if compatibilism is true, then God *can* control the free actions of creatures (since compatibilism includes the idea that free actions can be determined at the same time), so we must conclude that compatibilism is false (since God is not to blame for these free actions).

By way of conclusion: if compatibilism is the right account of freedom, then there is no problem with reconciling God's complete foreknowledge with human freedom. But compatibilism may not be the best account of freedom, and some philosophers think that incompatibilism is clearly better. So perhaps now we should consider the relationship between God's foreknowledge and human freedom as described by the incompatibilist.

4. INCOMPATIBILISM AND GOD'S KNOWLEDGE: ONE ARGUMENT

By way of reminder, incompatibilists believe that if an action is free, then it cannot be determined at the same time. If this is the correct approach to freedom, then what should we say about God's foreknowledge? Is it possible for God to know what a person will do freely in the future, even before the person has made a choice?

Many philosophers have argued that the answer to this question is "no," that not even God could know about a future, undetermined event such as a free choice. There are two main ways to argue for this conclusion. It will be helpful to consider each one carefully.

The first argument against the compatibility of God's knowledge and human freedom is very similar to the first argument against compatibilism discussed above, and it centers around the nature of freedom. It will be helpful to display it in the following format:

P1. You have no choice now about how events in the past turned out (this is the so-called "fixity" of the past).

P2. God knew long ago that you would read this chapter right now (for example) (this is the assumption of divine omniscience).

P3. You have no choice now about the fact that God knew long ago that you would read this chapter right now (from P1 and P2).

P4. If P implies Q and you have no choice about P, then you have no choice about Q.

P5. God's knowing long ago that you would read this chapter right now implies that you would read this chapter right now (by the definition of knowledge).

Conclusion. You have no choice now about reading this chapter right now (for example) (from P3, P4, and P5).

This argument attempts to show that if you assume that God knew long ago what you would do now (this assumption occurs in P2), then it follows that what you do now is not free. The argument can also be reversed: if we assume instead that what you do right now is free, then the argument attempts to show that it is not possible that God knew long ago what you would do now. Either way, the argument concludes that it is impossible for God to foreknow a free action. (This argument is defended in detail in Hasker 1989.)

Many philosophers find this argument compelling, but some philosophers think that it can be resisted. Is it true, for example, that it is impossible to change the past? Well, yes, it is impossible to change the past, in the sense that it is impossible to make the past be different from what it was. The phrase "the past" refers to what actually happened prior to the present moment, whatever that turns out to be. For the same reasons, it is impossible to change the future, since "the future" refers to whatever actually happens after the present moment, whatever that turns out to be. But is it possible to prevent the past? In other words, is it possible to perform an action now such that, were you to perform it, the past would have been different?

Let's consider again the suggestion that you are now freely reading this chapter. According to P2, God knew long ago that you would be reading right now. And if P1 is true, then you have no choice now about this fact concerning the past. But is that right? If you are really free right now in reading this chapter, then you could have decided not to read instead. And if you had decided not to read instead, then what would God have thought long ago? Presumably, if God knows the future, then God's past belief would have been different too. In other words, maybe we should say this: at this moment, you can do something (namely, stop reading) such that if you do it, then God's past beliefs about the future will have always been different from what they were in fact.

This reply to the argument seems to suggest that God's past beliefs "track" our future free choices, so that whatever we decide to do, then that is what God believed we would do. As St. Augustine noticed, typically we do not assume that whenever a

136

person knows something in the present time, that person determines what is known. For example, I can know that you are reading right now without bringing it about that you are reading right now. In the same way, perhaps God knows what we are going to do in the future, without bringing it about that we will do those things. So God's foreknowledge may be compatible with our freedom after all. (See St. Augustine 1993.)

This seems to be the best reply to the argument, but to be honest, it's a strange reply. It's strange to think that we have this power now to do something such that if we did it, then the past would have been different always. However, philosophers who defend this idea often point out that independently of the question of God's knowledge, you already have the power to do something such that if you did it, then *it would have been true* always that you were going to do it. In other words, you have the same kind of "counterfactual power" over God's past beliefs as you do over past truths about the future. So maybe this is not so strange after all, although it still seems very puzzling.

Perhaps what makes it so puzzling is that it is hard to see *how* God could know in advance exactly what you are going to do right now, especially if what you decide is not determined in advance. In other words, simply saying that God knows the future, without saying how, is very mysterious. But theists already have a certain amount of mystery to deal with (God is beyond our comprehension), so perhaps they will not be disturbed by the fact that there is no clear mechanism to explain God's complete knowledge of the future. In the end, this argument for the conclusion that God's knowledge of the future is incompatible with freedom is compelling, but not absolutely decisive.

5. INCOMPATIBILISM AND GOD'S KNOWLEDGE: A SECOND ARGUMENT

A second argument for the conclusion that God's foreknowledge is incompatible with freedom goes like this:

P1. God knew long ago that you would read this chapter right now (for example) (this is the assumption of divine omniscience).

P2. A person S knows something only if it is impossible for S to be mistaken about it in those circumstances.

P3. It is impossible for God to be mistaken in those circumstances about the fact that you would read this chapter right now (for example) (from P1 and P2).

P4. A person S acts freely only if it is possible for S to do something else in those circumstances (from the definition of incompatibilism).

Conclusion. You do not read this chapter freely right now (for example) (from P3 and P4).

As before, this argument starts with the assumption of divine foreknowledge and draws a conclusion about human freedom. But it could be reversed as well: if we assumed instead that a given choice was free, then we could argue that since the person in question could do something else in those circumstances, it follows that God's past belief could be mistaken, in which case God's past belief (even if it is true) would not count as knowledge. (One version of this argument is developed in detail in Davison 1991.)

The crucial question for this argument concerns P2: why should anyone accept it? Earlier we said that in order to have knowledge, a person's belief must be true in a nonaccidental way. But we did not say that a person must be unable to be wrong in the circumstances. Why should we believe this? Well, some philosophers have accepted P2 because of arguments like the following one.

Suppose that a fair lottery drawing will occur tomorrow, and that one hundred tickets have been sold. Only one ticket will win, and let's imagine you have bought one ticket for yourself. What are the odds in favor of your winning the lottery? A hundred to one, of course. So there is a 99 percent chance that you will lose. Suppose that you know that there have been one hundred tickets sold, and so you are very pessimistic about your ticket's chances of winning. In fact, let's say that you believe that your ticket will lose tomorrow.

To continue the story, let's imagine that tomorrow arrives, the drawing takes place, and your ticket loses, just like you believed it would. So far, you satisfy two of the criteria for knowing yesterday that your ticket would lose today: you believed that your ticket would lose, and it was true that your ticket would lose. However, should we go ahead and say that you *knew* that your ticket would lose? After all, there was some chance that you would win—you could have been wrong in believing that your ticket would lose. Because of this, many philosophers would say that you did not really know that your ticket would lose, even though your belief was very reasonable and actually turned out to be true. (This argument occurs in Dretske 1971.)

If this argument is correct, then it seems that the actual number of tickets in the lottery doesn't matter very much. As long as there is some chance that your ticket will win, you do not actually know that your ticket will lose. And this suggests strongly that in order to know something, it must be impossible for a person to be mistaken about it in the circumstances.

If we return to the case of God's foreknowledge, imagine how things look to God from the perspective of long ago. Imagine that God knows that at some future moment, you will be faced with the choice of either reading this chapter or not reading it, and God knows that your choice will be free. Suppose that God believes that you will read this chapter, and it turns out to be true. Should we say that God knew that you would read this chapter now? According to the lottery example, the answer here is "no," because God could have been mistaken. Even if the odds of your reading this chapter right now were high, there was still a chance that you would decide not to read now, in which case God's belief would be wrong. So even if

God's belief is true, and reasonable, it does not qualify as knowledge.

Does this argument show, then, that it is impossible even for God to foreknow human free actions? Not exactly. For one thing, not everyone will accept P2, despite the lottery argument developed above. And someone could try to argue that the circumstances mentioned in P2 are different from the circumstances mentioned in P4.

Still, this argument does bring into sharp focus the question about how God could foreknow the outcome of a future free choice, given the very real possibility that something else might happen instead. Once again, though, some theists are inclined to say that although it is mysterious to us, God somehow has a way of knowing what will happen in the future. Nontheists or those who are not impressed by the appeal to mystery will not find this move to be very plausible, of course. So it seems safe to say that this second argument for the conclusion that not even God could foreknow free actions is rather plausible.

6. COULD GOD BE OUTSIDE OF TIME?

So far, we have considered two arguments for the conclusion that it is impossible for God to foreknow free actions, when freedom is understood in the incompatibilist's way. Are there any arguments on the other side, arguments trying to show that God could foreknow free actions?

One popular suggestion throughout history is the idea that God exists outside of time altogether, which enables God to see past, present, and future events all at once. On this suggestion, it is misleading to say that God *fore*knows a future free action, because God's knowledge doesn't really occur *prior to* the free action in time, strictly speaking. After all, if God is outside of time altogether, then nothing belonging to God's essential nature occurs before, during, or after any event that occurs in time.

St. Thomas Aquinas used a famous analogy to describe God's relationship to time in a way that suggests a model for God's knowledge of free actions. (The analogy occurs in his *Summa Theologica*, Part 1, question XIV, article 13, reply to objection 3.) He imagines a wagon train passing through a valley, one wagon at a time. Passengers in the wagons can only see the wagons right in front of theirs, and the wagons right behind theirs. These passengers correspond to human beings, who live in time, and thus have access only to the present moment, the immediate past, or the immediate future.

In addition to the wagon train passing through the valley, in St. Thomas' analogy there is a person sitting on top of a mountain who is watching the entire wagon train from above. Unlike the passengers sitting on the wagons, who have a very limited view of the wagon train, this person can see all of the wagons together, including the relationships in which they stand to one another. This person represents God, of course. The idea is that since God is outside of time (not in between any two wagons), God can see all of history at once, including the distant past and the distant future.

Does this suggestion help? Does St. Thomas' analogy make sense? Does this approach provide a good reason for thinking that God could know what human persons will freely choose to do in the future?

In order to answer this question, we need to see whether or not the arguments we discussed earlier still apply to the suggestion that God exists outside of time altogether. The first argument stated that if God knew something in the past, and you had no choice now about the past, then you had no choice now about what God knew would happen in the future. If we now suggest that God is outside of time, then we can no longer talk about what God knew in the past. But we can talk instead about what God knows from the perspective of eternity. And now the argument can be restated:

P1. You have no choice now about how events look from the perspective of eternity.

P2. God knows from the perspective of eternity that you are reading this chapter right now (for example) (this is the assumption of divine omniscience).

P3. You have no choice now about the fact that God knows from the perspective of eternity that you are reading this chapter right now (from P1 and P2).

P4. If P implies Q and you have no choice about P, then you have no choice about Q.

P5. God's knowing from the perspective of eternity that you are reading this chapter right now implies that you are reading this chapter right now (by the definition of knowledge).

Conclusion. You have no choice now about reading this chapter right now (for example) (from P3, P4, and P5).

In this version of the argument, we have substituted "God knows from the perspective of eternity" for "God knew in the past." The main question here concerns P1: is it just as plausible as the premise that you have no choice now about how events in the past turned out?

It is hard to know what to say here. For some reason, it does seem that what is true from the perspective of eternity might be subject to my current choices in a way that the past is not. This suggests that viewing God as existing outside of time altogether might help to explain how God knows the future in every detail.

On the other hand, it seems very strange to say that what I freely decide to do tomorrow will bring it about that something is true from the perspective of eternity. If I myself haven't decided yet what to do tomorrow, for example, then how could God (or anyone else, for that matter) know what I will freely decide to do tomorrow, whether from the perspective of eternity or any other perspective? And if I were to do something else instead, so that God would believe something different from the perspective of eternity, then does this mean that I have some kind of power over what God thinks from the perspective of eternity? This is puzzling indeed.

Our second argument against the possibility that God knows in advance what people freely choose to do can also be recast in terms of the perspective from eternity:

P1. God knows from the perspective of eternity that you are reading this chapter right now (for example) (this is the assumption of divine omniscience).

P2. A person S knows something only if it is impossible for S to be mistaken about it in those circumstances.

P3. It is impossible for God to be mistaken in those circumstances about the fact that you are reading this chapter right now (for example) (from P1 and P2).

P4. A person S acts freely only if it is possible for S to do something else in those circumstances (from the definition of incompatibilism).

Conclusion. You do not read this chapter freely right now (for example) (from P3 and P4). This argument seems just as strong as the earlier version that involved God's past knowledge (instead of God's timeless knowledge from the perspective of eternity). As we noted earlier, though, although this argument is plausible, it is not absolutely decisive. If there is some way to resist P2, or some way to argue that the circumstances mentioned in P2 and P4 are different, then perhaps this argument can be answered. So to some degree, our earlier arguments for the conclusion that God could not foreknow human free actions remain standing even under the assumption that God exists outside of time altogether.

Some philosophers have objected to the idea that God exists outside of time for reasons that are independent of our question. (For a helpful summary of these reasons, see Hasker 1989.) For example, some philosophers think that if God exists outside of time, then it makes no sense to say that God does things at particular times (like creating the world at the first moment of time, or causing things to happen in the world at particular times) or to say that God could be united with a human nature (as traditional Christians believe the second person of the Trinity was, in the person of Jesus of Nazareth) (see Davis 1983). Other philosophers argue that the idea of God existing outside of time seems to stem from Greek philosophical thought, whereas the idea of God existing in time is more faithful to the biblical depiction of God's nature (see Wolterstorff 1975). In other words, even though appealing to the idea that God exists outside of time altogether might help to answer the question of how God could know about the free choices of creatures in the future, it might introduce new problems of its own. (Exploring this question fully would take us beyond the scope of this essay.)

7. IS FOREKNOWLEDGE USELESS TO GOD?

As we noted at the beginning of this essay, all of the major theistic religious traditions hold that God is omniscient, which means that God knows everything that can be known. As a result, the vast majority of theists throughout history have held that God foreknows free human actions. But what good is it to know the future? Would having foreknowledge of human free actions help God to exercise providential control over the world, for example?

Many theists have believed so. The idea is that if God knows what the future holds, then it can be prevented. However, a little reflection shows that this conclusion is mistaken.

In order to foreknow something, it must be a truth about the future. And the future is just whatever will in fact happen after the present moment. So if God (or anyone else) foreknows that something will happen, then it is too late to do anything about it. In particular, it is impossible to prevent anything that anyone foreknows will occur. (If it were prevented, then it would not actually have been part of the future, and so it could not have *ever* been foreknown, because it would have never been true in the first place.) (This argument is stated clearly in Hasker 1989.)

All major theistic traditions have held that God is omniscient, but they have also held that God is omnipotent (all-powerful) and provident. To be provident, God must exercise some degree of control over the world in order to achieve good purposes. (For more on this, see Davison 1999.) The argument just mentioned above shows that having foreknowledge of human free choices is not enough for providential planning. In order to determine the future (at least in part), God needs to have knowledge of *what would happen* if certain steps were taken, not just *what will actually happen* in the future.

It will be helpful to consider an example in order to make this point more clear. Suppose that I am playing with my new chemistry set and mixing chemicals at random. If I mix a certain combination of chemicals, then there will be an explosion that will kill me. God knows this, of course, and doesn't want me to die in this way. Suppose also that God knows what the future holds, so that God foreknows that I will (in fact) mix the chemicals and cause the explosion and die. If that is so, then it is too late even for God: since God knows that it is true, then it is true, and that's the end of it.

However, if God were to prevent me from mixing the chemicals, then God never could have foreknown that I was going to mix them together (since a person can foreknow only that which will in fact take place). What we want to say here is that God knows that *if* I am placed in certain circumstances, *then* I will choose freely to mix those chemicals together so as to cause the explosion to occur. Then God can make sure that I am never in those circumstances, and in this way God can prevent me from ever causing the explosion to occur. In other words, God needs to know not just what will in fact happen, but what would happen if free persons were placed in certain circumstances.

Luis de Molina, an influential Jesuit theologian (1535–1600 A.D.), realized that this was true, and so he formulated an account of God's knowledge that explained how God can foreknow free human actions and also how God can be provident. Molina's theory (often called "Molinism") involves distinguishing three different kinds of knowledge that God possesses. (For more on Molina, see Freddoso's introduction to Molina 1988, Craig 1987, and Flint 1988.)

Natural knowledge is God's knowledge of necessary truths, truths over which God has no control at all (such as "1 + 1 = 2," for instance). *Free knowledge* is God's knowledge of contingent truths over which God has complete control (such as "There exists a physical universe"). Finally, *Middle knowledge* is God's knowledge of contingent truths over which God has no control at all (such as "If you were to hear a siren right now, then you would freely stop reading this chapter and look out the nearest window instead").

Middle knowledge is so-called because it is "in between" natural knowledge and free knowledge: like free knowledge, it is contingent, and like natural knowledge, it is beyond God's control. According to Molina, God considers the items of natural knowledge and middle knowledge when deciding what kind of world to create. For instance, earlier we mentioned God's desire that I should not blow myself up with my new chemistry set. Molina would say that God knew (through middle knowledge) that if I were placed in some circumstances, then I would freely blow myself up, whereas if I were placed in other circumstances, I would freely not do this. God cannot choose which circumstances are the ones in which I would blow myself up or vice versa, though, because that depends upon what I would freely choose to do. In this regard, the items of God's middle knowledge are both contingent (that is, they could have been otherwise) and also beyond God's control.

So Molina thinks that God's middle knowledge includes knowledge of what every possible creature would do in every possible situation. This gives God a

measure of control over a world containing free creatures, since God need only place them in the right circumstances in order to get the desired results. However, on Molina's account, God is also constrained to
some degree by what free creatures would decide to do.
For instance, it might just turn out that there are no
circumstances in which I would freely do a certain
thing, so God would be unable to bring it about that I
do that thing freely. (God could bring it about directly
that I do that thing, of course, but God could not bring
it about that I do it *freely*: since we are talking about
freedom in the incompatibilist's sense, it is impossible
even for God to *make* someone do something *freely* in
this sense. For more on this, see Plantinga 1974.)

Molina's picture also explains how God could
have complete foreknowledge concerning the future,
including the future free choices of human beings.
Here is how it works: from middle knowledge, God
would know what every possible creature would do in
every possible situation. And from free knowledge,
God would know in which future situations actual
creatures would be placed. Finally, from these two
things, God can infer what actual creatures will
freely choose to do in those situations. Isn't this a
neat explanation?

It certainly is. And since many philosophers
accept the argument mentioned above for the conclusion that foreknowledge alone is useless for
God's providence, many philosophers are tempted
to embrace Molina's theory of middle knowledge.
But it is important to realize that although Molina's
theory can easily explain how God has foreknowledge of free human actions, it has a hard time explaining how God gets middle knowledge in the
first place.

In order to see why this is so, let's consider again
Molina's view of the nature of middle knowledge. Logically prior to the creation of the world, even if no free
creatures actually exist, God still knows what every possible creature would freely do in every possible situation.

But how does God know these things? Surely it is at least as puzzling (if not more so) to say that God knows what every possible creature would freely do in every possible situation than it is to say that God knows what actual creatures will freely do in the future. The argument against foreknowledge developed in section 5, for example, clearly applies here just as well as it did there.

Of course, it is always open to the theist to claim that God has this knowledge, even though we do not understand how it is possible. There are many mysterious things in life, and perhaps this is one of them. But nontheists are not likely to find this explanation very satisfying.

8. WHAT IF GOD DOESN'T KNOW?

On the basis of all of the arguments discussed above (and many others besides these), some philosophers who are theists have simply concluded that it is not possible for God to foreknow free actions. However, they do not regard this conclusion as unwelcome or unsettling. Instead, they argue that God is still omniscient (since God knows everything that it is possible to know) and that God is still provident. Many of these philosophers call their approach "The Open Future View" (see Rice 1985, Hasker 1989, Pinnock 1994, and Basinger and Basinger 1994, for example).

Proponents of the Open Future View like to emphasize the fact that according to their view, God still knows everything that is possible. And God also knows what will probably happen in the future. But God doesn't know every single detail. In particular, God doesn't know how free creatures will choose to act in specific circumstances. But God is very resourceful (this is an understatement, of course), and although creating free creatures involves taking a risk of sorts, God will not be taken off guard or be thwarted in the long run.

Most traditional theists view the Open Future

View as a departure from the traditional way of thinking about God's knowledge and providence, but defenders of the Open Future View argue that this is a mistake. Who is right about this? Theists need to consider the arguments on both sides before making up their minds, but that task falls beyond the scope of this paper.

9. CONCLUSION

We have discovered that it is important to clarify the ideas of knowledge and freedom. Once those ideas become clear, it is obvious that God could foreknow the free actions of creatures in the compatibilist's sense of "free." However, there are several plausible arguments for the conclusion that God could not foreknow the free actions of creatures in the incompatibilist's sense of "free." These arguments are not absolutely irresistible, though, and some theists think that an appeal to the timelessness of God or to God's middle knowledge will help to explain God's foreknowledge. These moves generate new puzzles of their own, though, so that in the end it is not clear whether they are worthwhile moves to make. Some theists say that God simply does not know the future free choices of creatures, but they are quick to add that their view is faithful to the major theistic traditions on all important points.

What conclusion should you draw from all of this? Now that you have finished reading this chapter freely, do you have a clearer idea? Do you think that God knew long ago that you would finish this chapter now, or not? Only you can decide for yourself what to believe.

REFERENCES

Aquinas, St. Thomas. *Summa Theologica* (available in many editions).

St. Augustine, *On Free Choice of the Will*, translated by Thomas Williams (Hackett Publishing Company, 1993).

David Basinger and Randall Basinger (editors), *Four Views on Sovereignty and Human Freedom* (InterVarsity Press, 1986).

William L. Craig, *The Only Wise God* (Baker Book House, 1987).

Stephen T. Davis, *Logic and the Nature of God* (William B. Eerdmans Publishing Company, 1983).

Scott A. Davison, "Divine Providence and Human Freedom" in Michael Murray (editor), *Reason for the Hope Within* (William B. Eerdmans Publishing Company, 1999), pp. 217–237.

Scott A. Davison, "Foreknowledge, Middle Knowledge, and 'Nearby' Worlds," *International Journal for Philosophy of Religion*, Volume 30, Number 1 (August 1991), pp. 29–44.

Daniel Dennett, *Elbow Room: The Varieties of Free Will Worth Wanting* (MIT Press, 1985).

Fred Dretske, "Conclusive Reasons" in *The Australasian Journal of Philosophy* 49 (1971), pp. 1–22, reprinted in *Knowledge: Readings in Contemporary Epistemology* (Oxford University Press, 2000), pp. 42–62.

John Martin Fischer (editor), *Moral Responsibility* (Cornell University Press, 1986).

Thomas P. Flint, "Two Accounts of Providence" in Thomas V. Morris (editor), *Divine and Human Action* (Ithaca: Cornell University Press, 1988), pp.147–81.

William Hasker, *God, Time, and Knowledge* (Cornell University Press, 1989).

J. L. Mackie, *The Miracle of Theism* (Oxford University Press, 1982).

Luis de Molina, *On Divine Foreknowledge* (Liberi arbitri cum gratiae donis, divina praescientia, providentia, praedestinatione et reprobatione concordia, Disputations 47–53), translated with an introduction by Alfred J. Freddoso (Ithaca: Cornell University Press, 1988).

Clark H. Pinnock (editor), *The Openness of God : A Biblical Challenge to the Traditional Understanding of God* (InterVarsity Press, 1994).

Alvin I. Plantinga, *God, Freedom, and Evil* (William B. Eerdmans Publishing Company, 1974).

Richard Rice, *God's Foreknowledge and Man's Free Will* (Bethany House Publishers, 1985).

William L. Rowe, *Philosophy of Religion* (Wadsworth Publishing Company, 1978).

Richard Swinburne, *The Existence of God* (Oxford University Press, 1979).

Peter van Inwagen, *An Essay on Free Will* (Oxford University Press, 1983).

Nicholas Wolterstorff, "God Everlasting" in Clifton J. Orlebeke and Lewis B. Smedes (editors), *God and the Good* (William B. Eerdmans Publishing Company, 1975).

Religion and the Queerness of Morality

George I. Mavrodes

Many arguments for the existence of God may be construed as claiming that there is some feature of the world that would somehow make no sense unless there was something else that had a stronger version of that feature or some analogue of it. So, for example, the cosmological line of argument may be thought of as centering upon the claim that the way in which the world exists (called "contingent" existence) would be incomprehensible unless there were something else—that is, God—that had a stronger grip upon existence (that is, "necessary" existence).

Now, a number of thinkers have held a view something like this with respect to morality. They have claimed that in some important way morality is dependent upon religion—dependent, that is, in such a way that if religion were to fail, morality would fail also. And they have held that the dependence was more than psychological, that is, if religion were to fail, it would somehow be *proper* (perhaps logically or perhaps in some other way) for morality to fail also. One way of expressing this theme is by Dostoevsky's "If there is no God, then everything is permitted," a sentiment that in this century has been prominently echoed by Sartre. But perhaps the most substantial philosophical thinker of the modern period to espouse this view, though in a rather idiosyncratic way, was Immanuel Kant, who held that the existence of God was a necessary postulate of "practical" (that is, moral) reason.[1]

On the other hand, it has recently been popular for moral philosophers to deny this theme and to maintain that the dependence of morality on religion is, at best, merely psychological. Were religion to fail, so they apparently hold, this would grant no sanction for the failure of morality. For morality stands on its own feet, whatever those feet may turn out to be.

Now, the suggestion that morality somehow depends on religion is rather attractive to me. It is this suggestion that I wish to explore in this paper, even though it seems unusually difficult to formulate clearly the features of this suggestion that make it attractive. I will begin by mentioning briefly some aspects that I will not discuss.

First, beyond this paragraph I will not discuss the claim that morality cannot survive psychologically without the support of religious belief. At least in the short run, this proposal seems to me false. For there certainly seem to be people who reject religious belief, at least in the ordinary sense, but who apparently have a concern with morality and who try to live a moral life. Whether the proposal may have more force if it is understood in a broader way, as applying to whole cultures, epochs, and so forth, I do not know.

Second, I will not discuss the attempt to define some or all moral terms by the use of religious terms, or vice versa. But this should not be taken as implying any judgment about this project.

Third, beyond this paragraph I shall not discuss the suggestion that moral statements may be entailed by religious statements and so may be "justified" by religious doctrines or beliefs. It is popular now to hold that no such alleged entailment can be valid. But the reason usually cited for this view is the more general doctrine that moral statements cannot be validly deduced from nonmoral statements, a doctrine usually traced to Hume. Now, to my mind the most important problem raised by this general doctrine is that of finding some interpretation of it that is both significant and not plainly false. If it is taken to mean merely that there is *some* set of statements that entails no moral statement, then it strikes me as probably true, but trivial. At any rate, we should then need another reason to suppose that religious statements fall in this category. If, on the other hand, it is taken to mean that one can divide the domain of statements into two classes, the moral and the nonmoral, and that none of the latter entail any of the former, then it is false. I, at any rate, do not know a version of this doctrine that seems relevant to the religious case and that has any reasonable likelihood of being true. But I am not concerned on this occasion with the possibly useful project of deducing morality from religion, and so I will not pursue it further. My interest is closer to a move in the other direction, that of deducing religion from morality. (I am not quite satisfied with this way of putting it and will try to explain this dissatisfaction later on.)

For the remainder of this discussion, then, my project is as follows. I will outline one rather common nonreligious view of the world, calling attention to what I take to be its most relevant features. Then I shall try to portray some sense of the odd status that morality would have in a world of that sort. I shall be hoping, of course, that you will notice that this odd status is not the one that you recognize morality to have in the actual world. But it will perhaps be obvious that the "worldview" amendments required would move substantially toward a religious position.

First, then, the nonreligious view. I take a short and powerful statement of it from a 1903 essay by Bertrand Russell, "A Free Man's Worship."

That man is the product of causes which had no prevision of the end they were achieving; that his origin, his growth, his hopes and fears, his loves and his beliefs are but the outcome of accidental collocations of atoms; that no fire, no heroism, no intensity of thought and feeling, can preserve an individual life beyond the grave; that all the labors of the ages, all the devotion, all the inspiration, all the noonday brightness of human genius, are destined to extinction in the vast death of the solar system, and that the whole temple of man's achievement must inevitably be buried beneath the debris of a universe in ruins—all these things, if not quite beyond dispute, are yet so nearly certain that no philosophy which rejects them can hope to stand. Only within the scaffolding of these truths, only on the firm foundation of unyielding despair, can the soul's habitation henceforth be safely built.[2]

For convenience, I will call a world that satisfies the description given here a "Russellian world." But we are primarily interested in what the status of morality would be in the actual world if that world should turn out to be Russellian. I shall therefore sometimes augment the description of a Russellian world with obvious features of the actual world.

What are the most relevant features of a Russellian world? The following strike me as especially important: (1) Such phenomena as minds, mental activities, consciousness, and so forth are the products of entities and causes that give no indication of being mental themselves. In Russell's words, the causes are "accidental collocations of atoms" with "no prevision of the end they were achieving." Though not stated explicitly by Russell, we might add the doctrine, a commonplace in modern science, that mental phenomena—and indeed life itself—are comparative latecomers in the long history of the earth. (2) Human life is bounded by physical death and each individual comes to a permanent end at his physical death. We might add to this the observation that the span of human life is comparatively short, enough so that in some cases we can, with fair confidence, predict the major consequences of certain actions insofar as they will affect a given individual throughout his whole remaining life. (3) Not only each individual but also the human race as a species is doomed to extinction "beneath the debris of a universe in ruins."

So much, then, for the main features of a Russellian world. Because the notion of benefits and goods plays an important part in the remainder of my discussion, I want to introduce one further technical expression—"Russellian benefit." A Russellian benefit is one that could accrue to a person in a Russellian world. A contented old age would be, I suppose, a Russellian benefit, as would a thrill of sexual pleasure or a good reputation. Going to heaven when one dies, though a benefit, is not a Russellian benefit. Russellian benefits are only the benefits possible in a Russellian world. But one can have Russellian benefits even if the world is not Russellian.

In such a case there might, however, also be other benefits, such as going to heaven.

Could the actual world be Russellian? Well, I take it to be an important feature of the actual world that human beings exist in it and that in it their actions fall, at least sometimes, within the sphere of morality—that is, they have moral obligations to act (or to refrain from acting) in certain ways. And if they do not act in those ways, then they are properly subject to a special and peculiar sort of adverse judgment (unless it happens that there are special circumstances that serve to excuse their failure to fulfill the obligations). People who do not fulfill their obligations are not merely stupid or weak or unlucky; they are morally reprehensible.

Now, I do not have much to say in an illuminating manner about the notion of moral obligation, but I could perhaps make a few preliminary observations about how I understand this notion. First, I take it that morality includes, or results in, judgments of the form "N ought to do (or to avoid doing)_____" or "It is N's duty to do (or to avoid doing)_____." That is, morality ascribes to particular people an obligation to do a certain thing on a certain occasion. No doubt morality includes other things as well—general moral rules, for example. I shall, however, focus on judgments of the sort just mentioned, and when I speak without further qualification of someone's having an obligation I intend it to be understood in terms of such a judgment.

Second, many authors distinguish prima facie obligations from obligations "all things considered." Probably this is a useful distinction. For the most part, however, I intend to ignore prima facie obligations and to focus upon our obligations all things considered, what we might call our "final obligations." These are the obligations that a particular person has in some concrete circumstance at a particular place and time, when all the aspects of the situation have been taken into account. It identifies the action that, if not done, will properly subject the person to the special adverse judgment.

Finally, it is, I think, a striking feature of moral obligations that a person's being unwilling to fulfill the obligation is irrelevant to having the obligation and is also irrelevant to the adverse judgment in case the obligation is not fulfilled. Perhaps even more important is the fact that, at least for some obligations, it is also irrelevant in both these ways for one to point out that he does not see how fulfilling the obligations can do him any good. In fact, unless we are greatly mistaken about our obligations, it seems clear that in a Russellian world there are an appreciable number of cases in which fulfilling an obligation would result in a loss of good to ourselves. On the most prosaic level, this must be true of some cases of repaying a debt, keeping a promise, refraining from stealing, and so on.

And it must also be true of those rarer but more striking cases of obligation to risk death or serious injury in the performance of a duty. People have, of course, differed as to what is good for humans. But so far as I can see, the point I have been making will hold for any candidate that is plausible in a Russellian world. Pleasure, happiness, esteem, contentment, self-realization, knowledge—all of these can suffer from the fulfillment of a moral obligation.

It is not, however, a *necessary* truth that some of our obligations are such that their fulfillment will yield no net benefit, within Russellian limits, to their fulfiller. It is not contradictory to maintain that, for every obligation that I have, a corresponding benefit awaits me within the confines of this world and this life. While such a contention would not be contradictory, however, it would nevertheless be false. I discuss below one version of this contention. At present it must suffice to say that a person who accepts this claim will probably find the remainder of what I have to say correspondingly less plausible.

Well, where are we now? I claim that in the actual world we have some obligations that, when we fulfill them, will confer on us no net Russellian benefit—in fact, they will result in a Russellian loss. If the world is Russellian, then Russellian benefits and losses are the only benefits and losses, and also then we have moral obligations whose fulfillment will result in a net loss of good to the one who fulfills them. I suggest, however, that it would be very strange to have such obligations—strange not simply in the sense of being unexpected or surprising but in some deeper way. I do not suggest that it is strange in the sense of having a straightforward logical defect, of being self-contradictory to claim that we have such obligations. Perhaps the best thing to say is that were it a fact that we had such obligations, then the world that included such a fact would be absurd—we would be living in a crazy world.

Now, whatever success I may have in this paper will in large part be a function of my success (or lack thereof) in getting across a sense of that absurdity, that queerness. On some accounts of morality, in a Russellian world there would not be the strangeness that I allege. Perhaps, then, I can convey some of that strangeness by mentioning those views of morality that would eliminate it. In fact, I believe that a good bit of their appeal is just the fact that they do get rid of this queerness.

First, I suspect that morality will not be queer in the way I suggest, even in a Russellian world, if judgments about obligations are properly to be analyzed in terms of the speaker rather than in terms of the subject of the judgment. And I more than suspect that this will be the case if such judgments are analyzed in terms of the speaker's attitude or feeling toward some action, and/or his attempt or inclination to incite a similar attitude in someone else. It may be, of course, that there is something odd about the supposition that human beings, consciousness, and so forth, could arise at all in a Russellian world. A person who was impressed by that oddity might be attracted toward some "teleological" line of reasoning in the direction of a more religious view. But I think that this oddity is not the one I am touching on here. Once given the existence of human beings with capacities for feelings and attitudes, there does not seem to be anything further that is queer in the supposition that a speaker might have an attitude toward some action, might express that attitude, and might attempt (or succeed) in inciting someone else to have a similar attitude. Anyone, therefore, who can be satisfied with such an analysis will probably not be troubled by the queerness that I allege.

Second, for similar reasons, this queerness will also be dissipated by any account that understands judgments about obligations purely in terms of the feelings, attitudes, and so forth of the subject of the judgment. For, given again that there are human beings with consciousness, it does not seem to be any additional oddity that the subject of a moral judgment might have feelings or attitudes about an actual or prospective action of his own. The assumption that morality is to be understood in this way takes many forms. In a closely related area, for example, it appears as the assumption—so common now that it can pass almost unnoticed—that guilt could not be anything other than guilt *feelings*, and that the "problem" of guilt is just the problem generated by such feelings.

In connection with our topic here, however, we might look at the way in which this sort of analysis enters into one plausible-sounding explanation of morality in a Russellian world, an explanation that has a scientific flavor. The existence of morality in a Russellian world, it may be said, is not at all absurd because its existence there can be given a perfectly straightforward explanation: morality has a survival value for a species such as ours because it makes possible continued cooperation and things of that sort. So it is no more absurd that people have moral obligations than it is absurd that they have opposable thumbs.

I think that this line of explanation will work only if one analyzes obligations into feelings, or beliefs. I think it is plausible (though I am not sure it is correct) to suppose that everyone's having feelings of moral obligation might have a survival value for a species such as Man, given of course that these feelings were attached to patterns of action that contributed to such survival. And if that is so, then it is not implausible to suppose that there may be a survival value for the species even in a moral feeling that leads to the death of the individual who has it. So far so good. But this observation, even if true, is not relevant to the queerness with which I am here concerned. For I have not suggested that the existence of moral feelings would be absurd in a Russellian world; it is rather the existence of moral *obligations* that is absurd, and I think it important to make the distinction. It is quite possible, it seems to me, for one to feel (or to believe) that he has a certain obligation without actually having it, and also vice versa. Now, beliefs and feelings will presumably have some effect upon actions, and this effect may possibly contribute to the survival of the species. But, so far as I can see, the addition of actual moral obligations to these moral beliefs and feelings will make no further contribution to action nor will the actual obligations have an effect upon action in the absence of the corresponding feelings and beliefs. So it seems that neither with nor without the appropriate feelings will moral obligations contribute to the survival of the species. Consequently, an "evolutionary" approach such as this cannot serve to explain the existence of moral obligations, unless one rejects my distinction and equates the obligations with the feelings.

And finally, I think that morality will not be queer in the way I allege, or at least it will not be as queer as I think, if it should be the case that every obligation yields a Russellian benefit to the one who fulfills it. Given the caveat expressed earlier, one can perhaps make some sense out of the notion of a Russellian good or benefit for a sentient organism in a Russellian world. And one could, I suppose, without further queerness imagine that such an organism might aim toward achieving such goods. And we could further suppose that there were certain actions—those that were "obligations"—that would, in contrast with other actions, actually yield such benefits to the organism that performed them. And finally, it might not be too implausible to claim that an organism that failed to perform such an action was defective in some way and that some adverse judgment was appropriate.

Morality, however, seems to require us to hold that certain organisms (namely, human beings) have in addition to their ordinary properties and relations another special relation to certain actions. This relation is that of being "obligated" to perform those actions. And some of those actions are pretty clearly such that they will yield only Russellian losses to the one who performs them. Nevertheless, we are supposed to hold that a person who does not perform an action to which he is thus related is defective in some serious and important way and an adverse judgment is appropriate against him. And that certainly does seem odd.

The recognition of this oddity—or perhaps better, this absurdity—is not simply a resolution to concern ourselves only with what "pays." Here the position of Kant is especially suggestive. He held that a truly moral action is undertaken purely out of respect for the moral law and with no concern at all for reward. There seems to be no room at all here for any worry about what will "pay." But he also held that the moral enterprise needs, in a deep and radical way, the postulate of a God who can, and will, make happiness correspond to virtue. This postulate is "necessary" for practical reason. Perhaps we could put this Kantian demand in the language I have been using here, saying that the moral enterprise would make no sense in a world in which that correspondence ultimately failed.

I suspect that what we have in Kant is the recognition that there cannot be, in any "reasonable" way, a moral demand upon me, unless reality itself is committed to morality in some deep way. It makes sense only if there is a moral demand on the world too and only if reality will in the end satisfy that demand. This theme of the deep grounding of morality is one to which I return briefly near the end of this paper.

The oddity we have been considering is, I suspect, the most important root of the celebrated and somewhat confused question, "Why should I be moral?" Characteristically, I think, the person who asks that question is asking to have the queerness of that situation illuminated. From time to time there are philosophers who make an attempt to argue—perhaps only a halfhearted attempt—that being moral really is in one's interest after all. Kurt Baier, it seems to me, proposes a reply of this sort. He says:

> Moralities are systems of principles whose acceptance by everyone as overruling the dictates of self-interest is in the interest of everyone alike though following the rules of a morality is not of course identical with following self-interest. . . .

> The answer to our question "Why should we be moral?" is therefore as follows. We should be moral because being moral is following rules designed to overrule self-interest whenever it is in the interest of everyone alike that everyone should set aside his interest.[3]

As I say, this seems to be an argument to the effect that it really is in everyone's interest to be moral. I suppose that Baier is here probably talking about Russellian interests. At least, we must interpret him in that way if his argument is to be applicable in this context, and I will proceed on that assumption. But how exactly is the argument to be made out?

It appears here to begin with a premise something like

(A) It is in everyone's best interest (including mine, presumably) for everyone (including me) to be moral.

This premise itself appears to be supported earlier by reference to Hobbes. As I understand it, the idea is that without morality people will live in a "state of nature," and life will be nasty, brutish, and short. Well, perhaps so. At any rate, let us accept (A) for the moment. From (A) we can derive

(B) It is in my best interest for everyone (including me) to be moral.

And from (B) perhaps one derives

(C) It is in my best interest for me to be moral.

And (C) may be taken to answer the question, "Why should I be moral?" Furthermore, if (C) is true, then moral obligation will at least not have the sort of queerness that I have been alleging.

Unfortunately, however, the argument outlined above is invalid. The derivation of (B) from (A) *may* be all right, but the derivation of (C) from (B) is invalid. What does follow from (B) is

(C') It is in my best interest for me to be moral *if everyone else is moral.*

The argument thus serves to show that it is in a given person's interest to be moral only on the assumption that everyone else in the world is moral. It might, of course, be difficult to find someone ready to make that assumption.

There is, however, something more of interest in this argument. I said that the derivation of (B) from (A) may be all right. But in fact is it? If it is not all right, then this argument would fail even if everyone else in the world were moral. Now (A) can be interpreted as referring to "everyone's best interest" ("the interest of everyone alike," in Baier's own words) either collectively or distributively; that is, it may be taken as referring to the best interest of the whole group considered as a single unit, or as refer-ring to the best interest of each individual in the group. But if (A) is inter-preted in the collective sense, then (B) does not follow from it. It may not be in *my* best interest for everyone to act morally, even if it is in the best interest of the group as a whole, for the interest of the group as a whole may be advanced by the sacrificing of my interest. On this interpretation of (A), then, the argument will not answer the question "Why should I be moral?" even on the supposition that everyone else is moral.

If (A) is interpreted in the distributive sense, on the other hand, then (B) does follow from it, and the foregoing objection is not applicable. But another objection arises. Though (A) in the collective sense has some plausibility, it is hard to imagine that it is true in the distributive sense. Hobbes may have been right in supposing that life in the state of nature would be short, etc. But some lives are short anyway. In fact, some lives are short just because the demands of morality are observed. Such a life is not bound to have been shorter in the state of nature. Nor is it bound to have been less happy, less pleasurable, and so forth. In fact, does it not seem obvious that *my* best Russellian interest will be further advanced in

160

a situation in which everyone else acts morally but I act immorally (in selected cases) than it will be in case everyone, including me, acts morally? It certainly seems so. It can, of course, be observed that if I act immorally then so will other people, perhaps reducing my benefits. In the present state of the world that is certainly true. But in the present state of the world it is also true, as I observed earlier, that many other people will act immorally *anyway*, regardless of, what I do.

A more realistic approach is taken by Richard Brandt.[4] He asks, "Is it *reasonable* for me to do my duty if it conflicts seriously with my personal welfare?" After distinguishing several possible senses of this question, he chooses a single one to discuss further, presumably a sense that he thinks important. As reformulated, the question is now: "Given that doing x is my duty and that doing some conflicting act y will maximize my personal welfare, will the performance of x instead of y satisfy my reflective preferences better?" And the conclusion to which he comes is that "the correct answer may vary from one person to another. It depends on what kind of person one is, what one cares about." And within Russellian limits Brandt must surely be right in this. But he goes on to say, "It is, of course, no defense of one's failure to do one's duty, before others or society, to say that doing so is not 'reasonable' for one in this sense." And this is just to bring the queer element back in. It is to suppose that besides "the kind of person" I am and my particular pattern of "cares" and interests there is something else, my duty, which may go against these and in any case properly overrides them. And one feels that there must be some sense of "reasonable" in which one can ask whether a world in which that is true is a reasonable world, whether such a world makes any sense.

This completes my survey of some ethical or metaethical views that would eliminate or minimize this sort of queerness of morality. I turn now to another sort of view, stronger I think than any of these others, which accepts that queerness but goes no further. And one who holds this view will also hold, I think, that the question "Why should I be moral?" must be rejected in one way or another. A person who holds this view will say that it is simply a fact that we have the moral obligations that we do have, and that is all there is to it. If they sometimes result in a loss of good, then that too is just a fact. These may be puzzling or surprising facts, but there are lots of puzzling and surprising things about the world. In a Russellian world, morality will be, I suppose, an "emergent" phenomenon; it will be a feature of certain effects though it is not a feature of their causes. But the wetness of water is an emergent feature, too. It is not a property of either hydrogen or oxygen. And there is really nothing more to be said; somewhere we must come to an end of reasons and explanations. We have our duties. We can fulfill them and be moral, or we can ignore them and be immoral. If all that is crazy and absurd—well, so be it. Who are we to say that the world is not crazy and absurd?

Such a view was once suggested by William Alston in a criticism of Hasting Rashdall's moral argument for God's existence.[5] Alston attributed to Rashdall the view that "God is required as a locus for the moral law." But Alston then went on to ask, "Why could it not just be an ultimate fact about the universe that kindness is good and cruelty bad? This seems to have been Plato's view." And if we rephrase Alston's query slightly to refer to obligations, we might be tempted to say, "Why not indeed?"

I say that this is perhaps the strongest reply against me. Since it involves no argument, there is no argument to be refuted. And I have already said that, so far as I can see, its central contention is not self-contradictory. Nor do I think of any other useful argument to the effect that the world is not absurd and crazy in this way. The reference to Plato, however, might be worth following for a moment. Perhaps Plato did think that goodness, or some such thing related to morality, was an ultimate fact about the world. But a Platonic world is not very close to a Russellian world. Plato was not a Christian, of course, but his world view has very often been taken to be congenial (especially congenial compared to some other philosophical views) to a religious understanding of the world. He would not have been satisfied, I think, with Russell's "accidental collocations of atoms," nor would he have taken the force of the grave to be "so nearly certain." The idea of the Good seems to play a metaphysical role in his thought. It is somehow fundamental to what *is* as well as to what ought to be, much more fundamental to reality than are the atoms. A Platonic man, there-fore, who sets himself to live in accordance with the Good aligns himself with what is deepest and most basic in existence. Or to put it another way, we might say that whatever values a Platonic world imposes on a man are values to which the Platonic world itself is committed, through and through.

Not so, of course, for a Russellian world. Values and obligations cannot be deep in such a world. They have a grip only upon surface phenomena, probably only upon man. What is deep in a Russellian world must be such things as matter and energy, or perhaps natural law, chance, or chaos. If it really were a fact that one had obligations in a Russellian world, then something would be laid upon man that might cost a man everything but that went no further than man. And that difference from a Platonic world seems to make all the difference.

This discussion suggests, I think, that there are two related ways in which morality is queer in a Russellian world. Or maybe they are better con-strued as two aspects of the queerness we have been exploring. In most of the preceding discussion I have been focusing on the strangeness of an overriding demand that does not seem to conduce to the *good* of the person on whom it is laid. (In fact, it does not even promise his good.) Here, however, we focus on the fact that this demand—radical enough in the human life on which it is laid—is *superficial* in a Russellian world. Something that reaches close to the heart of my own life, perhaps even demanding the sacrifice of that life, is not deep at all in the world in which (on a Russellian view) that life is lived. And that, too, seems absurd.

This brings to an end the major part of my discussion. If I have been successful at all you will have shared with me to some extent in the sense of the queerness of morality, its absurdity in a Russellian world. If you also share the conviction that it cannot in the end be absurd in that way, then perhaps you will also be attracted to some religious view of the world. Perhaps you also will say that morality must have some deeper grip upon the world than a Russellian view allows. And, consequently, things like mind and purpose must also be deeper in the real world than they would be in a Russellian world. They must be more original, more controlling. The accidental collocation of atoms cannot be either primeval or final, nor can the grave be an end. But of course that would be only a beginning, a sketch waiting to be filled in.

We cannot here do much to fill it in further. But I should like to close with a final, and rather tentative suggestion, as to a direction in which one might move in thinking about the place of morality in the world. It is suggested to me by certain elements in my own religion, Christianity.

I come more and more to think that morality, while a fact, is a twisted and distorted fact. Or perhaps better, that it is a barely recognizable version of another fact, a version adapted to a twisted and distorted world. It is something like, I suppose, the way in which the pine that grows at timberline, wind blasted and twisted low against the rock, is a version of the tall and symmetrical tree that grows lower on the slopes. I think it may be that the related notions of sacrifice and gift represent (or come close to representing) the fact, that is, the pattern of life, whose distorted version we know here as morality. Imagine a situation, an "economy" if you will, in which no one ever buys or trades for or seizes any good thing. But whatever good he enjoys it is either one which he himself has created or else one which he receives as a free and unconditional gift. And as soon as he has tasted it and seen that it is good he stands ready to give it away in his turn as soon as the opportunity arises. In such a place, if one were to speak either of his rights or his duties, his remark might be met with puzzled laughter as his hearers struggled to recall an ancient world in which those terms referred to something important.

We have, of course, even now some occasions that tend in this direction. Within some families perhaps, or even in a regiment in desperate battle, people may for a time pass largely beyond morality and live lives of gift and sacrifice. On those occasions nothing would be lost if the moral concepts and the moral language were to disappear. But it is probably not possible that such situations and occasions should be more than rare exceptions in the daily life of the present world. Christianity, however, which tells us that the present world is "fallen" and hence leads us to expect a distortion in its important features, also tells us that one day the redemption of the world will be complete and that then all things shall be made new. And it seems to me to suggest an "economy" more akin to that of gift and sacrifice than to that of rights and duties. If something like that should be true, then perhaps morality, like the Marxist state, is destined to wither away (unless perchance it should happen to survive in hell).

Christianity, then, I think is related to the queerness of morality in one way and perhaps in two. In the first instance, it provides a view of the world in which morality is not an absurdity. It gives morality a deeper place in the world than does a Russellian view and thus permits it to "make sense." But in the second instance, it perhaps suggests that morality is not the deepest thing, that it is provisional and transitory, that it is due to serve its use and then to pass away in favor of something richer and deeper. Perhaps we can say that it begins by inverting the quotation with which I began and by telling us that, since God exists, not everything is permitted; but it may also go on to tell us that, since God exists, in the end there shall be no occasion for any prohibition.

Notes

1   Perhaps, however, Kant was not entirely clear on this point, for in some places he talks as though it is only the *possibility* of God's existence that is a necessary postulate of morality. For a discussion of this point see M. Jamie Ferreira, "Kant's Postulate: The Possibility or the Existence of God?" *Kant-Studien* 17, no. 1 (1983): 75–80.

2   In Bertrand Russell, *Mysticism and Logic* (New York: Barnes & Noble, 1917), pp. 47–8.

3   Kurt Baier, *The Moral Point of View* (Ithaca: Cornell University Press, 1958), p. 314.

4   Richard Brandt, *Ethical Theory* (Englewood Cliffs, N J: Prentice-Hall, 1959), pp. 375–8.

5   William P. Alston, ed., *Religious Belief and Philosophical Thought* (New York: Harcourt, Brace & World, 1963), p. 25.